Introduction to Economic Evaluation in Oral Health Care

Carlos Zaror • Rodrigo Mariño
Editors

Introduction to Economic Evaluation in Oral Health Care

Springer

Editors
Carlos Zaror
Department of Paediatric Dentistry
and Orthodontics
Faculty of Dentistry
Universidad de La Frontera
Temuco, Chile

Rodrigo Mariño
Melbourne Dental School
University of Melbourne
Melbourne, VIC, Australia

ISBN 978-3-030-96288-3 ISBN 978-3-030-96289-0 (eBook)
https://doi.org/10.1007/978-3-030-96289-0

This Springer imprint is published by the registered company Springer Nature Switzerland AG
The registered company address is: Gewerbestrasse 11, 6330 Cham, Switzerland

Foreword

I am very pleased to have the privilege to provide a foreword for *Introduction to Economic Evaluation in Oral Health Care* edited by Associate Professor Carlos Zaror and Professor Rodrigo Mariño, and published by Springer.

In recent times, no matter where you live in the world, the routine of life has been impacted by biologic forces which at the time of writing are still largely uncontrolled. No country, community, or individual has been spared the impact of the COVID-19 pandemic. Dramatic, often unexpected changes in the political, economic, social, technical, and environmental landscape, continue to affect how health and oral health is prioritised, delivered, and managed. The means by which health professionals acquire knowledge and skills, and communicate with patients and peers are all impacted. In the face of some vocal ill-informed opposition, now more than ever, society needs strong, evidence-based decisions, and respect for research and science to drive the most effective use of health resources in order to meet the multiple challenges we face.

In health service provision, we are interested in differentiating the health benefits of different programmes aimed at addressing particular health needs. Our work is motivated by the principles of improving equality of access to healthcare and driving a better quality of life for all. But to achieve this, we have a responsibility to provide research-informed evidence that will convince those holding the purse strings that this is the most economic means of addressing the issue under consideration.

Economic evaluation is playing a growing role in testing and informing policies and programmes in health. It is very welcome to see the authors of this book demonstrating how this evaluation does exactly that.

Health economics is helping tool in oral health and a field that has gained preponderance in the last few decades. This book is aimed at oral health professionals and students who do not have any existing knowledge in the field of economic evaluation. It is certainly the first book that attempts to achieve this for oral health.

I congratulate Associate Professor Carlos Zaror and Professor Rodrigo Mariño in bringing together such an authoritative selection of authors and experts in the field to discuss and demonstrate how economic evaluation can be applied to oral health.

The book emphasises the explanation of basic concepts and specifically their application to oral health situations. The approach taken in this book provides an accessible, practical, and engaging read for a broad range of oral health practitioners and researchers.

Mike Morgan
Professor and Dean, Faculty of Dentistry
University of Otago
Dunedin, New Zealand

Preface

The aim of this book is to explain the concepts and tools required to conduct economic evaluations in oral health and to allow practitioners with little or no formal training or experience in economic evaluation to enter into this process. Therefore, providing the foundation for applying economic evaluation principles to oral health programs (e.g., dental caries prevention programs), as well as more advanced technical information for those interested in acquiring knowledge of health economics within the context of oral health care.

This is the first book on economic evaluation specifically for oral health professionals. However, it should be useful for any health professionals, decision makers, and health economists interested in enhancing their practical understanding of economic evaluation in the field of oral health.

The book describes the different types of economic evaluation and discusses their role and application in oral health care. Different chapters introduce the basic concepts required to conduct economic evaluations, such as scope of the problem, selection of alternatives for comparison, description of the perspective of the analysis and the time horizon, measurement and evaluation of costs and health effects, decision modelling techniques, and presentation and interpretation of the results. It also includes a discussion on such issues as reasons for conducting an economic evaluation and what the literature tells us about economic evaluation in oral health.

The book provides information on how to assess the literature related to economic evaluation and how to use it to inform decision-making in oral health policies. It has an applied orientation. Each chapter includes practical examples in the area of oral health, as well as distinctive aspects of the management of an economic evaluation in the oral health field.

Throughout the chapters readers are exposed to real examples of economic evaluation to support learning and understanding. Worked examples about how to conduct the main types of economic evaluation in the field of oral health are described in detail, such as cost-effectiveness analysis (CEA), cost-benefit analysis (CBA), and cost-utility analysis (CUA). Therefore, the emphasis is placed on developing practical solutions to existing problems and situations.

In summary, this book offers general and practical guidelines to oral health practitioners and researchers interested in conducting economic evaluations in the field of oral health.

Temuco, Chile
Melbourne, VIC, Australia

Carlos Zaror
Rodrigo Mariño

Abbreviations

ACE	Assessing Cost-Effectiveness methodology
ADA	American Dental Association
ART	Atraumatic Restorative Treatment
BNF	British National Formulary
CADTH	Canadian Agency for Drugs and Technology in Health
CARIES-QC	Caries Impacts and Experiences Questionnaire for Children
CASP	Critical Appraisal Skills Programme
CBA	Cost-Benefit Analysis
CDC	Centers for Disease Control and Prevention
CEA	Cost-Effectiveness Analysis
CHEC	Consensus on Health Economic Criteria
CHEERS	Consolidated Health Economic Evaluation Reporting Standards
Child-OIDP	Child Oral Impacts on Daily Function
CHU9D	Child Health Utility Index 9 Dimensions
CLP	Chilean Pesos
CPSTF	Community Preventive Services Task Force
CR	Composite Resin
CRF	Case Report Form
CRFs	Common Risk Factors
CUA	Cost-Utility Analysis
CWF	Community Water Fluoridation
DCE	Discrete Choice Experiments
DMFT	Decayed, Missing, or Filled Teeth index
DMFS	Decayed, Missing, and Filled Surfaces index
DALY	Disability-Adjusted Life Years
EAC	Equivalent Annual Cost
EBD	Evidence-Based Dentistry
EE	Economic Evaluation
EQ-5D	EuroQol's Five Dimensions
FFS	Fee-for-Service
FiCTION	Fillings in Children's Teeth: Indicated or Not?
FONASA	Chilean National Health Fund

FPM	First Permanent Molars
FV	Fluoride Varnish
GBD	Global Burden of Disease
GDP	Gross Domestic Product
GOHAI	Geriatric Oral Health Assessment Index
HALY	Health-Adjusted Life Years
HRQoL	Health-Related Quality of Life
HTA	Health Technology Assessment
HUI	Health Utilities Index
HVGIC	High Viscosity Glass-Ionomer Cements
HYE	Healthy Years Equivalents
ICER	Incremental Cost-Effectiveness Ratio
INAHTA	International Network of Agencies for Health Technology Assessment
IQWIG	Institute for Quality and Efficiency in Health Care
ISPOR	Pharmacoeconomics and Outcomes Research
MCDA	Multi-Criteria Decision Analysis
NCDs	Non-Communicable Diseases
NHANES	National Health and Nutrition Examination Survey
NHMRC	Australian National Health and Medical Research Council
NHS	National Health System
NICE	National Institute for Health and Clinical Excellence
NMB	Net Monetary Benefit
NSW	New South Wales
OHIP	Oral Health Impact Profile
OHRQoL	Oral Health-Related Quality of Life
PBAC	Pharmaceutical Benefits Advisory Committee
PHARMAC	Pharmaceutical Management Agency
PHC	Public Health Care
PPP	Purchasing Power Parity
PROM	Patient-Reported Outcome Measures
QALY	Quality-Adjusted Life Years
QAPY	Quality-Adjusted Prosthesis Year
QATY	Quality-Adjusted Tooth Years
QHES	Quality of Health Economic Studies
QoL	Quality of Life
RACFs	Residential Aged Care Facilities
RCT	Randomized Controlled Trial
ROI	Return on Investment
SDGs	Sustainable Development Goals
SF-36	36-item short-form health survey
SF-6D	Short-Form Six Dimensions
STB	Supervised Toothbrushing
TTO	Time Trade-Off
UDA	Units of Dental Activity

USD	United States Dollar
VBHC	Value-Based Health Care
WHO	World Health Organization
WTP	Willingness-to-Pay
YHEC	York Health Economics Consortium

Contents

Contributors

Alonso Carrasco-Labra, PhD Center for Integrative Global Oral Health, School of Dental Medicine, University of Pennsylvania, Philadelphia, PA, USA

Marianela Castillo-Riquelme, MSc, PhD(c) School of Public Health, Universidad de Chile, Santiago, Chile

Thomas Davidson, MSc, PhD Department of Health, Medicine and Caring Sciences, Linköping University, Linköping, Sweden

Gerardo Espinoza-Espinoza, DDS, MSc Department of Public Health, Universidad de La Frontera, Temuco, Chile

Center for Research in Epidemiology, Economics and Oral Public Health (CIEESPO), Faculty of Dentistry, Universidad de La Frontera, Temuco, Chile

Lan Gao, PhD, MMed Deakin Health Economics, Institute for Health Transformation, School of Health & Social Development, Faculty of Health, Deakin University, Burwood, VIC, Australia

Ann S. Goldman-Hawes, MPH, PhD Department of Epidemiology, The George Washington University Milken Institute of Public Health, Washington, DC, USA

Susan O. Griffin, PhD Division of Oral Health, Centers for Disease Control and Prevention, Atlanta, GA, USA

Tara Homer, MSc Population Health Sciences Institute, Newcastle University, Newcastle Upon Tyne, UK

Kari Jones, PhD Division of Oral Health, Centers for Disease Control and Prevention, Atlanta, GA, USA

Rodrigo Mariño, PhD Melbourne Dental School, The University of Melbourne, Melbourne, VIC, Australia

Bernardo Martorell, MD Director of Primary Health Care, La Pintana Municipality of Chile, Universidad de Santiago, Santiago, Chile

Marj Moodie, DrPH, BA(Hons), Dip Ed, DipTRP Deakin Health Economics, Institute for Health Transformation, Faculty of Health, Deakin University, Burwood, VIC, Australia

Mauricio Baeza Paredes, DDS, MSc, PhD(c) Department of Conservative Dentistry, Faculty of Dentistry, Universidad de Chile, Santiago, Chile

School of Public Health, Universidad de Chile, Santiago, Chile

Catherine de La Puente, MSc Department of Health Technology Assessment and Evidence-Based Health, Ministry of Health Chile, Santiago, Chile

John Rogers, BDS, MPH, PhD Melbourne Dental School, The University of Melbourne, Melbourne, VIC, Australia

Jing Shen, PhD Newcastle University, Newcastle Upon Tyne, UK

Laura Ternent, MSc, PHD Population Health Sciences Institute, Newcastle University, Newcastle Upon Tyne, UK

Utsana Tonmukayakul, DDS, MPH, MEcon Deakin Health Economics, Institute for Health Transformation, School of Health & Social Development, Faculty of Health, Deakin University, Burwood, VIC, Australia

Christopher R. Vernazza, PhD Newcastle University, Newcastle Upon Tyne, UK

Carlos Zaror, DDS, MSc, PhD Department of Paediatric Dentistry and Orthodontics, Faculty of Dentistry, Universidad de La Frontera, Temuco, Chile

Center for Research in Epidemiology, Economics and Oral Public Health (CIEESPO), Faculty of Dentistry, Universidad de La Frontera, Temuco, Chile

About the Editors

Carlos Zaror, DDS, MSc, PhD is an associate professor and head of the Department of Paediatric Dentistry and Orthodontics, Faculty of Dentistry, at Universidad de la Frontera in Temuco, Chile. Currently, he is also head of the Center for Research in Epidemiology, Economics and Oral Public Health (CIEESPO) at the same university.

Prof. Zaror has a dental degree from the University of Frontera, is a specialist in pediatric dentistry from Universidad de Chile, and holds a Master of Clinical Epidemiology from Universidad de La Frontera and a PhD in methodology of biomedical research and public health from the Universitat Autònoma de Barcelona, Spain.

His work focuses on health technology assessment in the field of oral health. This has allowed him to contribute to public policies, developing research for the Chilean Ministry of Health and providing expert input into public health issues. He has also participated in the preparation of protocols and clinical practice guidelines for the Chilean Ministry of Health.

Prof. Zaror has published more than 80 papers in scientific journals, and he has been awarded several oral public health research projects and serves as associate editor of *BMC Oral Health* and the *International Journal of Interdisciplinary Dentistry*.

Rodrigo Mariño, CD, MPH, PhD is a public health dentist, Professorial Fellow at the Melbourne Dental School, The University of Melbourne, Australia, where he has worked since 2004. Prof. Mariño has a dental degree from the University of Chile, a master's degree in public health from the University of Minnesota, and a PhD from the University of Melbourne.

Prof. Mariño also has an honorary appointment with the Faculty of Dentistry, Universidad de la Frontera in Temuco, Chile, and holds a position at the Population Oral Health and Research, Dental Services, Monash Health, Melbourne, Australia.

Prof. Mariño's research strongly focuses on oral health promotion and reducing inequalities in oral health status. Prof. Mariño has excellent research expertise in social epidemiology, health economics, dental workforce issues, public health, migrant health, information and communication technology, gerontology, and population oral health. He has established links and maintains continuous contact and research activities with major research and academic groups in Australia and overseas. Prof. Mariño has published more than 160 papers in scientific journals, several major research reports, and 39 book chapters.

Prof. Mariño was the founder and first president of the e-Oral Health Research Network, IADR, and serves on the editorial boards of *BMC Oral Health*, *Dental Traumatology*, and *Gerodontology*. Prof. Mariño has also been a consultant to the Pan American Health Organization/World Health Organization in Washington, DC.

Chapter 1
Overview of Health Economics

Carlos Zaror and Rodrigo Mariño

1.1 Introduction

Economic evaluations (EE) are commonly used in decision-making processes for health programs. Health programmers and planners need to make recommendations and policies, for example, for the introduction of new forms of health technology (e.g., preventive programs, pharmaceutical products, diagnostic equipment, or therapeutic devices). The introduction of new technologies has represented in many cases significant benefits, in terms of prevention, safety, and improvements in health and quality of life. At a basic level, to choose between competing technologies, two characteristics of an intervention must be considered: these are its outcomes and its cost. Based on cost and outcome, planners must select the option that offers the best results.

However, the correct incorporation and dissemination of technologies has proven to be a challenge for all health systems and in many cases is a serious problem. Therefore, since available resources are limited, delivering health services involves making decisions. As Alan Williams put it, "...We are in a fortunate, yet painful situation to have at our disposal more beneficial activities than we can fund ... the explicit decision to allocate resources to one patient is inevitably an implicit decision to deny them to another patient" (Williams 1988). This implies that it is necessary to determine what interventions should be offered and how the health system

C. Zaror (✉)
Department of Paediatric Dentistry and Orthodontics, Faculty of Dentistry, Universidad de La Frontera, Temuco, Chile

Center for Research in Epidemiology, Economics and Oral Public Health (CIEESPO), Faculty of Dentistry, Universidad de La Frontera, Temuco, Chile
e-mail: carlos.zaror@ufrontera.cl

R. Mariño
Melbourne Dental School, The University of Melbourne, Melbourne, VIC, Australia
e-mail: r.marino@unimelb.edu.au

C. Zaror, R. Mariño (eds.), *Introduction to Economic Evaluation in Oral Health Care*, https://doi.org/10.1007/978-3-030-96289-0_1

should be organized to achieve optimal health benefit using available resources and respecting people's expectations.

This leads us to a fundamental concept of health economics, the concept of opportunity cost (Gafni and Birch 2003). This is defined as the benefits that must be foregone by not allocating resources to the next best activity. The resources that will be consumed when implementing one technology will no longer be available to implement another; therefore, the system will lose the benefits that it could have obtained from its implementation. It is important to consider that the "lost" benefits of not having been able to implement an intervention should be less than those that will be obtained with the chosen intervention, that is, the performance of the chosen intervention must present the better opportunity cost. Therefore, health systems should allocate their available resources in the best possible way among the possible technologies to minimize the opportunity cost, sacrificing the least amount of benefits and obtaining the greatest possible benefits using those available resources.

The effectiveness and safety of any given intervention by itself may not be enough to decide on its implementation. Cost-effectiveness, as well as the political, organizational, social, ethical, and legal impacts, must be considered, especially when applied within the public health context (Vallejos et al. 2014). The goal of EE, as of any public health measure, is to maximize the health of the population. For this purpose, health service managers, programmers, and planners are required to select the interventions with highest impact, based on evidence and prioritizing of high-risk groups. It is now well established and recognized that EE is a central component of the objective evaluation of new technology/therapies and preventive programs that seek to replace current treatments or practices (Niessen and Douglass 1984).

Current standards for the evaluation of evidence in public health interventions include considerations of effectiveness but also require that – for the use of resources – the benefits and costs of interventions are described and evaluated so that they can be weighed against other options (Vallejos et al. 2014). Nonetheless, the allocation of economic resources between competing health treatments may also have an emotional or political burden, so decision-makers prefer to use rational evaluative methods aimed at maximizing the efficient use of health funds (Vallejos et al. 2014).

In the context of diminishing public resources for oral health care and increasingly sophisticated treatment options, decision-makers may not have enough information to identify the financial benefit per monetary unit of resources required for most health interventions. The need to understand health and healthcare systems and how to best allocate scarce resources requires decision-makers to apply the full range of methods and skills to assure these resources are used wisely (Glied and Teutsch 2016). It is in this context that economic evaluations are relevant, as they provide information that managers weigh, alongside other evidence.

This chapter presents the basic concepts and framework of economic evaluation. The chapter presents a description of the main types of economic evaluation, provides guidelines for selecting the most appropriate type of economic evaluation, and describes the main stages of an economic evaluation study. This chapter is not intended to be a comprehensive description of all relevant theories.

1.2 Economic Evaluations

Evaluation has been defined as "the systematic collection of information about the activities, characteristics, and outcomes of programs to make judgments about the program, improve program effectiveness, and/or inform decisions about future program development" (U.S. Department of Health and Human Services 2011).

This definition establishes first and foremost that the collection of data for evaluative purposes must be done in a systematic way. Additionally, another component of the definition specifies that the purposes of evaluation are to make judgements, improve effectiveness, and make decisions about the program.

However, making judgements and assessing effectiveness by themselves do not provide sufficient bases to initiate a program in most healthcare situations (U.S. Preventive Services Task Force 1996). Current standards for evaluating evidence on public health interventions include considerations of effectiveness but also demand that the benefits and costs of public health interventions should be described and evaluated, so they can be weighed against other options for the use of resources (Rychetnik and Frommer 2001).

Economics is defined as "the science which studies human behavior as a relationship between ends and scarce means which have alternative uses," and its objective is to maximize human welfare or utility (Robbins 1935). Health economics is a branch of economics that studies the production and distribution of health and healthcare. Thus, an *economic evaluation* is "the comparative analysis of alternative actions in terms of their costs and their consequences in order to assist in policy decision" (Drummond et al. 2005). There are several important components to this definition. The first is that an economic evaluation must compare alternative interventions. It cannot be said that an intervention is cost-effective if it is not compared to another intervention. Second, an economic evaluation measures not only costs but also results or consequences. Third, the technique should be considered as one input to the decision-making process as to whether a program is worthwhile doing. Finally, the technique represents only one dimension within a broader, integrated, and cyclical decision-making and evaluation process (Drummond et al. 2005).

An economic evaluation is not a substitute for decision-making processes but should be used in combination with other evidence as part of those processes. Therefore, before conducting an economic assessment, health programmers should be certain that the program can work (*efficacy*); that the program works for a given place or situation (*effectiveness*); and that the program reaches those it aims to reach (*equity*) (Goodacre & McCabe 2002; Shiell et al. 2002).

Additionally, other factors reflecting the immediate trade-offs and broad implications of providing a service are relevant to the goals and the practical constraints confronted by every decision-maker. These might include ethical issues, political reality, policy priorities, and availability of resources to implement the program.

Thus, the development of any new treatment or program should ideally result from a sequence of studies, ranging from basic research to community trials. To evaluate an intervention, we do not only use quantitative methods. Often a quantitative evaluation is complemented by an evaluation conducted in a qualitative manner.

Then comes the question whether it should be used, given other needs under a fixed budget (economic evaluation). It is important to clarify that the economic evaluations in health focus on measures of effectiveness and non-efficacy, since what is relevant is the magnitude of the effect of a certain intervention when implemented in routine conditions.

1.3 Types of Economic Evaluation

The term cost-effectiveness tends to be used sometimes generically to refer to any type of economic evaluation done in health; however, there are different types of EE. Drummond and collaborators (Drummond et al. 2005) describe three economic evaluation techniques, incorporating the two features that must be present in a true economic evaluation: (a) comparison of at least two alternatives and (b) examination of both costs and consequences of these alternatives. These techniques are:

- Cost-effectiveness analysis (CEA)
- Cost-benefit analysis (CBA)
- Cost-utility analysis (CUA)

If the economic evaluation does not compare the costs and consequences of two or more alternatives, it should be designated as partial. The partial economic evaluation involves studies of (1) cost description, (2) cost consequence description, and (3) cost analysis. The description of costs is characterized in that it does not compare alternative courses of action, its main purpose being the report of costs associated with a specific intervention. The description of cost consequence, on the other hand, adds to the above the description of outcomes; however, it does not consider the evaluation of therapeutic alternatives either. Cost analysis does compare different courses of action but examines only the relationship between costs to the detriment of the consequences (Drummond et al. 2005) (See Fig. 1.1).

1.3.1 Cost-Effectiveness Analysis

The CEA is the approach most often used in health economic evaluation including oral health (Mariño et al. 2020) and compares the costs and effects of two or more alternative interventions (e.g., two caries prevention modalities, or even between dental caries preventions and dental caries treatment techniques). In this case, health effects are measured in health units (e.g., caries averted, years of life gained, mortality avoided, etc.), and it is common in both alternatives. However, an important requirement is that benefits of the strategies to be evaluated must not be equivalent in terms of quantity. The measure of health benefit that we need to carry out a CEA

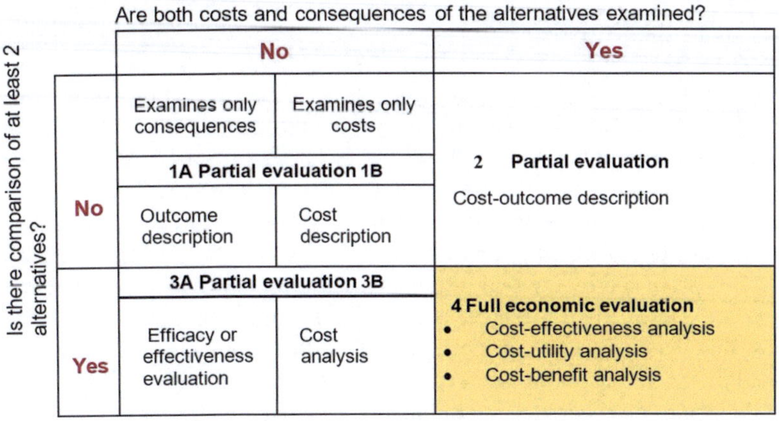

Fig. 1.1 Types of economic evaluation
Original drawing

will depend on the objective of the program or treatment to be evaluated. For example, if we want to evaluate an oral cancer screening program, the effectiveness will be measured by the number of cases detected early; on the other hand, if we want a preventive treatment for dental caries, the effectiveness will be measured as cavities avoided. To the extent that there is evidence, final outcomes should be chosen over the intermediate ones. As in the example of early detection of oral cancer, if we want to produce goods valued by the population, we need information on final outcomes such as the reduction in mortality.

We could use CEA to decide the most efficient (the least expensive) way to achieve our goals.

CEAs have the limitation of being one-dimensional, that is, they evaluate only one dimension of benefits. Typically, interventions produce more than one clinical outcome (caries incidence or effect adversed); however, the final result cannot be summarized in a single value. This not only makes the process of choosing the outcome to evaluate difficult, since it must try to choose the most representative outcome of the intervention, but it also limits the possibilities of comparison between different interventions. The latter is another limitation in CEA, that is, they do not allow us to compare interventions in different areas or even in similar areas if different cost-effectiveness measures were chosen.

Cost-minimization analysis is a special case of CEA, where programs under comparison get the same outcome and do not differ in their effectiveness, except that one costs less.

1.3.2 Cost-Benefit Analysis

When the consequences of two or more programs are not the same or the result cannot be reduced to a common effect among alternatives (e.g., dental caries prevention and oral cancer prevention), it is not possible to perform a CEA. In these cases, analysts use CBA to assign economic value to the outcomes and calculate the economic benefits of the intervention. To do this, it is necessary to translate into monetary terms all the effects and benefits, that is, the monetary value attached to the health states produced by the two interventions.

CBAs are useful when it is necessary to have a common denominator of interventions that have different effects. The fact that both benefits and costs are expressed in the same unit makes it easier for the final outcomes to be analyzed not only in the health field but also in comparison to other social impact programs such as education, transport, or environment (Zarate 2010). Thus, a CBA of a health intervention might try to measure not only the monetary value of any health benefits gained by the patient but also the value to society of other consequences, such as the ability to take paid employment (Gray et al. 2011). Therefore, the CBA allows evaluation of whether it is justified to invest resources in the provision of a certain treatment, regardless of what the alternatives are.

There are three methods for assigning a monetary value to health benefits: the human capital, where the health of the person is valued based on their present and future capacity to generate income; revealed preferences, seeking to infer the assessment of health from the decisions that individuals make in practice; and willingness to pay, where it is determined how much society is willing to spend to obtain a certain health benefit or avoid the costs of a certain disease. However, the concept of placing explicit monetary values on health or on life and the variability and methodological uncertainty around the valuations themselves are the main limitation of the CBA.

1.3.3 Cost-Utility Analysis

The CUA, which is a variant of the studies of cost-effectiveness, determines the effects on health in an aggregate measure that takes into account the quantity and quality of life and that reflects the preferences (utilities) of patients in the face of different health states. Utility is a satisfaction measure by which individuals value the choice of certain goods or services in economic terms. This is expressed as cost per healthy year of quality of life gained by patients or their families (e.g., quality-adjusted life years [QALY] per intervention unit) after the implementation of the program. In oral health the concept of quality-adjusted tooth years (QATY) was introduced as an outcome measure to provide an outcome measure which could be compared across treatments (Antczak-Bouckoms and Weinstein 1987). Their great advantage is that they allow us to summarize all the effects of the interventions in a single value; therefore, they are useful when the interventions have multiple consequences of interest or when we are interested in obtaining an outcome that allows the comparison of alternatives that are not related to each other and do not share the same consequences.

1.4 Considerations for Selecting the Appropriate Type of Economic Evaluation

The choice of economic evaluation to be undertaken depends upon the question that is being asked, which will depend on the type of decision to be made. Questions involving allocative efficiency (What would be the best program to implement?) are more concerned with the broader healthcare resources available and deciding what should be the focus of attention. For example, decisions need to be made about whether health programs are more meritorious than those related to education. Within the health arena, the question may relate to the proportion of a budget spent on primary vs. secondary care, etc.

Once it has been determined what to do, technical efficiency (how to do it) may be more relevant. For example, if it has been decided to allocate funding to a school oral healthcare program, technical efficiency would indicate what mix of programs would get the best outcomes for the available expenditure.

Additionally, the context of where a program is to be implemented may also influence the type of economic evaluation. For example, programs may be implemented system wide, within an organizational setting, or within a program setting.

The nature of the benefits/outcomes may influence the type of economic evaluation selected. When the question being asked is about quality of life, rather than merely the effectiveness of the program, it suggests that CUA rather than CEA may be more appropriate. On the other hand, when non-health sector impacts are important and all benefits can be measured in monetary unit equivalents, then CBA might be more relevant than CEA.

1.5 Steps to Conduct an Economic Evaluation

As discussed previously, there are a number of forms of economic evaluation, each of which is suited to a different purpose. Every evaluation has unique challenges. Still, it is possible to identify the main steps which are common to most forms of economic evaluation. In outline, an economic evaluation can be divided into six different steps, although not all of the common economic evaluation methods involve all six steps (Splett 1996).

The following six steps for cost-effectiveness analysis serve as a good outline of the economic evaluation process (Fig. 1.2).

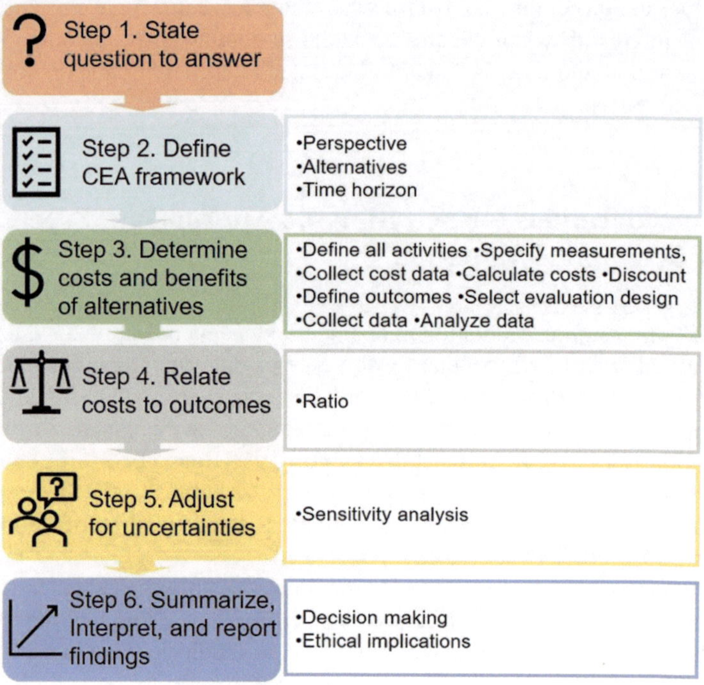

Fig. 1.2 Steps for economic evaluation
Original drawing

1.5.1 Step 1: Define the Problem or Question to Answer

Like all forms of scientific enquiry, formulating a research question is the most important step in the research design and development and therefore is the first step in identifying the purpose of the economic evaluation. The economic evaluation has to answer a well-defined evaluation question, which represents an uncertainty about the efficiency of alternative interventions. The nature of the question that the economic evaluation seeks to answer will determine both the study design and the analysis technique. The research question must be formulated in a clear and concise manner that specifies the interventions or strategies to be compared, the target population, and the analysis perspective (MINSAL 2013).

In identifying the context and intent of the study, the evaluator should clearly:

- Define the current situation and describe which aspects are going to be affected by the proposal put forward
- Describe the context of the economic evaluation; identify whether it is part of a clinical trial, a retrospective database analysis, etc.
- Indicate why the economic evaluation is being undertaken
- Define treatment protocols (e.g., duration of treatments) and scenarios

- Define the target population (e.g., patients), clearly indicating the criteria for inclusion or exclusion of any specific groups or individuals

1.5.2 Step 2: Define the Framework for the Economic Evaluation

1.5.2.1 Perspective of the Economic Analysis

The analysis perspective is the point of view from which the analysis will be focused, such as that of the society, the financier of the health services, insurance companies, hospitals, primary care units, health provider, etc. (Meltzer 2001). The choice of one or the other perspective has important implications for the rest of the elements of the analysis, as it will guide or decide which costs and outcomes should be included in the analysis (García-Altes et al. 2011). For example, if the Department of Health funded a program, they would consider the costs they experience; costs incurred by the patient may be irrelevant from their perspective (Russell et al. 1996). Table 1.1 shows the types of costs to be included according to the perspective.

Table 1.1 Main perspectives and types of costs to be included in each economic evaluation

	Perspective of economic evaluation				
Examples of costs	Patient	Healthcare provider	Hospital	Payer	Society
Direct medical					
Healthcare provider time	Yes	Yes	Yes	Yes	Yes
Other healthcare personnel time (e.g., nurse, technician)	No	Yes	Yes	Yes	Yes
Drugs	Yes	No	Yes	Yes	Yes
Health supplies and devices (e.g., syringes, ultrasound)	No	No	Yes	Yes	Yes
Laboratory tests	No	No	Yes	Yes	Yes
Direct nonmedical					
Administration	No	No	Yes	Yes	Yes
Physical facility (e.g., clinic, office)	No	No	Yes	No	Yes
Utilities (e.g., telephone, electricity)	No	Yes	No	Yes	Yes
Patient's travel costs	Yes	No	No	No	Yes
Temporary hired caregiver	Yes	No	No	No	Yes
Indirect					
Time off from work to visit healthcare provider	Yes	No	No	No	Yes
Time off work while ill and recuperating	Yes	No	No	No	Yes
Hire a temporary household help while ill	Yes	No	No	No	Yes

For these reasons, results from analyses done under different perspectives may not be comparable. The vast majority of economic evaluations are carried out from the funder's point of view; however, some health economists recommend a societal viewpoint (Drummond and Jefferson 1996). This perspective requires measurement of all costs and benefits to the community, no matter to whom they accrue (Russell et al. 1996; Glied and Teutsch 2016). However, in practice many of these costs and benefits are difficult to measure, and a pragmatic view should prevail (Russell et al. 1996). The societal perspective is the one that represents the public interest rather than that of any other groups (Russell et al. 1996). On the other hand, if a program puts at risk a sector of the population, a CEA conducted from the societal perspective should include any harm done as well as the benefits and all related costs.

1.5.2.2 Alternatives Being Compared

As the economic analysis is based on a comparison of alternatives, its selection becomes an important piece of information. As indicated, a true or complete economic evaluation compares at least two alternatives (Drummond et al. 2005). The choice of alternatives is often crucial to the net results, and all reasonable alternatives should be included. The alternatives being compared should be described in detail with a clear and specific statement of the primary objective of each alternative. It is recommended to use as a comparator the standard practice or the most effective practice available at the time (Ministerio de la Protección Social 2010). The option "do nothing" can be considered in certain scenarios (Drummond et al. 2005). This alternative does not mean that there are no costs and no consequences, rather it involves the "status quo." For example, in the case of community water fluoridation, the status quo would involve patients with dental caries seeking treatment and that has a cost. The EE would evaluate change in cost and consequences as a result of the introduction of community water fluoridation.

The selection criteria will consider the availability of the intervention, its habitual use, the identification by the population according to criteria of relevance, or the presence of uncertainty regarding its efficiency (García-Altes et al. 2011). In this sense, the chosen alternatives must be justified in the local context for which the decision is expected to be made (health system, patients, aspects of clinical practice, etc.). In the case of an oral health evaluation, the appropriate comparison is with the form of treatment or prevention which the dental health program under consideration is most likely to replace in practice, the most commonly used alternative, or the next most effective option.

1.5.2.3 Time Horizon

The time horizon is the relevant period for the normal course of the intervention (Splett 1996). Costs and health effects do not always take place in the same period of time. This is especially important in public health interventions, because the costs of the intervention take place in the early years, and the health effects do not appear until much later (García-Altcs ct al. 2011). It must be clearly established when the program begins and the appropriate time horizon to track the key outcomes. The time period to be covered by an evaluation must be enough to allow for the full effects of the program on costs and outcomes. Benefits realized in the future should be counted in the analysis if they can be directly related to actions taken during the period of analysis used for estimating costs (MINSAL 2013). In general, it will be longer for interventions associated with chronic diseases and shorter for acute conditions. Most international guidelines about EE recommend lifetime time horizon for chronic disease (Ministerio de la Protección Social 2010; NICE 2014).

1.5.3 Step 3: Determine Costs and Consequences/Benefits of Alternatives

In order to perform an economic evaluation, costs and health effects must be identified, measured, and then compared. There are several formats to estimate costs and benefits in economic evaluation, such as prospective, retrospective, and models. Most studies use the "model" format. This modelling is based, as much as possible, on real data and real values. When this is not possible, it uses assumptions. Consideration must be given to those assumptions; they must be clearly presented and will form the basis of the sensitivity analysis (Meltzer 2001).

1.5.3.1 Determine Costs

As we mentioned previously, the stage of identifying the costs or resources used is closely related to the perspective from which the analysis will be carried out (Table 1.1). This process, of quantifying costs, must be approached in a systematic and careful manner (Russell et al. 1996); therefore, the precision with which costs are measured is one of the main determinants of the quality of an economic evaluation.

Costs covered would include all supplies and material used by the program, capital costs, administrative costs, opportunity costs, volunteer labor, staff salaries, shared office space, etc., required for implementation of the program, and costs incurred by patients and their families. That is, there will be costs involved in organizing and providing the service; costs to the individuals; and costs external to the individual and services during the provision of the program or services (e.g., opportunity costs) (Meltzer 2001). Costs must be expressed in appropriate physical units and then calculated in monetary terms using market costs (Niessen and Douglass 1984; Horowitz and Heifetz 1979).

Drummond et al. (2005) suggest that three categories of cost must be taken into account in an economic evaluation:

1. Health resources costs, which consist of the costs of organizing and operating the program, for example, medication, equipment, hospitalization, etc.
2. Patient and family costs: these include transport and travel expenses to and from the community health center or hospital, co-payments, and time to seek and receive attention (time is one of the most important resources in a family).
3. Other sectors: volunteers, caregivers, childcare, etc.

Cost analysis involves three main stages: identification, measurement, and valuation. Identification consists of listing the likely resource effects of the intervention as comprehensively as possible; therefore, it covers the types of resource use that are relevant for the disease and the intervention studied and the level of detail that has to be measured and valued. The measurement of resource use is used to determine the quantities of resources used as part of a given intervention. The final stage refers to valuation of these resource effects.

In Chap. 3 we will go into more detail and show examples of how to do costing in an economic evaluation.

1.5.3.2 Determine Consequences

Consequences/benefits are the services, capabilities, and qualities of each alternative system and can be viewed as the return on an investment (Meltzer 2001). Consequences/benefits include direct costs being avoided, such as expenditure on oral health and lost or reduced productivity. Benefits also include improved health status and improvements in the quality of life of patients. An intervention may also bring other benefits (Russell et al. 1996), for example, better nutrition, improved social contacts, enjoyment of food, etc.

Economic evaluation relies on the results of epidemiologic and clinical studies to establish the effectiveness of an intervention. This is important as poor evidence of effectiveness has the potential to mislead resource allocation decision-makers.

The process of identifying beneficial consequences should also be done in a systematic way. Identifying consequences involves (Splett 1996):

- Defining the key outcome or consequence of interest; this is related to the objectives of the intervention.
- Specifying the outcome indicator; this is the precise way the outcome is measured, for example, sound teeth, birth weight, year of life added, etc.

There are three main categories of benefits:

- Benefits can be measured in terms of effects (e.g., years of life gained) or health states preferences in a CUA or by willingness to pay in a CBA.
- Healthcare programs can create other values not necessarily related to an improvement in health status. This refers to the fact that patients can gain value just from the process of receiving attention.

- Healthcare programs can save resources. These savings are the reflection of costs and are measured and valued in the same manner. In fact, savings are costs not spent on the alternative program.

While most costs can be quantified in monetary terms, many benefits cannot. Putting a value on benefits may look simply, but it might be very difficult to do. This is particularly so when some of these outcomes cannot be quantified in monetary terms; this is a common case in dentistry. For example, what should the value of losing a tooth be? How many dollars should be added to the effect of a preventive program because it leads to intact teeth, rather than to perfectly restored ones (Niessen and Douglass 1984; Horowitz and Heifetz 1979)? The preference for an early cure or for sound teeth is difficult to quantify in monetary terms, although there are attempts to do this by using a quality of life measure. However, in dentistry there is no consistently used QALY equivalent. Therefore, if we do not give adequate consideration to a lot of factors and we just consider the savings in cost of treatments of dental caries as the tangible benefit, the results, both the cost and benefits, of any dental preventive method will either be overestimated or underestimated.

Analysts include in the cost of prevention some of the visible costs of the program and assume that if a program can reduce the cost of treatments, other benefits are assured in that way. An alternative way to quantify intangible benefits can be by using a subjective, qualitative rating system (National Institutes of Health 1998).

Intangible benefits of preventive programs in dentistry can include freedom from pain, a dentition free of dental decay, improved social acceptability, psychological value of retaining teeth (aesthetic, taste or speech), less time missed from work or school, reduction of prevalence of malocclusion, prevention of future dental problems, extraction, and treatments or improved quality of life (Niessen and Douglass 1984; Horowitz and Heifetz 1979).

In Chap. 4 we will delve into how to measure outcomes in an economic evaluation.

1.5.3.3 Discounting

When the time horizon exceeds 12 months, an adjustment must be made because of the temporal distribution of costs (Drummond et al. 2005; Splett 1996). This is achieved through a procedure called "discounting," which transforms past or future costs and benefits to their "present value." The discount is based on the idea that today's money has greater value than the same amount of money in the future. This is valid, even with an inflation rate or a bank interest rate of 0%, as there is an opportunity benefit in postponing cost payments, as available funds can be used for other purposes (Meltzer 2001). For more information see Chap. 3.

1.5.4 Step 4: Relating Outcomes to Costs

After collecting and appropriately measuring costs and outcomes, CEA, CBA, and CUA comparisons of costs and benefits are expressed in a single ratio (Drummond et al. 2005). In this way, the comparative alternatives can be ordered from the lowest to the highest cost ratio per unit of effect and the one with the lowest ratio chosen. This ratio takes the form of a price, a monetary unit cost per unit of effect, such as cost per life year extended, the cost per QALY, or in dental health programs, cost per DMFS avoided or cost per "quality-adjusted tooth year" (Fyffe and Nuttall 1995).

The results of economic evaluation are summarized through the incremental cost-effectiveness ratio (ICER). This is calculated from the quotient between the differences in cost and effectiveness of the evaluated alternatives. Therefore, the ICER informs how much more we have to pay to obtain an additional effectiveness unit (Drummond et al. 2005) (Box 1.1).

Box 1.1

$$\text{Incremental Cost} - \text{Effectiveness Ratio} = \text{Cost Difference} / \text{Difference in Outcome}$$

where

$$\text{Cost difference} = \left(\text{Cost of intervention} - \text{Cost of alternative}\right)$$
$$\text{Incremental resources required } by \text{ the intervention}$$

$$\text{Difference in outcome} = \begin{pmatrix} \text{Effectiveness of intervention} \\ -\text{Effectiveness of alternative} \end{pmatrix}$$
$$\text{Incremental health effect gained } by \text{ using the intervention}$$

Economists like to use both average cost-effectiveness ratios (i.e., cost per unit of outcome for each intervention) and incremental cost-effectiveness ratios (i.e., incremental cost per additional unit of benefits comparing one intervention with another).

In Chap. 6 we will delve into how to interpret the results of an economic evaluation.

1.5.5 Step 5: Sensitivity Analysis

Although in economic analysis we should use the best available data, in most evaluations there is a degree of uncertainty about the accuracy of the underlying data, which needs to be combined with subjective estimates. To evaluate these uncertainties, the stability of the conclusions, and the assumptions made, analysts redo the analysis changing assumptions and estimations (Petitti 2000). If the basic conclusion does not vary when a particular feature or assumption is changed, there is more confidence in the results. If, however, a relatively small change in the value of an input parameter changes the results for the alternative selected, then the analysis is considered to be sensitive to that parameter. More effort has to be invested in reducing the uncertainties and in improving the exactitude of critical variables.

An analysis of the possible range of costs and outcomes, given the uncertainty surrounding our estimate of the true costs and benefits, is called a "sensitivity analysis." Since an economic evaluation might be a key document in the review process, reviewers want assurance that the analysis is reliable (National Institutes of Health 1998). The objective of this analysis is to verify how the results of the study would vary if the values of the variables considered changed.

We should always use the best available information in economic analyses. In most evaluations it is possible that assumptions are used in the primary analysis, which introduces some degree of uncertainty about the accuracy of the underlying data. Since the values, for both cost and outcome/effectiveness, are based on literature, consultation with experts, or an "educated guess."

There are three types of uncertainty:

- Methodological uncertainty: variability of analytical approaches to economic evaluation (perspective, type of analysis, discount, etc.)
- Structural uncertainty: related to the decisions, simplifications, and assumptions required for the construction of a model (number of branches of the tree, the defined health states, the duration of the cycle in a Markov model, etc.)
- Parameter uncertainty: the fact that the true value of the parameters is unknown

The sensitivity analysis process requires three steps (National Institutes of Health 1998):

(a) Identification of input parameters with the greatest influence on the outcome
(b) Repetition of the cost analysis with changed parameters
(c) Evaluation of the results

(a) <u>Identification of Input Parameters with the Greatest Influence on the Outcome</u>

In principle, all the variables included in the analysis are potential candidates for sensitivity analysis (Drummond et al. 2005). Nonetheless, in general, the variables that are most controversial must be chosen for sensitivity analysis, as the credibility of the conclusions of the analysis is based on assumptions about these variables (Drummond et al. 2005). For example, it is always important to do a sensitivity analysis for the discount rate.

Typically, analysts consider a range of values for each important variable and examine the sensitivity of the results to variations in each variable. Good candidates for sensitivity analysis are those with significant cost factors and those with a wide range of maximum and minimum estimated values. The reasons for the ranges used in the analysis must be included and justified. These ranges should be based on evidence and logic (Drummond et al. 2005).

(b) Repetition of the Cost Analysis

Sensitivity analysis can be done in several ways. The simplest way is a univariate (one-way) sensitivity analysis; the assumed values are tested one at a time, while the others are kept fixed. However, it could be two ways, three ways, or n-ways, depending on the number of variables that are combined in the sensitivity analysis. For example, in a two-way sensitivity analysis, the expected outcome is determined for every possible combination of reasonable estimates of two variables (Weinstein et al. 1996; Petitti 2000; Drummond and Jefferson 1996).

A different approach is the "threshold analysis." In threshold analysis the value of one variable is changed and analyses repeated until the alternative decision strategies are found to have equal outcomes and there is no benefit of one alternative over the other in terms of estimated outcome (Petitti 2000; Drummond et al. 2005).

(c) Evaluate the Results of the Sensitivity Analysis

This evaluation is done by comparing the original set of inputs and the outcome to the results obtained by varying the input parameters. When the assumed value of a variable affects the conclusions of the analysis, that analysis is said to be "sensitive." When the conclusions do not change, the analysis is said to be "insensitive" to the variable.

1.5.6 Step 6: Interpret and Report the Findings

A complete economic evaluation is one that compares the results of one alternative (cost-effectiveness ratio) with the results of another, to determine the benefits of one treatment over the other (Laupacis et al. 1992). As we have already mentioned, the main results of economic evaluations are expressed as incremental ratios (e.g., incremental cost-effectiveness ratio). These results are usually presented graphically on a cartesian plane (Fig. 1.3). In brief, for decision-making, there are four possible outcomes for an economic evaluation. Firstly, when the new treatment or intervention is less effective and more costly than the current or comparator alternative and secondly when the new treatment or intervention has an improved outcome and costs savings. In these two situations, the decision is unambiguous and clear, a new treatment, intervention, or technology should be rejected and accepted, respectively. However, in some cases the decision may not be as simple or as clear, for example, when the innovation is more effective but also more costly or vice versa. In these cases, the choice depends on a number of additional considerations (Drummond et al. 2005; Laupacis et al. 1992). For more details on how to interpret the results, refer to Chap. 6.

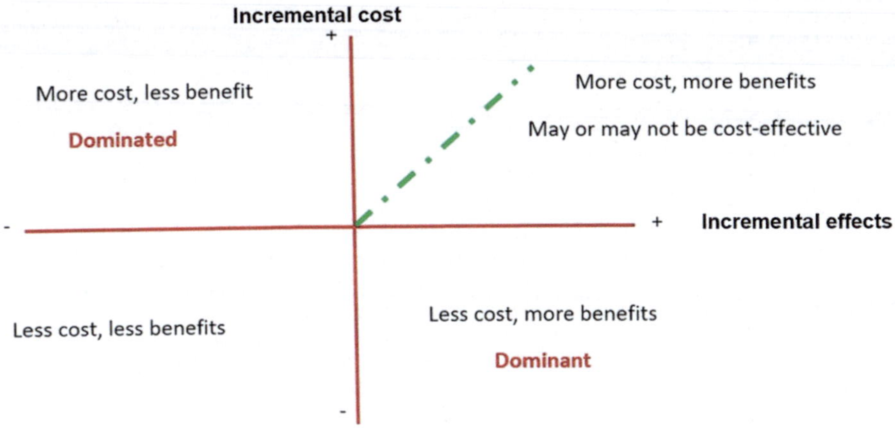

Fig. 1.3 Cost-effectiveness plane

1.6 Final Remarks

Economic evaluations are commonly used in decision-making processes about health programs; however, less examples exist in the oral health literature. If, as health professionals, we want to be able to define the final use of resources in relation to the needs of the population, we must prepare ourselves to deal with basic principles of economic evaluation. We hope that this chapter provides the starting point and that readers will be motivated to expand their current knowledge and efforts to include an economic evaluation in future endeavors, thus contributing to a solid body of economic information in oral health. The effective use of economic evaluations will in turn make important research information accessible and relevant to a broad audience of policy makers, researchers, practitioners, and community leaders.

References

Antczak-Bouckoms AA, Weinstein MC (1987) Cost-effectiveness analysis of periodontal disease control. J Dent Res 66:1630–1635

Drummond MF, Jefferson TO (1996) Guidelines for authors and peer reviewers of economic submissions to the BMJ. BMJ 313:275–283

Drummond MF, Sculpher MJ, Torrance GW, O'Brien BJ, Stoddart GL (2005) Methods for the economic evaluation of health care Programmes, 3rd edn. Oxford University Press, London

Fyffe HE, Nuttall NM (1995) Decision processes in the management of dental disease. Part 1: QALYs, QATYs and dental health state utilities. Dent Update 22:67–71

Gafni A, Birch S (2003) NICE methodological guidelines and decision making in the national health service in England and Wales. PharmacoEconomics 21:149–157

García-Altes A, Navas E, Soriano MJ (2011) Evaluación económica de intervenciones de salud pública. Gac Sanit 25(Suppl 1):31

Glied S, Teutsch SM (2016) How can economics advance prevention? Am J Prev Med 50(5 Suppl 1):S4–S5

Goodacre S, McCabe C (2002) An introduction to economic evaluation. Emerg Med J 19(3):198–201

Gray AM, Clarke PM, Wolstenholme JL, Wordsworth S (2011) Applied methods of cost-effectiveness analysis in health care, 1st edn. Oxford University Press, New York

Horowitz HS, Heifetz SB (1979) Methods of assessing the cost-effectiveness of caries preventive agents and procedures. Int Dent J 29:106–117

Laupacis A, Feeny D, Detsky A, Tugwell P (1992) How attractive does a new technology have to be to warrant adoption and utilization? Tentative guidelines for using clinical and economic evaluations. Can Med Assoc J 146:473–481

Mariño R, Ravisankar G, Zaror C (2020) Quality appraisal of economic evaluations done on oral health preventive programs – A systematic review. J Public Health Dent 80(3):194–207

Meltzer MI (2001) Introduction to health economics for physicians. Lancet 358:993–998

Ministerio de la Protección Social (2010) Guía metodológica para el desarrollo de guías de atención integral en el sistema general de seguridad social en salud. Colombia. https://www.minsalud.gov.co/salud/Documents/Gu%C3%ADa%20Metodológica%20para%20la%20elaboración%20de%20gu%C3%ADas.pdf. Accessed 30 Aug 2019

Ministerio de Salud de Chile (MINSAL) (2013) Revisión de la Literatura sobre la inclusión del criterio de costo-efectividad en guías de práctica clínica. http://www.repositoriodigital.minsal.cl/bitstream/handle/2015/775/3831.pdf?sequence=1&isAllowed=y. Accessed 30 Aug 2019

National Institutes of Health (1998) Cost-benefit analysis guide for NIH IT projects. Office of the Deputy Chief Information Officer. https://slideplayer.com/slide/5672379/. Accessed 22 Jan 2021

NICE (2014) The guidelines manual. https://www.nice.org.uk/process/pmg20/chapter/introduction. Accessed 30 Aug 2019

Niessen LC, Douglass CW (1984) Theoretical considerations in applying benefit-cost and cost-effectiveness analyses to preventive dental programs. J Public Health Dent 44:156–168

Petitti B (2000) Meta-analysis, decision analysis, and cost-effectiveness analysis: methods for quantitative synthesis in medicine, 2nd edn. Oxford University Press, New York

Robbins L (1935) An essay on the nature and significance of economic science, 2nd edn. Macmillan, London

Russell LB, Gold MR, Siegel JE, Daniels N, Weinstein MC (1996) The role of cost-effectiveness analysis in health and medicine. Panel on cost-effectiveness in health and medicine. JAMA 276:1172–1177

Rychetnik L, Frommer M (2001) A proposed schema for evaluating evidence on public health interventions. In touch. Public Health Association of Australia, Sydney. http://www.phaa.net.au/intouch/intouch01/august01.pdf. Accessed 30 May 2019

Shiell A, Donaldson C, Mitton C, Currie G (2002) Health economic evaluation. J Epidemiol Community Health 56(2):85–88

Splett P (1996) The practitioner's guide to cost-effectiveness analysis of nutrition interventions. https://www.ncemch.org/NCEMCH-publications/NtrnCstEff_Anl.pdf. Accessed 30 Aug 2019

U.S. Department of Health and Human Services, Centers for Disease Control and Prevention (2011) Introduction to program evaluation for public health programs: a self-study guide. https://www.cdc.gov/eval/guide/cdcevalmanual.pdf. Accessed 30 Aug 2019

U.S. Preventive Services Task Force (1996) Guide to clinical preventive services, 2nd edn. U.S. Department of Health and Human Services, Office of Disease Prevention and Health Promotion, Washington, DC

Vallejos C, Bustos L, de la Puente C, Reveco R, Velasquez M, Zaror C (2014) The main methodological aspects in health technology assessment. Rev Med Chil 142(Suppl 1):S16–S21

Weinstein MC, Siegel JE, Gold MR, Kamlet MS, Russell LB, for the Panel on Cost-Effectiveness in Health and Medicine (1996) Recommendations of the Panel on Cost-Effectiveness in Health and Medicine. JAMA 276:1339–1342

Williams A (1988) Priority setting in public and private health care: a guide through the ideological jungle. J Health Econ 7(2):173–183

Zarate V (2010) Evaluaciones económicas en salud: Conceptos básicos y clasificación. Rev Med Chil 138(Suppl 2):93–97

Chapter 2
Why Carry Out an Economic Evaluation in Oral Health Care?

Susan O. Griffin and Kari Jones

2.1 Real-World Questions Regarding Oral Health Policy, Programs, and Interventions

2.1.1 Question 1: How to Reduce Untreated Dental Disease Among Adults

A publicly available analysis of National Health and Nutrition Examination Survey (NHANES) data collected in 2011–2016 indicated that about 40% of working-age, dentate US adults living in low-income households had untreated dental caries (CDC 2019). This value is more than twice that among higher-income adults. Similar to most population surveys, NHANES dentists use visual/tactile assessment, so diagnosed caries is likely cavitated and thus symptomatic (Kassebaum et al. 2015). Prevalence and disparities in untreated caries between low- and higher-income adults have remained stable among working-age adults since 1999–2004 (Griffin et al. 2019). Prevalence of untreated decay among low-income, dentate, older adults aged 65+ years is lower than that for working-age adults (prevalence = 29%) but still is more than twice that among their higher-income counterparts (CDC 2019). The trend in disparities by income among older adults since 1999–2004, however, differs from that for working-age adults—disparities among older adults by income level have increased (Griffin et al. 2019). An additional concern regarding older adults is that their risk for tooth decay may be increasing as successive generations are retaining more of their natural teeth. Between 1999–2004

The findings and conclusions in this report are those of the author(s) and do not necessarily represent the official position of the Centers for Disease Control and Prevention.

S. O. Griffin (✉) · K. Jones
Division of Oral Health, Centers for Disease Control and Prevention, Atlanta, GA, USA
e-mail: sig1@cdc.gov; Kari.Jones@ihsmarkit.com

C. Zaror, R. Mariño (eds.), *Introduction to Economic Evaluation in Oral Health Care*, https://doi.org/10.1007/978-3-030-96289-0_2

and 2011–2016, the percentage of adults aged 65+ years who had not lost all their natural teeth increased from 73% to 83%, and the mean number of retained teeth among these adults increased from 19 to 21 (CDC 2019).

The high prevalence of tooth decay among low-income adults of all ages is likely the result of financial barriers (Vujicic et al. 2016). Many poor and older adults do not have access to public dental benefits. Fee-for-service or "original" Medicare, the US public health insurance program for older adults and some individuals with disabilities, does not cover routine preventive or restorative dental services (Medicare 2020); some Medicare Advantage plans (Medicare Part C) include coverage for dental services (KFF 2017). Medicaid, the public health insurance program for certain categories of eligible low-income persons that is administered by the states and jointly funded by states and the federal government, typically does not cover comprehensive dental services—in 2015, only 11 states did so (CHCS 2015).

What can be done to address this health issue? The status quo could be maintained, or evidence-based solutions described in the literature as having been effective include (1) Medicaid coverage of routine dental services, which if implemented in all states could affect all eligible enrollees regardless of age (Decker and Lipton 2015); (2) a Medicare dental benefit, which, if added, could affect all beneficiaries regardless of income (Chavez et al. 2019); and (3) introduce innovative practice models that could include increasing use of teledentistry, with lower-cost providers such as dental hygienists triaging patients in need of restorative care to dentists (Khan and Omar 2013).

2.1.2 *Question 2: How to Reduce Unmet Treatment Needs Among School children*

Let us next consider a community that has identified unmet dental treatment needs as one of the primary causes of school absenteeism and poor school performance. The community has decided to explore options to increase access to preventive and restorative dental care. They are considering four evidence-based programmatic approaches. Under approach 1, children would be screened for dental caries by dental hygienists in each school and then referred to participating dentists for preventive and needed restorative care (CPSTF 2017b). In approach 2, teams of dental hygienists and assistants would provide sealants and fluoride varnish using portable dental equipment onsite at the school and then inform parents about their child's unmet treatment needs (CPSTF 2017b). In approach 3, children would receive preventive and restorative care by dentists in a van onsite at the school (Gupta et al. 2019). With approach 4, which has some evidence of effectiveness, the community would implement a policy requiring all children to be screened by a dentist prior to registering for school. A referral network would be established for children who did not have a dental home (CDHP 2019).

2.1.3 Question 3: An Insurance Company Serving Veterans Is Examining How to Reduce Oral Cancer Incidence and Mortality in Their Insured Population

The company estimates that about 50% of its enrollees are over age 50 years and are current or past smokers. Options include retaining the status quo or considering implementing one of the following evidence-based programs: (1) reimburse dentists to screen all adult patients (AAOM 2010; ADA 2019) and (2) reimburse dentists as well as primary care providers to screen for and counsel adult patients regarding tobacco use and alcohol misuse (USPSTF 2013).

What criteria should be used to identify the best course of action in the above scenarios? To evaluate the economic impacts of competing alternatives, decision-makers would typically want to know the population's risk for the disease, related treatment costs, and the relative effectiveness and costs of the competing alternatives (Haddix et al. 2003). To allocate their scarce resources most efficiently, they would benefit from knowing which of the alternatives offers the highest value (i.e., the greatest gain in health per dollar spent). In the next section we discuss key reasons for conducting an economic evaluation and illustrate how an economic evaluation could help determine potential costs, benefits, and the value of a possible intervention, using public dental insurance for adults as an example.

2.2 Key Benefits from Conducting an Economic Evaluation

Economic evaluations can inform decision-makers on which policies, programs, and interventions would offer the highest value. The overarching goal of all economic analyses is to determine how to use limited resources as efficiently as possible (Haddix et al. 2003). Efficiency in economics is typically defined as either achieving the greatest level of outcome (e.g., health gain, improvement in quality of life) for a given amount of resources (e.g., money) or using the least amount of resources to achieve a given level of outcome (Nicholson and Snyder 2016). An economic evaluation can help us to (1) identify the burden (e.g., cost and reduced quality of life) of oral diseases; (2) quantify how much of the burden could be prevented with various interventions, policies, and programs; (3) quantify the cost of various alternatives and the most efficient manner in which to implement and deliver them; and (4) quantify the trade-offs from implementing various alternatives and identify those that offer the highest value. Each of the first three components, which are necessary to identify the highest-value alternative, in themselves could provide useful information that policymakers and other stakeholders can consider in decision-making (Haddix et al. 2003). In this section we expand upon these key reasons to conduct an economic evaluation, provide examples from the published literature, and use hypothetical data from a hypothetical country to illustrate some of the calculations needed for decision-makers to evaluate alternatives. We assume that in this hypothetical country, public health insurance for the low-income enrollees is administered regionally and for older adults nationally. Low-income retirees would be eligible for both types of public insurance. Decision-makers in this country consider two evidence-based policy options to address the dental needs of public health insurance enrollees—adding dental benefits to public insurance for persons with low income (Decker and Lipton 2015) and adding benefits for retirement-age persons (Willink et al., 2016). The assumptions used in these calculations are provided in Table 2.1.

2.2.1 *Quantify Cost/Burden of Oral Condition*

The burden, or the magnitude of the health problem, can be expressed in monetary terms (commonly referred to as the cost of illness) or by the loss in health or well-being attributable to the problem (e.g., loss in quality of life) (Haddix et al. 2003). The two policy options in our illustrative example in this section address slightly different, but overlapping, populations. A decision-maker evaluating the costs and outcomes to society from providing public dental insurance to all low-income or to all retirement-age adults, compared to not providing insurance, likely would want to know the burden of untreated dental disease in these two populations in order to inform the assessment of the options (Haddix et al. 2003). Providing dental benefits also can improve periodontal health and reduce tooth loss (Burt and Eklund 2005), but for ease of illustration we will limit our discussion to caries. When estimating the burden of disease, it is important to specify the time frame (Sanders et al. 2016). Again, to simplify calculations we assume that all new caries is treated at the end of 1 year and there are no additional costs thereafter, so we will use a time frame of 1 year. Let's further assume that our hypothetical country has 74 million low-income adults with a caries incidence of 38.7% and 37 million retirement-age adults with a

Table 2.1 Assumptions used in exercise to evaluate providing public dental insurance to working-age and retirement-age adults in hypothetical country

Two policies being considered: Provide public dental insurance to all low-income adults (*n* = 74 million (M)) Provide public dental insurance to all elderly adults (*n* = 37 M)
All new caries remains untreated for 1 year
Caries incidence among low-income and elderly without insurance is 38.7% and 15.9%, respectively
Restorative dental costs per person ($600) are three times higher than preventive services costs ($200)
Each case of caries is associated with productivity losses of $18
Without public dental insurance, the probability of receiving preventive care among low-income adults of all ages is 30% and for elderly adults (regardless of income) is 48%.
With public dental insurance, restorative visits and associated costs decrease by 25%, but preventive visits and associated costs increase by 50%

caries incidence of 15.9%. The number of cases of caries that remain untreated for 1 year would be 28.6 million and 5.9 million for low-income and retirement-age adults, respectively. Information on untreated dental caries cases alone is likely insufficient for decision-makers to evaluate the two options. Before proceeding to the next paragraph of the exercise, jot down what additional information decision-makers might want to know when considering these two policy options.

Information about the burden of untreated disease (i.e., caries) could also be useful to the decision-maker (Haddix et al. 2003). In terms of impact, persons with untreated caries may experience pain and infection that can limit their food choices. The Global Burden of Disease project uses a common metric, disability-adjusted life year (DALY), to quantify the loss in quality of life for health conditions in all regions and for most countries in the world (GBD 2016). With this information, decision-makers can rank diseases on their relative burden. DALYs, the loss in well-being attributable to having the condition for 1 year, can range in value from 0, representing perfect health, to 1, representing death. The Global Burden of Disease has estimated disability weights for three oral conditions: severe tooth loss (having 8 or fewer natural teeth) with a disability weight of 0.073; severe periodontitis (a clinical attachment loss of more than 6 mm or a gingival pocket depth of more than 5 mm) with a disability weight of 0.0079; and untreated dental caries with a disability weight of 0.012 (Marcenes et al. 2013). The total DALYs, or equivalent loss in annual quality of life attributable to the disease in the population of interest, will depend on the disability weight associated with one case of the disease and the annual number of cases (WHO).

Returning to our two hypothetical options to reduce caries among adults, if we multiply the annual number of cases in our hypothetical country (recall we are assuming that caries remains untreated for 1 year) by the disability weight for untreated caries, the annual DALYs attributable to having untreated dental caries for a year among low-income and older adults would be 0.34 million and 0.07 million, respectively (Table 2.2).

As an outcome measure and by themselves, DALYs do not provide an estimate of the monetary costs associated with an illness (WHO). The items to include in estimating these costs will depend on the perspective of the study (i.e., who is internalizing the cost). At a bare minimum, costs estimated from the payer perspective include treatment (also known as direct) costs. The most expansive perspective is societal, where all relevant and measurable costs incurred by society are included. Thus, the costs to society would include both the direct treatment costs and indirect

Table 2.2 Outcomes for hypothetical country under status quo, no public dental insurance

	Untreated caries cases (M)	DALYS (M)	Preventive costs (M)	Restorative costs (M)	Indirect productivity losses (M)	Total costs (M)
Low income	28.6	0.34	$4440	$17,160	$515	$22,115
Elderly	5.9	0.07	$3552	$3540	$106	$7198

M is millions, *DALYs* is disability-adjusted life years

costs, such as lost productivity (Haddix et al. 2003). Persons may miss work to obtain restorative care, and symptoms arising from untreated caries may also result in missed workdays or being less productive at work. The Global Burden of Disease provides global and regional estimates of lost productivity attributable to the three oral conditions it tracks (Righolt et al. 2018). The estimated global productivity losses in 2015 US dollars attributable to untreated dental caries were $22.1 billion, to severe periodontitis $28.9 billion, and to severe tooth loss $126.7 billion (Righolt et al. 2018).

Critical pieces of information needed to estimate the cost of illness (i.e., untreated caries among low-income and retirement-age adults in this exercise) are the number of new cases and the associated cost per case (Haddix et al. 2003). Using a societal perspective, let's assume that the per-person cost of restorative care per case of caries is $600 US dollars and the loss in productivity associated with one case of caries is $18 US dollars (Table 2.1). The annual cost burden for caries among low-income and retirement-age adults would be, respectively, $17,675 million ($17,160 million + $515 million from Table 2.2) and $3646 million ($3540 million + $106 million from Table 2.2).

In estimating the cost of dental diseases, some studies (e.g., GBD 2015; Righolt et al. 2018) examine total dental expenditures instead of costs associated with specific dental conditions such as dental caries. Several published analyses, however, have estimated the cost of illness for severe early childhood caries from the Medicaid (payer) perspective (Kanellis et al. 2000; Griffin et al. 2000; Bruen et al. 2016). Because very young children are more likely to receive care for multiple, complex dental restorations under general anesthesia than other age groups, these studies have focused on the number of caries-related hospital operating room encounters and associated costs (Kanellis et al. 2000; Griffin et al. 2000; Bruen et al. 2016). The most recent analysis of Medicaid claims data in six states (Bruen et al. 2016) found that 0.5% of enrolled children received caries-related treatment in an operating room at an average cost in 2010 and 2011 of about $2500 per case.

Knowledge of the relative burden of diseases can help to prioritize public health spending. For example, if a state legislature had budgeted $20 million US dollars to improve children's health, the set of policy/programs/interventions from which to choose could be daunting. Understanding the burden of various diseases and conditions among children could help narrow the list of interventions to consider. For example, the United States Preventive Services Task Force (USPSTF) makes recommendations regarding the effectiveness of various preventive services delivered in healthcare settings (Kemper et al. 2018). The recommendations of the USPSTF influence how insurance companies in the USA set copays (i.e., how much of the cost of an intervention must be paid out of pocket by the patient; Griffin et al. 2014). Services provided by dentists are not evaluated by the USPSTF (Kemper et al. 2018). Oral health services currently recommended by the USPSTF include primary care providers prescribing fluoride supplements to children whose household tap water has low fluoride content and providing fluoride varnish to children under age 5 years (USPSTF 2014). Many recommendations by the USPSTF are rated "I," meaning that there is insufficient evidence to recommend the service—almost half of all recommendations regarding childhood screening have an "I" rating, including primary care providers conducting caries risk assessments in very young children (Kemper et al. 2018). Conducting studies to assess effectiveness of an intervention is costly (Kemper et al. 2018). Efforts to prioritize effectiveness research could include an assessment of the relative burden of diseases related to the interventions under consideration (GBD 2015).

2.2.2 *Quantify How Much of the Burden Could Be Averted with Intervention*

Once the burden in terms of health outcomes and costs has been documented, a possible follow-up question to consider is, "How much disease and associated costs could be prevented by each of the proposed alternatives?" To answer this question, we would need to know the cost of the illness and how effective the intervention/program/policy is in preventing it.

The Community Preventive Services Task Force (CPSTF) identifies population health interventions that have been shown to "improve health directly; prevent or reduce risky behaviors, disease, injuries, complications, or detrimental environmental or social factors; or promote healthy behaviors and environments" based on available scientific evidence (CPSTF 2019a). These recommendations can inform decision-makers as they consider public health policies and interventions and their associated cost (CPSTF 2019b). Two population-level oral health interventions currently recommended by the CPSTF are community water fluoridation (CPSTF 2017a) and school-based sealant programs (CPSTF 2017b). The CPSTF and its scientists conduct systematic reviews of economic evaluations of interventions the CPSTF has deemed to be effective. The systematic review of six economic evaluations of water fluoridation conducted between 2001 and 2013 (Ran et al. 2016) found that the annual benefit from the societal perspective (averted treatment and productivity costs) from water fluoridation in 2013 US dollars ranged from $5.49 to $93.19 per person. The systematic review of economic evaluations of school dental sealant programs (Griffin et al. 2017) found that the annual averted treatment and productivity losses per child attributable to sealant programs in 2014 US dollars from six studies ranged from $18.78 to $233.86.

Studies have used claims data to evaluate the effectiveness of implementing various policies and interventions by comparing outcomes and treatment costs for persons exposed to the intervention compared to those not exposed (CDC 1999; Blackburn et al. 2017). Thus, significant averted treatment costs and outcomes could imply the intervention was effective. For example, an analysis of Louisiana Medicaid claims data for children, aged 1–5 years, found that children living in parishes (equivalent to a county in other US states) without fluoridated drinking water were three times as likely to receive restorative dental care in a hospital operating room and had dental treatment costs twice as high as children living in parishes with fluoridated drinking water (CDC 1999). Another analysis of Alabama Medicaid claims data published in 2017 in JAMA Pediatrics (Blackburn et al. 2017) compared caries-related treatment visits and expenditures between enrolled children who had received a caries-preventive service from a dentist or primary care provider prior to age 2 and those children who had not. The difference in the treatment expenditures between the two groups would provide an estimate of averted caries treatment costs associated with receiving preventive dental services prior to age 2 years. The findings disproved the hypothesis, which was surprising—compared to children who did not receive early preventive care, caries-related visits and annual treatment costs were significantly higher for a child who received early preventive care from a dentist and were not statistically different for those receiving early care from a primary care provider. It is important to keep in mind that treatment and control groups in claims data are not randomly assigned, and thus they may be subject to selection bias, that is, there may be factors that influence whether a child is in the treatment group and which could also be affecting outcomes and costs (Jensen et al. 2015). For example, very young children who visit the dentist may have a higher caries risk than children who don't. There are methods, however, to reduce selection bias (e.g., propensity scores, instrumental variables, regression discontinuity models). The JAMA Pediatrics study, for example, used propensity scores to match children in the intervention and treatment groups.

Selection bias in claims data also can result from differences among providers who provide treatment. For example, dentists who place sealants may be less likely to place restorations on incipient caries that could possibly remineralize in the absence of the restoration. If this were the case, then part of the averted treatment costs could be due to dentists' treatment decisions as opposed to sealant effectiveness. Weintraub and colleagues found that delivering dental sealants to Medicaid-enrolled, North Carolina children at high risk for caries was associated with lower future restorative costs. The researchers included an indicator variable for each dental provider to control for the effect of differences in dentists' treatment criteria (Weintraub et al. 2001).

Let's return to our hypothetical country trying to reduce untreated dental caries among adults and make a few more simplifying assumptions: (1) providing public dental insurance would increase consumption of preventive care by 50% and reduce the annual number of cases of untreated caries and associated costs by 25% (Table 2.1). From Table 2.3, we see that providing public dental insurance to low-income adults in the hypothetical country would reduce untreated caries cases to

Table 2.3 Outcomes for hypothetical country with public dental insurance

	Untreated caries cases (M)	DALYS (M)	Preventive costs (M)	Restorative costs (M)	Indirect productivity losses (M)	Total costs (M)
Low income	21.5	0.26	$6660	$12,870	$386	$19,916
Elderly	4.4	0.05	$5328	$2655	$80	$8063

M is millions, *DALYs* is disability-adjusted life years

21.5 million cases and DALYs to 0.26 million. It would further reduce restorative costs and productivity losses to $12,870 million and $386 million, respectively (Table 2.3). Averted adverse outcomes and costs would be the difference between providing public dental insurance and the status quo (Table 2.4) or 7.1 million averted cases, 0.09 million averted DALYs, and $4419 million in averted cost of illness ($4290 million in restorative costs + $129 million in productivity losses from Table 2.4). Providing public dental insurance to retirement-age adults in the hypothetical country could avert 1.5 million cases of untreated caries, 0.02 million DALYS, and $912 million in the cost of illness (Table 2.4).

Although information quantifying gains in health and averted costs from implementing various interventions provides better information for ranking intervention alternatives, we can still do better by using additional information to make more informed decisions. What else would you like to know if you had to determine which intervention to implement?

2.2.3 *Quantify Costs of Interventions and How to Deliver Them Most Efficiently*

Information on the cost of the intervention can be combined with information from the previous section on averted disease and cost of illness to determine whether the intervention offers good value (Haddix et al. 2003). This will be described in more detail in the next section. Cost information is critical to program efficiency (i.e., delivering the intervention at the lowest cost). In measuring costs, perspective again matters (Haddix et al. 2003). From the payer's perspective (e.g., insurance company) the primary cost incurred is the amount paid to the provider, e.g., reimbursement fee (Haddix et al. 2003). State Medicaid agencies in the USA typically pay the same amount for the same dental procedure (e.g., sealant) for a child regardless of how efficient the provider is (KFF 2018). On the other hand, a local program or dentist would want to know the cost of all resources used to deliver sealants because understanding these costs would be a key to sustainability (Griffin et al. 2018). An efficient program or dentist has lower costs and, as a result, will require less revenue to operate. Thus, an efficient school sealant program would be more likely to sustain

Table 2.4 Difference between outcomes for providing public dental insurance and status quo for hypothetical country

	Untreated caries cases (M)	DALYS (M)	Preventive costs (M)	Restorative costs (M)	Indirect productivity losses (M)	Total costs (M)
Low income	−7.1	−0.09	$2220	−$4290	−$129	−$2199
Elderly	−1.5	−0.02	$1776	−$885	−$27	$864

M is millions, *DALYs* is disability-adjusted life years

itself on Medicaid/private insurance reimbursements alone than would an inefficient program (Griffin et al. 2018).

An accurate understanding of the delivery process and resource costs can also be important in evaluating program efficiency over time (Griffin et al. 2018). The systematic reviews on economic evaluations of school sealant programs (Griffin et al. 2017) and community water fluoridation (Ran et al. 2016) conducted for the Community Preventive Services Task Force identified the key resource cost components and those components that had the greatest influence on total cost. Resource cost categories for school sealant programs included labor, equipment, sealant material and other disposable goods, travel, and administrative (Griffin et al. 2017). Because labor costs accounted for about two-thirds of total costs, using labor as efficiently as possible can have a large impact on costs (Griffin et al. 2017). Scherrer et al. (2007) simulated how school sealant programs could use their labor more efficiently. They found that for large programs, it would be more efficient to have one extra chair and dental assistant. This would allow teams of operators to move to an open chair rather than stay at the same chair while infection control barriers were being changed. Lower paid providers (e.g., dental assistants) could then change infection control barriers alone. For these larger programs, the lower costs associated with dental hygienists not having to wait for each barrier change could offset the cost of the extra assistant and chair (Scherrer et al. 2007).

Scherrer also showed that screening and sealing children at two different times instead of at the same seating would be more efficient for school sealant programs operating in states with practice acts that require a dentist to screen the child prior to dental hygienists/assistants placing sealants. Separating the screening process from providing sealants minimized the number of hours the highest cost labor input—the dentist—spent at the school.

For community water fluoridation, the CPSTF review identified three types of costs—one-time fixed investment in fluoridation facilities; recurrent fixed costs to maintain, operate, and monitor fluoridation; and variable recurrent costs including labor and chemicals (Ran et al. 2016). Because fixed costs accounted for the largest share of total cost, water system population had the most influence on total cost. Annual per capita costs were less than one dollar (2013 US dollars) for communities >20,000 people, compared to a range of $3.36–$24.38 for communities of smaller sizes.

Better understanding of different provider resource costs could become important to payers as well, given the shift in payments for dental care from fee-for-service (reimbursement per procedure) to capitated (reimbursement per person). To accurately allocate the capitated fee among various providers serving the same patient, knowledge of their relative contributions to total costs would be helpful (Griffin et al. 2018).

Cost analyses from the payer perspective have also been used to evaluate policies and can provide insight into barriers and facilitators of policy implementation. For example, to increase dental utilization among low-income children, policymakers have tried to stimulate the supply of dentists willing to accept publicly insured children by raising reimbursement rates for dental procedures. The impact of this policy was evaluated by Decker (2011). Using the reimbursement for dental prophylaxis as a proxy for dental fees, Decker found that increasing this fee from $20 to $30 US dollars would increase past 6-month dental use among youth by about 4 percentage points. In fact, youth in states where the Medicaid reimbursement was $30 or more had utilization rates that were not statistically different from privately insured children.

Now, let us return to our example of strategies to decrease untreated dental caries among adults. Recall that we assumed that providing public insurance increases the consumption of preventive care by 50%. The increase in preventive costs would thus measure the cost associated with providing public dental insurance. From Table 2.1, we see that the percentage of low-income and retirement-age adults receiving preventive dental care under the status quo is 30% and 48%, respectively, and that the annual cost to provide preventive care to a person is $200. From Table 2.2, we see that the annual cost of preventive care under the status quo is $4440 million for low-income and $3552 million for retirement-age adults. Providing public dental insurance would increase preventive care costs to $6660 million for low-income and to $5328 million for retirement-age adults (Table 2.3). The incremental cost of providing public dental insurance would thus be $2220 million for low-income and $1776 million for retirement-age adults (Table 2.4).

2.2.4 *Quantify Trade-Offs to Identify Highest-Value Alternative*

We have now come to the gold standard of economic evaluations—combining information on the cost and averted burden of various interventions/programs/policies to identify the alternative with the highest value. To illustrate, let's return to our example on how best to reduce untreated dental caries in adults. In the previous sections we found that the averted dental treatment costs of public dental insurance ($4419 million from adding averted treatment costs and productivity losses in Table 2.4) offset the increased preventive costs ($2220 million from Table 2.4) for low-income adults. Thus, this option saved society $2199 million (total costs in Table 2.4) in annual costs. In economic evaluation, strategy A would dominate strategy B if it has a higher health gain and lower cost (Haddix et al. 2003). Using this criterion, providing dental insurance to low-income adults in the hypothetical country would dominate the strategy of not providing dental insurance because public dental insurance was associated with lower costs, fewer cases of untreated caries, and improved quality of life (i.e., decreased DALYs in Table 2.4).

For retirement-age adults in this exercise, however, the decreases in cost of illness did not offset the increased cost of prevention. Providing public dental insurance to retirement-age adults would increase total costs by $864 million and decrease cases by 1.5 million and DALYS by 0.02 million (Table 2.4). This option, however, could still offer good value. The cost to avert one case of untreated caries would be $576 ($864/1.5) and to avert one DALY, $43,200 ($864/0.02). Our hypothetical country would have to compare the incremental costs and health gains from providing public dental insurance for older adults to other competing alternative uses of the resources required to provide dental insurance (Haddix et al. 2003). Why, in our example, was public dental insurance cost-saving for low-income but not for retirement-age adults? Likely factors include their higher caries risk and lower consumption of preventive care under the status quo.

This example was meant for illustrative purposes to provide insight regarding questions an economic analysis can address. Because of our simplified assumptions, this example cannot be used to evaluate actual policies. For example, it is unlikely that all cases of new caries will be treated within the year, and the costs of administering public dental insurance may vary between low-income adults and retirement-age adults. In the USA, for example, public insurance for persons aged 65+ years is administered by the federal government, whereas for low-income adults, it is jointly administered by each state and the federal government (KFF 2016).

There are several published analyses of interventions to prevent dental disease that can inform considerations about public funding. The findings of the CPSTF, for example, can be used by agencies funding public health research and programs (CPSTF 2019b). The two interventions currently funded by the CDC Division of Oral Health to improve oral health outcomes in states, territories, and tribes are community water fluoridation and school sealant programs, (NCCDPHP 2018). These are the only oral health interventions for which the CPSTF has found strong evidence to recommend (CPSTF 2019c). The CPSTF review of community water fluoridation found wide variation in annual averted costs per person estimated from the societal perspective in the six included studies. In all studies, however, the averted treatment costs exceeded the intervention costs (Ran et al. 2016). The review of school sealant programs found that school sealant programs were cost-saving when they provided services in schools where the children were at high risk for caries (Griffin et al. 2017).

2.3 Determining When to Implement Economic Analysis in Program Evaluation and the Most Appropriate Type of Analysis

Evaluation is a systematic method for collecting, analyzing, and using data to examine the effectiveness and efficiency of programs and, as importantly, to contribute to continuous program improvement.[1] As illustrated in Sect. 2.2, an economic evaluation always includes the component of costs (e.g., cost of illness, intervention, or per unit of health gained), with the ultimate goal of measuring efficiency (i.e., is health gain achieved at lowest cost). Data for an economic evaluation can be obtained prospectively (i.e., collection throughout the intervention time frame, which also could be concurrent with the collection of data to evaluate effectiveness)

[1] https://www.cdc.gov/eval/index.htm

or retrospectively (after the intervention is implemented using data sources such as claims or hospital records (O'Connell and Griffin 2011). The benefits of prospective data collection are that it allows for the ongoing review of data and for modification of data collection methods to ensure accuracy and to address identified reporting issues (O'Connell and Griffin 2011). In addition, concurrent evaluation of effectiveness and costs could help ensure that the economic evaluation was conducted with the same rigor (i.e., random assignment, concurrent control group, and consideration of all aspects of program implementation and service delivery) as the effectiveness study. It also may be less costly to collect cost data at the same time as effectiveness data, as opposed to designing a separate economic evaluation later.

When conducting the economic analysis simultaneously with other evaluation efforts, it is important to only include the costs of resources that typically are required to set up and administer the program (O'Connell and Griffin 2011). Costs associated with collecting and analyzing data for evaluation purposes that would not normally be incurred by a program should be excluded. It also is important to understand how the cost structure will vary over time (O'Connell and Griffin 2011). For example, if there are costs unique to starting the program (e.g., economies of scale or high fixed costs), or a learning curve associated with administering the program, then costs incurred during the first few years of operation may be significantly higher than costs incurred by an established program. An economic evaluation would be more accurate by including both start-up and steady-state costs (O'Connell and Griffin 2011).

On the other hand, there are interventions with strong evidence of effectiveness but insufficient evidence to determine cost-effectiveness (Carande-Kulis et al. 2000). Researchers may want to determine effectiveness before allocating resources to economic evaluation. The CPSTF often conducts separate systematic reviews for evaluations of effectiveness and economic evaluation, with economic evaluations typically only being conducted if there is evidence of effectiveness. Among the criteria used by the CPSTF to identify interventions for which to conduct systematic reviews of economic evaluations is strong evidence of effectiveness (Carande-Kulis et al. 2000).

Even when there is strong evidence of effectiveness and cost-effectiveness for an intervention in the literature, local programs may find it useful and more informative to periodically assess their cost-effectiveness using their own data (Griffin et al. 2018). For example, because of the large variation in reported SSP costs (range: $33–$163 per child in 2014 US dollars) in the CPSTF systematic review of economic analyses and the CPSTF finding that there is limited evidence of effectiveness and cost-effectiveness for sealant programs serving children with low-caries risk (Griffin et al. 2017; CPSTF 2017a), CDC's Division of Oral Health encourages local school sealant programs in their funded states to periodically assess their impact and costs (NCCDPHP 2018). Recognizing that following children longitudinally is costly and may not be feasible, CDC has developed a streamlined approach that requires participating programs to collect data on the number of children served, children's caries risk at baseline screening, 1-year sealant retention, and quantity of resources used to administer programs and deliver sealants in school settings. With these data, a web application, SEALS (https://www.cdc.gov/oralhealth/dental_sealant_program/seals.htm), developed by CDC can simulate the amount of caries that would have occurred with and without the program (i.e., averted caries) and the cost to provide services. The Division of Oral Health in the CDC can use these de-identified, standardized cost, and effectiveness estimates per sealant program to develop efficiency benchmarks, controlling for factors that are beyond a local school sealant program's control (e.g., state dental practice act).

Our examples in the previous sections illustrate the many types of questions an economic analysis can answer. In Sect. 2.2 we provided examples of two types of economic analysis: (1) cost (i.e., cost of intervention, cost of illness, and cost of intervention after netting out the cost of illness; see Chap. 3), and (2) cost-effectiveness (CEA; net cost per gained outcome; see Chap. 7). A cost-utility analysis (see Chap. 9) is a type of CEA that examines the net cost per gained increase in quality of life or well-being (Haddix et al. 2003). In our example in the previous section on providing public dental insurance to adults, net cost per averted DALY would be considered a cost-utility analysis, whereas net cost per averted case of untreated caries would not. Cost-utility analyses also can be easier to interpret than other cost-effectiveness analyses when comparing interventions with different health outcomes or evaluating an intervention that affects multiple outcomes—in cost-utility analyses the outcomes are all converted to a common metric, such as DALYs. Another type of economic analyses we have not yet described is a cost-benefit analysis. Whereas cost-effectiveness analyses measure the net cost per gained health or quality of life outcome, a cost-benefit analysis monetizes the gained outcomes as well as resource costs (Haddix et al. 2003). Typically, the gained outcome is monetized by how much individuals on average would be willing to pay for it (Haddix et al. 2003). One caveat to conducting a cost-benefit analysis is that it can be difficult and costly to monetize outcomes. An example of a cost-benefit analysis is provided in Chap. 8.

The evaluation question will largely determine which type of economic analysis is most appropriate for your evaluation. Table 2.5 provides a summary of what we have discussed in this chapter regarding selecting the most appropriate type of economic analysis for your evaluation question. As in any analysis, an important consideration is availability and quality of data to perform the analysis.

Table 2.5 Considerations for selecting the appropriate type of economic analysis

Question to address	Type of economic analysis
How much is the cost to implement a policy, program, or intervention? Is the intervention being delivered at minimum cost?	Cost of intervention
What is the absolute or relative magnitude of the problem?	Cost of illness
Is cost of implementing policy, program, or intervention offset by reductions in the cost of illness?	Net cost (typically conducted from payer perspective)
What is the net cost per gained health outcome from implementing the intervention?	Cost-effectiveness (utility) analysis
Is the dollar value of the benefit offset by the cost?	Cost benefit

References

American Academy of Oral Medicine. Oral Cancer Screening (2010) https://www.aaom.com/clinical-practice-statement%2D%2Doral-cancer-screening. Accessed 10 Aug 2020

American Dental Association (ADA) (2019) ADA expands policy on oral cancer detection to include oropharyngeal cancer. https://www.ada.org/en/publications/ada-news/2019-archive/september/ada-expands-policy-on-oral-cancer-detection-to-include-oropharyngeal-cancer. Accessed 10 Aug 2020

Blackburn J, Morrisey MA, Sen B (2017) Outcomes associated with early preventive dental care among Medicaid-enrolled children in Alabama. JAMA Pediatr 171(9):918–919

Bruen BK, Steinmitz E, Byshee T, Glassman P, Ku L (2016) Potentially preventable dental care in operating rooms for children enrolled in Medicaid. J Am Dent Assoc 147(9):702–708

Burt BA, Eklund SA (eds) (2005) Dentistry, dental practice, and the community. Elsevier/Saunders, St. Louis

Carande-Kulis VG, Maciosek MV, Briss PA, Teutsch SM, Zaza S et al (2000) Methods for systematic reviews of economic evaluations for the guide to community preventive services. Am J Prev Med 18(1S):75–91

Center for Health Care Strategies (CHCS) (2015) Medicaid adult dental benefits: an overview. https://www.ncsl.org/Portals/1/Documents/magazine/articles/2016/TRENDS_OralHealth.pdf. Accessed January 3, Accessed 10 Aug 2020

Centers for Disease Control and Prevention (CDC) (Griffin SO, Gooch BF, Tomar SL) (1999) Fluoridation and costs of Medicaid treatment for dental decay—Louisiana, 1995–1996. Morb Mortal Wkly Rep 48(34):753–757

Centers for Disease Control and Prevention (CDC) (Lin M Griffin SO, Gooch BF, Espinoza L, Wei L) (2019) Oral health surveillance report: trends in dental caries and sealants, tooth retention, and edentulism, United States, 1999–2004 to 2011–2016. https://www.cdc.gov/oralhealth/publications/OHSR-2019-index.html. Accessed 12 June 2020

Chavez EM, Calvo JM, Jones JA (2019) Oral health and older Americans: a Santa Fe Group White Paper. http://santafegroup.org/manage/wp-content/uploads/2018/01/Oral-Health-and-Older-Americans-A-Santa-Fe-Group-White-Paper.pdf. Accessed 10 Aug 2020

Children's Dental Health Project (CDHP) (2019) state dental screening laws for children: examining the trend and impact. https://s3.amazonaws.com/cdhp/Matt+Jacob/Dental+Screening+Law+Report+(Jan+2019).pdf. Accessed 10 Aug 2020

Community Preventive Services Task Force (CPSTF) (2017a) Dental caries (cavities): community water fluoridation dental caries (cavities): community water fluoridation. Community guide. https://www.thecommunityguide.org/findings/dental-caries-cavities-community-water-fluoridation. Accessed 11 June 2020

Community Preventive Services Task Force (CPSTF) (2017b) Dental caries (cavities): school-based dental sealant delivery programs. Community guide. https://www.thecommunityguide.org/findings/dental-caries-cavities-school-based-dental-sealant-delivery-programs. Accessed 11 June 2020

Community Preventive Services Task Force (CPSTF) (2019a) Develop evidence-based policies. https://www.thecommunityguide.org/about/policy-development. Accessed 14 Aug 2020

Community Preventive Services Task Force (CPSTF) (2019b) Inform funding decisions and fund proposals. https://www.thecommunityguide.org/about/funding-development. Accessed 13 Aug 2020

Community Preventive Services Task Force (CPSTF) (2019c) Oral health. https://www.thecommunityguide.org/topic/oral-health. Accessed 14 Aug 2020

Decker SL (2011) Medicaid payment levels to dentists and access to dental care among children and adolescents. JAMA 306(2):187–193

Decker SL, Lipton BJ (2015) Do Medicaid benefit expansions have teeth? The effect of Medicaid adult dental coverage on the use of dental services and oral health. J Health Econ 44:212–225

GBD 2015 Disease and Injury Incidence and Prevalence Collaborators (2016) Global, regional, and national incidence, prevalence, and years lived with disability for 310 acute and chronic diseases and injuries, 1990–2015: a systematic analysis for the Global Burden of Disease Study 2015. Lancet 388(10053):1545–1602

Griffin SO, Gooch B, Beltran E, Sutherland J, Barsley R (2000) Dental services, costs and factors associated with hospitalization for Medicaid-eligible children. J Public Health Dent 60(1):21–27

Griffin SO, Barker LK, Wei L, Li C-H, Albuquerque MS, Gooch BF (2014) Use of dental care and preventive services effective in preventing tooth decay among U.S. children and adolescents—Medical Expenditure Panel Survey (U.S.), 2003–2009 and National Health and Nutrition Examination Survey (U.S), 2005–2010. Morb Mort Wkly Rep 63(Suppl 2):54–60

Griffin SO, Naavaal S, Scherrer CR, Patel M, Chattopadhay S (2017) Evaluation of school-based dental sealant programs: a community guide systematic economic review. Am J Prev Med 52(3):407–415

Griffin SO, Jones K, Naavaal S, Arlotta D, Demopoulos C, O'Connell J (2018) Estimating the cost of school sealant programs with minimal data. J Public Health Dent 78(1):17–24

Griffin SO, Griffin PM, Li C-H, Bailey WD, Brunson D, Jones JA (2019) Changes in older adults' oral health and disparities: 1999–2004 and 2011–2016. J Am Geriatr Soc 67(6):1152–1157

Gupta D, Hakim M, Patel D, Stow LC, Shin K et al (2019) Reaching vulnerable populations through portable and mobile dentistry – current and future opportunities. Dent J (Basel) 7(3):75

Haddix AC, Teutsch SM, Corso P (2003) Prevention effectiveness: a guide to decision making and economic evaluation. Oxford University Press, New York

Jensen ET, Cook SF, Allen JK, Logie J, Brookhart MA, Kappelman MD, Dellon ES (2015) Enrollment factors and bias of disease prevalence estimates in administrative claims data. Ann Epidemiol 25(7):519–525.e2

Kaiser Family Foundation (KFF) (2016) Access to dental care in Medicaid: spotlight on nonelderly adults. http://files.kff.org/attachment/issue-brief-access-to-dental-care-in-medicaid-spotlight-on-nonelderly-adults. Accessed 15 Aug 2020

Kaiser Family Foundation (KFF) (2017) Medicare advantage 2017 spotlight: enrollment market update. https://www.kff.org/medicare/issue-brief/medicare-advantage-. Accessed 10 Aug 2020

Kaiser Family Foundation (KFF) (2018) Medicaid benefits: dental services 2018. https://www.kff.org/medicaid/state-indicator/dental-services/?currentTimeframe=0&sortModel=%7B%22colId%22:%22Location%22,%22sort%22:%22asc%22%7D. Accessed 15 Aug 2020

Kanellis MJ, Damiano PC, Momany ET (2000) Medicaid costs associated with the hospitalization of young children for restorative dental treatment under general anesthesia. J Public Health Dent 60(1):28–32

Kassebaum NJ, Bernabé E, Dahiya M, Bhandari B, Murray CJL et al (2015) Global burden of untreated caries: a systematic review and metaregression. J Dent Res 94(5):650–658

Kemper AR, Krist AH, Tseng C-W (2018) Challenges in developing U.S. Preventive Services Task Force Child Health recommendations. Am J Prev Med 54(1S1):S63

Khan SA, Omar H (2013) Teledentistry in practice: literature review. Telemed J E Health 19(7):565–567

Marcenes W, Kassebaum NJ, Bernabe E, Flaxman A, Naghavi M, Lopez A, Murray CJ (2013) Global burden of oral conditions in 1990–2010: a systematic analysis. J Dent Res 92(7):592–597

Medicare. Dental Services 2020. https://www.medicare.gov/coverage/dental-services#:~:text=Medicare%20doesn't%20cover%20most,plates%2C%20or%20other%20dental%20devices.&text=Some%20Medicare%20Advantage%20Plans%20(Part,vision%2C%20hearing%2C%20or%20dental. Accessed 10 Aug 2020

National Center for Chronic Disease Prevention and Health Promotion (NCCDPHP). Notice of Funding Opportunities 2018. State, territorial, and tribal actions to improve oral health outcomes (DP18-1810). https://www.cdc.gov/chronicdisease/programs-impact/nofo/index.htm. Accessed 10 Aug 2020

Nicholson W, Snyder CM (2016) Microeconomic theory: basic principles and extensions. Cengage Learning, Boston

O'Connell J, Griffin S (2011) Overview of methods in economic analyses of behavioral interventions to promote oral health. J Public Health Dent 71:S101–S118

Ran T, Chattopadhyay SK, the Community Preventive Services Task Force (2016) Economic evaluation of community water fluoridation: a community guide systematic review. Am J Prev Med 50(6):790–796

Righolt AJ, Jevdjevic M, Marcenes W, Listl S (2018) Global-, regional-, and country-level economic impacts of dental diseases in 2015. J Dent Res 97(5):501–507

Sanders GD, Neumann PJ, Russell LB et al (2016) Recommendations for conduct, methodological practices, and reporting of cost-effectiveness analyses: Second Panel on Cost-Effectiveness in Health and Medicine. JAMA 316(10):1093-103

Scherrer CR, Griffin PM, Swann JL (2007) Public health sealant delivery programs: optimal delivery and the cost of practice acts. Med Decis Mak 27(6):762–771

U.S. Preventive Services Task Force (USPSTF) (2013) Oral cancer screening. Available at: https://www.uspreventiveservicestaskforce.org/uspstf/recommendation/oral-cancer-screening. Accessed 11 June 2020

U.S. Preventive Services Task Force (USPSTF) (2014) Prevention of dental caries in children from birth through age 5 years. http://www.uspreventiveservicestaskforce.org/uspstf/uspsdnch.htm. Accessed 11 June 2020

Vujicic M, Buchmueller T, Klein R (2016) Dental care presents the highest level of financial barriers, compared to other types of health care services. Health Aff 35(12):2176–2182

Weintraub JA, Stearns SC, Rozier RG et al (2001) Treatment outcomes and costs of dental sealants among children enrolled in Medicaid. Am J Public Health 91(11):1988-81

Willink A, Schoen C, Davis K (2016) Dental care and Medicare beneficiaries: access gaps, cost burdens, and policy options. Health Aff (Millwood) 35(12):2241–2248

World Health Organization (WHO). health statistics and information systems: metrics. https://www.who.int/healthinfo/global_burden_disease/metrics_daly/en/. Accessed 10 Aug 2020

Chapter 3
Measuring Cost in Oral Health Care

Laura Ternent, Tara Homer, Jing Shen, and Christopher R. Vernazza

3.1 Costing in Oral Health

In economic analyses of healthcare interventions, costs have historically received less research attention compared to effectiveness (often in the form of utilities see Chap. 4). Given their prominence as the numerator of the cost-effectiveness ratio, there is no doubt that costs should be valued and measured as rigorously as effectiveness. Ambiguity or confusion in cost calculation could hinder our ability to examine cost-effectiveness accurately and may lead to biased results. A set of clearly defined costing methodology and terminology is therefore essential, and this should be understood along with some important concepts on costing in healthcare.

Firstly, the notion of cost used in economics analysis is *opportunity cost* – when we choose to use resources one way, we lose the *opportunity* to use the resources in another desirable way. The *cost* of this decision is the benefits we could have obtained had we used them in another way. Strictly, *opportunity cost* is the benefits foregone from the resources if they had been used in the next best alternative. This is the founding principle of how costs are valued in economic evaluation. Secondly, in any cost analysis it is essential to specify the *costing perspective* (i.e. whose costs are being counted). A narrow but commonly adopted perspective examines costs from the healthcare provider's perspective, for example, health system costs, e.g. National Health System (NHS) in the UK or the Veterans Administration in the USA. This narrow perspective is often widened for different analysis purposes. A common extension is to include condition-related costs to the patients and their families. Additionally, research suggests that an important cost of oral health conditions is productivity loss due to absenteeism and presentism, which extends the costing perspective further to employers (Breckons et al. 2018). In some cases, it

L. Ternent (✉) · T. Homer · J. Shen · C. R. Vernazza
Newcastle University, Newcastle Upon Tyne, England
e-mail: laura.ternent@newcastle.ac.uk; tara.homer@newcastle.ac.uk; jing.shen@ncl.ac.uk; Christopher.Vernazza@newcastle.ac.uk

C. Zaror, R. Mariño (eds.), *Introduction to Economic Evaluation in Oral Health Care*, https://doi.org/10.1007/978-3-030-96289-0_3

may also be relevant to include costs to the sectors beyond health, for example, interventions to improve the oral health of children may have an impact on school attendance and educational attainments; therefore, the intervention may have implications for costs to the education sector (Seirawan et al. 2012). The extensions of costs beyond the healthcare provider's perspective are commonly termed as a societal perspective. Lastly, in oral healthcare, where services may not be free at point of access regardless of the healthcare system, it is important to distinguish between costs and charges. Charges in oral healthcare are a contribution paid by patients towards the costs of dental goods or services, and the level of the contribution is usually set by the healthcare provider. Charges do not necessarily reflect the true cost of providing the good or service and, therefore, are not appropriate to use when calculating costs from the healthcare provider's perspective. However, charges may be relevant in the cost calculation if a patient or societal perspective is taken, as they would fall within the costs borne by the patients.

Understanding the costing perspective paves the way for the first step in defining the two main cost categories in economic evaluation: *direct cost* and *indirect cost.*

Direct Cost covers all goods, services, and other resources that are consumed in the provision of a healthcare good or service, as well as any associated aspect in the follow-up to the care. Direct cost can include costs to both the healthcare provider and the patients and their families, depending on the perspective chosen.

Indirect Costs (structural) represent administrative support resources and logistical support costs. This category could include the costs of electrical energy, maintenance costs, cleaning costs, and administrative support.

Indirect Costs *(productivity)* usually refer to productivity loss due to illness and this will include absenteeism and presentism.

Within the cost categories, particularly direct cost, costing terminologies are defined below with respect to their specific use in oral healthcare.

Total Cost is the sum of all costs being considered in an analysis. This would cover all costs related to delivering an oral healthcare intervention if only direct cost is considered and will also include productivity loss due to the oral health condition if indirect cost is also counted. Total cost is comprised of both fixed cost and variable cost components.

Fixed Cost is a cost that remains the same regardless of the quantity of output in the short term, i.e. a cost that is unrelated to the number of teeth or patients treated, for instance, the rental cost of the practice facility. Fixed cost may, however, vary with time.

Variable Cost is a cost that varies with the level of output, i.e. the cost related to the number of teeth or patients treated, for example, materials used in making a dental crown.

Average Cost is calculated by dividing total cost by the quantity of output, so it represents cost per patient or tooth treated.

Marginal Cost is the extra cost incurred from producing one more (or one less) of a unit of output, i.e. cost of treating one extra patient or tooth. In the short term it is equal to variable cost, but in longer term some costs considered fixed in the short term can be changed.

Incremental Cost is calculated when comparing more than one treatment strategies and represents the difference in average total cost between treatment strategies.

In addition to understanding the costing terms, a set of steps is typically followed to assemble costs in order to calculate those specific costs. There are broadly two methodologies of gathering costs: the bottom-up approach (micro-costing) and the top-down approach (Brouwer et al. 2001).

The *bottom-up costing approach* involves first identifying the resources used in providing the good or service, then obtaining information on each resource identified (usually via participating clinical practices), and summing up all resources required on a per patient basis. This approach is time-consuming but is likely to produce the most accurate estimation of cost in question. However, this may only be possible if the economic evaluation is undertaken alongside a clinical trial, where details on the resources used are collected.

The *top-down costing approach* generally relies on information obtained from routine data sources, and such data are typically based on national averages. This approach is less time-consuming but may not capture the true costs of an intervention. This approach may be the only option when undertaking a decision analytic modelling study where only routinely collected data are available to use.

In many costing studies a blended approach is common. For example, for intervention costs a micro-costing approach might be used and a top-down approach used for health service use (e.g. primary care visits).

Finally, there are a few additional issues to consider.

Costs should be considered for as long as it is relevant. When the costs and benefits of an intervention last more than a year, discounting should then be applied. *Discounting* reflects people's time preferences – cost arising in the future impinges on us less than costs that arise now, and typically the same amount of money is valued more highly now than in the future. Appropriate rates of discounting should be adopted depending on the purpose of the study and the audience the study is conducted for. Internationally recommended rates vary between countries but typically lie within the range of 3–5% per annum (Drummond et al. 2005).

In gathering costs for different resources, it is likely that prices may be taken from different price years. It is then important to convert all costs into a common price year, and this requires applying the appropriate *inflation* index. Commonly used inflation indices include those produced by respective country's national statistics bureau or specifically for the healthcare system, for example, the Hospital and

Community Health Services Pay and Price Inflation Index in the UK (Homer et al. 2020).

When identifying resources used in an intervention, it is likely capital outlays and overheads, for instance, a dental chair or an X-ray machine, will be encountered which are not an intervention specific item but may need to be costed. These are typically referred to as capital costs, and they include opportunity cost and depreciation of the item over time. The common way of measuring and valuing capital costs is to annuitise the initial capital outlay over the useful life of the asset, though other methods are also used (Brouwer et al. 2001).

3.2 The FiCTION Case Study

The Filling Children's Teeth: Indicated or Not? (FiCTION) study was a multi-centre, three-arm, parallel group, patient-randomised controlled trial set in general dental practices in England, Scotland, and Wales. The aim of the study was to evaluate three treatment strategies to manage caries in the primary teeth of children aged 3–7 years with at least one primary molar tooth with carious lesions extending into dentine (Innes et al. 2020). The three strategies were conventional with best practice prevention (C+P), biological with best practice prevention (B+P) and best practice prevention alone (PA). The C+P strategy involved local anaesthetic, the removal of carious tissue and filling placement. The B+P strategy involved sealing-in decay, selective carious tissue removal and fissure sealants. PA involved dietary and tooth-brushing advice, fluoride varnish application, and fissure sealants to prevent further carious lesions.

Generally, trials have scheduled follow-up visits to collect data on outcomes at specific timepoints, but FiCTION was a pragmatic trial with follow-up visits based on each practices' recall schedule, in order that the treatments compared were arguably more representative of how dental care is provided in the UK.

3.2.1 Costing Methods

Two costing exercises were undertaken as part of this study: micro-costing and charges to the UK NHS (Homer et al. 2020). The micro-costing exercise involved collecting data on all of the treatments provided (operative and preventive) at each visit, the length of each visit, and the dental personnel providing treatment. In the UK, dentists can have an NHS contract and/or a private practice. The methods of reimbursement for dentists differ between the different countries that make up the UK. In England and Wales, reimbursements are based on contracts to provide an agreed annual number of "Units of Dental Activity" (UDA). There are three bands of UDA reimbursement: band 1 (worth 1 UDA) covers diagnosis, treatment planning, preventive treatments, and X-rays; band 2 (worth 3 UDAs) covers operative treatments including fillings and extractions; and band 3 (worth 12 UDAs) covers complex treatments, which include laboratory element (e.g. bridges). In Scotland and Northern Ireland, a "fee-for-service" (FFS) system is in operation. The FFS system reimburses dentists for each treatment provided within each course of treatment so each type of service provided (e.g. composite filling) has its own fee.

As with other countries, dentists in the UK receive co-payments from patients for dental treatments provided; however, children are excluded from these co-payments under NHS contracts so these costs were not considered.

3.2.2 *Perspective*

The perspective of the study was that of the UK NHS in the primary analysis. A wider perspective accounting for parents' time and out-of-pocket expenses was incorporated in a sensitivity analysis.

3.2.3 *Data Collection*

Study-specific data collection tools were developed to capture costs relevant to the perspective chosen. The costs for the primary analysis were the costs associated with managing caries in primary teeth. A trial case report form (CRF) was developed and completed by a dental professional at every visit. The CRF collected information on staff present, main treatment provided (preventive and operative), any other treatment provided (e.g. inhalation sedation), and medication prescribed. Parental questionnaires, collecting direct and indirect costs to parents, were completed by the child's parent/guardian at every visit. When developing a study-specific data collection tool, compromises need to be made on the level of data required and the respondent burden.

3.2.4 *Micro-costing*

3.2.4.1 Staff Costs

The start and end times of the visit were collected on the CRF to estimate the total length of each visit. How long preventive interventions were provided for was also collected on the CRF. The rationale for this was because different dental professionals could provide different interventions during the same visit. The distinction between the staff and the length of time of each treatment was to ensure that the costs applied were representative of the staff present. Staff costs were collected from online sources (PSSRU/NHS pay scales) and inflated to account for employers' national insurance and pension costs. This annual salary cost, which included annual and administrative leave, was converted into a cost per minute, assuming a 37.5 h working week. This staff unit cost was multiplied by the number of minutes treatments were provided, as reported in the CRF.

To prevent overburdening respondents, information on all of the staff present at each visit was not collected in the CRF. It was assumed, based on clinical advice, that a dental nurse would be present for the full duration of a visit, so this cost was incorporated into the total staff costs per visit.

3.2.4.2 Treatment Costs

Information on restoration materials, local anaesthetic, other procedures (e.g. extractions), and number of surfaces treated were collected on the CRF to identify what treatments were provided. The researcher, using clinical input and dental teaching resources, identified the individual resources required to provide each treatment. The resources were split into consumable and reusable items.

3.2.4.3 Costing Consumable Items

Costs associated with consumable items were collected from online dental suppliers, and a VAT rate of 20% was applied. VAT, also known as valued added tax, is a tax levied on the sale of goods and services. The use of online suppliers as the source of costs meant that potential economies of scale experienced by larger practices were not considered, but it reduced the burden on practices and potential selection bias if the data were to be collected at a practice level. Consumable items are usually purchased in bulk so these costs needed to be broken down to estimate a unit cost per item. Table 3.1 is an illustrative example of how a unit cost per item was identified and how these unit costs were used to estimate the total cost of consumable items used at every visit.

3.2.4.4 Costing Reusable Items

The equivalent annual cost of consumable items was estimated to account for purchasing, using, and maintaining an asset over its lifespan. It was assumed that there was no residual value associated with these assets. In some instances, capital assets may be traded in or sold to generate additional revenue; in these instances the residual value needs to be included in the equivalent annual cost calculation. Additionally, if there are significant operating costs associated with capital items, such as annual maintenance fees, these also need to be considered. The inclusion/exclusion of the residual value and operating costs of consumable items is study dependent.

Similar to how the cost of consumable items was estimated, the cost of reusable items was collected from online sources, and VAT was applied to the total cost. The

Table 3.1 Example of how consumable items were costed

Estimating the unit cost of consumable items						
Item	No. of units	Cost	VAT*	Total cost	Cost/unit	Cost/item**
Disposable gloves	100	£5.25	£1.05	£6.30	£0.06	£0.12
Disposable masks	50	£3.45	£0.69	£4.14	£0.08	£0.08
Disposable bibs	500	£15.95	£3.19	£19.14	£0.04	£0.04
Tissues	7200	£25.95	£5.19	£31.14	£0.00	£0.01
Disposable cups	5000	£36.85	£7.37	£44.22	£0.01	£0.01
Mouthwash tablets	1000	£7.95	£1.59	£9.54	£0.01	£0.01
3 in 1 tips	200	£34.75	£6.95	£41.70	£0.21	£0.21
Sheaths	250	£11.65	£2.33	£13.98	£0.06	£0.06

*VAT is 20%; ** cost/item is the cost per unit multiplied by the number of items needed, e.g. the GPD would need two disposable gloves which would cost 12p (6p*2)

Estimating the total cost of consumable items used at every visit				
Single use items	Unit cost	No. of units	Cost (£)	Item
Gloves	£0.13	1	£0.12	1 pair
Gloves (nurse)	£0.13	1	£0.12	1 pair
Masks	£0.08	1	£0.08	1 mask
Masks (nurse)	£0.08	1	£0.08	1 mask
Bibs (child)	£0.11	1	£0.04	1 bib
Tissues	£0.01	3	£0.03	3 tissues
Disposable cups (water)	£0.01	1	£0.01	1 cup
Tablets (for the water)	£0.01	1	£0.01	1 tablet
3 in 1 tips	£0.21	1	£0.21	1 tip
Sheaths	£0.06	1	£0.06	1 sheath
Total cost of consumable items used at every visit			**£0.76**	

total cost was divided by the number of items purchased if it was more than one. The equivalent annual cost (EAC) was estimated using following equation, where n = expected time span of the asset:

$$EAC = \frac{asset\ price * discount\ rate}{1-(1+discount\ rate)^{-n}}$$

It was assumed in the primary analysis that the lifespan of dental equipment would be 3 years; this assumption was explored in sensitivity analyses. The recommended discount rate in the UK, 3.5%, was applied.

Reusable dental items are also sterilised after every use so the cost of autoclaving each item was estimated and added to the cost per use for each reusable item.

The unit costs associated with every consumable and reusable item were estimated using the methods above. Depending on the treatment recorded on the CRF, the appropriate unit costs of all the resources required to provide that treatment were added together to estimate the total cost of providing treatment at that visit.

3.2.4.5 Other Treatment Costs

If a child had a radiograph, inhalation sedation, or was referred for further treatment, this was collected on the CRF. The cost of radiographs was estimated based on the cost of a film; capital equipment costs were not included in this analysis. Capital costs were assumed to be fixed where the capital equipment would last for a considerable number of years and be used intensively so that the cost per image would be very small.

The cost of inhalation sedation was taken from another study which had undertaken a micro-costing exercise, and this unit cost (excluding staff costs to prevent double counting) was inflated to the same price year as the other costs collected for the trial (Curtis and Burns 2018).

A patient referral form was created to identify what treatment the child had, who provided this treatment, and where this was provided. This information was collected by a clinical researcher on the trial. Each referral was categorised into "packages of care" and assigned a unit cost based on the information collected in the patient referral form.

3.2.4.6 Medication Costs

Medication costs were sourced from the British National Formulary (BNF) for every painkiller and antibiotic recorded in the CRF (British National Formulary 2018). When information on dose, frequency, and/or duration were missing, BNF recommendations were used.

3.2.4.7 Capital Costs

While it is important to consider capital costs, large capital items, such as the dental chair, were not included in the FiCTION study. The rationale for this was that it was assumed that the capital equipment would last for a considerable number of years and be used intensively, so that the cost per use would be very small.

The inclusion or omission of capital costs will be study dependent and based on the magnitude of these costs and their opportunity costs.

3.2.5 Charges to the NHS

As previously mentioned, in the UK dentists are reimbursed by the NHS for providing treatments to NHS patients (i.e. not private patients). There are two reimbursement strategies: UDAs and FFS.

3.2.5.1 Units of Dental Activity (UDAs)

Information on UDA contracts for the English practices in the FiCTION trial was available from the NHS Business Services Authority website. The UDA value per practice was estimated based on the value of the practice's contractual payments divided by the number of contracted UDAs. For the four Welsh practices, their UDA values were not available online, so they were collected via personal communication. A UDA was reimbursed based on a completed course of treatment, but as the CRF did not collect information on whether a visit was related to a previous visit, a course of treatment definition had to be created. Clinical input, clinical guidelines, and reimbursement guidelines were used to define a course of treatment. Sensitivity analyses explored any uncertainty in these assumptions to ensure they were robust. The difference in costs between two of the arms (C + P and B + P) decreased in the UDA analysis, which was expected, as treatments in both of these arms were reimbursed at band 2 (three UDAs per course of treatment). Also, the difference between prevention and the other two arms increased as prevention is reimbursed at band 1 (one UDA per course of treatment).

3.2.5.2 Fee-for-Service (FFS)

In Scotland, dentists are reimbursed based on the treatment provided. So similarly to the micro-costing exercise, a unit cost, from the Statement of Dental Remuneration, was applied to every treatment and every visit. In some instances (e.g. clinical examination), reimbursements were based on a course of treatment, so the same assumptions used in the UDA analysis to define a course of treatment were used in the FFS analysis.

The inclusion of the UDA and FFS values in analysis increased the average total costs, as additional costs not considered in the micro-costing exercise are included in NHS charges (e.g. capital costs); however, the overall conclusions remained similar.

3.2.6 Parent Costs

The parental questionnaires completed at every visit contained information on direct (e.g. childcare, pain medication) and indirect (e.g. time off paid work) costs to parents. Unit costs for over-the-counter medications and childcare were taken from online sources. The median wage rate in the UK was used to estimate parent's time off work. The inclusion of parent costs had minimal effect on our overall conclusions. Co-payments were not considered in this analysis as there is no co-payment in the UK for child patients.

3.2.7 Discounting

Children were followed up for up to 3 years post-randomisation as part of the study; hence costs were discounted at the recommended rate of 3.5% (NICE 2013). The child's randomisation date and visit date were used to estimate when a visit occurred and what discount rate (if the visit wasn't in year 1) needed to be applied. Similarly, UDAs were discounted based on when a course of treatment started.

3.2.8 Missing Data

As follow-up visits were based on the practice's recall, the only visits considered in the analysis were visits with an associated CRF. It was assumed that a child did not have a visit and hence incurred no costs if there was no CRF. This assumption could have led to an underestimation of the average total costs for each arm; however, it was considered to be reflective of current practice as children don't always attend the dentist at regular intervals. On average, children had seven visits over their follow-up period.

Of those with a completed CRF, the completion of data within the CRF was relatively high (~95%). Assumptions on missing data (e.g. staff present, length of visit) were based on other information in the CRF, information from previous visits, and clinical advice. More robust methods of imputation, such as multiple imputation, could have been used, but given the percentage of missing data was so low, the imputation method chosen would have had a minimal impact on conclusions.

3.2.9 Sensitivity Analysis

Deterministic sensitivity analyses were undertaken to explore any uncertainty in the assumptions made when estimating costs. These analyses included varying the unit cost estimates in the micro-costing exercise and exploring different timeframes underpinning a course of treatment in the UDA analysis. Overall, while these analyses varied the point estimate results, incrementally they made very little to no difference, confirming the robustness of the results.

3.2.10 Conclusion

Overall, a robust costing exercise was undertaken for this study to capture the intrinsic nature of dental treatments and dental reimbursements in the UK. Study-specific data collection tools were created to capture as much detail as possible while trying to minimise the burden on respondents. Using two costing methodologies (micro-costing and top-down costing) allowed us to identify the "actual" difference in treatment costs based on the resources required to provide the treatment and the difference in treatment costs based on current reimbursement rates, which is arguably more important to the healthcare provider, the NHS.

3.3 Handling Uncertainty

For all costing studies (and economic evaluations) it is important to consider the uncertainty or lack of precision of our estimates of costs. This section will focus on parameter uncertainty. Structural uncertainty (e.g. in economic modelling) is addressed in Chap. 5.

Parameter uncertainty is uncertainty of the true value of an input, in this case costs, for example, the uncertainty of the cost of a medical device or treatment, uncertainty around staff costs associated with delivering treatments, the lifespan of a medical device, or discount rate. These costs may vary due to different clinical settings, different countries, or uncertainty due to ambiguity in how services are delivered.

Parameter uncertainty is usually assessed via deterministic sensitivity analysis. This can be either one way or multi-way. One-way sensitivity analysis involves changing the value of one input parameter at a time and examining the impact of a change on the results. This is the most simplistic form of sensitivity analysis, and while it will provide some indication of the uncertainty or robustness of results and conclusions drawn, it is likely to underestimate the overall uncertainty of results (Drummond et al. 2005). Multi-way sensitivity analysis is an extension of one-way sensitivity analysis, where a number of parameters are changed at the same time, and the impact of the change is examined on the results (Drummond et al. 2005).

There are a number of ways input parameters can be varied, for example, by an extreme sensitivity analysis, taking the extreme values of a parameter (high and low), or within a plausible range of values. How that plausible range is identified will vary. For example, it could be from clinical/expert input.

3.4 Presenting Results

For all cost analyses, clear reporting procedures should be followed. This should always be transparent but will also need to consider the audience, for example, policy makers, clinical professionals, academics, patients, and their level of understanding. At a minimum, all sources of data should be reported. This includes unit costs and resource use (mean and standard deviations or an appropriate measure of variance). Total costs should be reported and an appropriate disaggregated level of costs presented. This will be determined by the question being addressed and the audience who will be using the results. All assumptions in the costing methods and the perspective of the analysis (patient, healthcare provider, societal) should be stated. The horizon of costs and discount rate used, if applicable, should be reported. Currency and cost year should be stated.

Where appropriate, relevant checklists, e.g. CHEERS (Husereau et al. 2013), and guidelines (NICE 2013; Philips et al. 2004) (e.g. NICE, WHO) should be followed.

3.5 Some Issues in Costing in Dentistry

Most aspects of costing will be no different in oral health than for any other application of health economics. However, there are a few areas where oral health presents particular challenges, and these stem from some common aspects of dental care including the issues raised by patient co-payments and the small, independent status of many dental clinics. These two issues have important implications for the perspective considered, the treatment of patient co-payments, and difficulties in collecting and aggregating data across multiple independent organisations. While these implications are not unique to dental care, with similarities occurring in general medical practice, for example, it is worth outlining these here as they will commonly be faced by those undertaking costings in dentistry.

3.5.1 Perspectives to Take

While patient perspectives are always important in understanding the non-health service costs of healthcare (e.g. travel, childcare, lost productivity), in dentistry, co-payments are more likely to feature, and so the patient perspective remains important. In many health systems worldwide, dentistry is often treated as a peripheral aspect of the health system and is therefore either not covered in some public systems and private health insurance schemes or requires a co-payment from the patient covering some of the cost of the provision of oral healthcare services. This means that the patient could be argued to have a greater vested interest in any healthcare decisions at a system level, and this increases the value of studying patient-level perspectives in oral health.

Another feature of many healthcare systems is that much of dentistry in many countries is undertaken in small community-based clinics which run as independent businesses contracted to provide dental care by third party payers, such as public systems or private insurers. In some settings wider federations of clinics have formed often run by corporate dental providers with contracts either still held at the individual clinic or alternatively at federation level. Each of these businesses has to remain financially solvent, and so each will have to make decisions, sometimes within parameters set by third party payers, which economic evaluations may play a part in. Therefore, in many cases, it will be useful to consider splitting the healthcare provider perspective into two separate analyses, a system-wide level and also a clinic-level analysis. In addition, for those decision-makers at a system level, they will have an interest in ensuring that sufficient clinics remain financially viable and so will also have a use for clinic-level analysis alongside the usual utility in terms of understanding variation and also designing remuneration or contractual systems to ensure this is reflected.

3.5.2 Patient Co-payments and Charges

As already noted, in many settings there will be a co-payment for dentistry that will involve the patient paying a charge. However, the nature and details of these charges vary greatly between systems (Hunger et al. 2016). This may even extend to different arrangements within a country in different provinces, states, or devolved administrations. In addition, within a system the charges may vary by different dental provider type, for example, between primary care general dental clinics and hospital-provided specialist dentistry. Often the payments may reflect the remuneration system for the dental team, particularly where a very granular fee per item scale is used, where there may be different charges for each treatment item, but in other settings there may be a limited number of charges, even to the extent that a single flat fee may be charged per dental visit. In addition, charges may be different for different individuals. A common case is that those on low income or particular age groups (especially children) are fully covered (i.e. they are exempt from any charges) or may have a reduced charge to pay. This may also impact on payer charges so that where patients pay less, the payer may or may not pay a different amount to individual clinics. Finally, in private settings, dental clinics will almost certainly set their own patient charges (for those not covered by insurance), and so charges may vary across individual clinics.

It would be impossible to describe in detail how to deal with the different patient charges in each different context, but those undertaking or appraising economic evaluations are recommended to consider patient charges very carefully. It would be useful to consult with those working in the system to fully understand the intricacies of each system. In addition, the context in which any evaluation is undertaken should be fully reported so that the audience can understand how patient charges were dealt with and to allow the audience to understand the generalisability to their own setting, as well as the applicability of the approach taken to the question posed. In addition, where charges vary across clinics, the aggregation of these charges should be considered carefully due to the possibility of outliers skewing the overall data. Some of the techniques for dealing with variance and uncertainty in costs considered in Section "Handling Uncertainty" may be useful here.

Where charges are different for different sections of the population, subgroup analyses may be appropriate at the patient perspective level. Finally, when considering healthcare provider perspectives, if the patient charge revenue returns to the dental clinic or dental system directly, it will be important to consider deducting this from the cost to the health service or clinic.

3.5.3 Determining and Aggregating Costs Across Clinics

In many health systems, the majority of dentistry is delivered in multiple relatively small independent dental clinics. While many economic evaluations face problems of multiple centres being involved, there are usually some aspects of commonality, and some level of data is collected and available. In dental care collecting and dealing with costs are sometimes more difficult, for example, dental clinics may never have collected cost information, and it is less likely that any cost data are already published. This usually means that a micro-costing approach at individual clinic level may be required involving measuring time taken and consumables as well as overhead and capital costs. Where economic evaluation is being undertaken alongside a trial, this may be relatively easy though can be resource intensive, but where a model-based evaluation is being undertaken, access to clinics may not be as easy. In these cases, it may be necessary to rely on expert opinion, but it will be important to make clear any assumptions made (Brocklehurst and Tickle 2011).

Costs collected directly from clinics may vary considerably across clinics, and careful consideration will need to be given to the number of clinics and procedures sampled to give the relevant level of certainty of costs across the system (Brocklehurst and Tickle 2011). It is likely that a mean of costs across different procedures and/or clinics will be used for the primary analysis, but as detailed in the following section, the variance and uncertainty can be dealt with using a variety of statistical techniques and also sensitivity analysis.

References

Breckons M, Shen J, Bunga J, Vale L, Durham J (2018) DEEP study: indirect and out-of-pocket costs of persistent orofacial pain. J Dent Res 97(11):1200–1206

British National Formulary. Series British National Formulary https://www.medicinescomplete.com/mc/bnf/current/. Accessed 20 Aug 2018

Brocklehurst PR, Tickle M (2011) Is skill mix profitable in the current NHS dental contract in England? Br Dent J 210(7):303–308

Brouwer W, Rutten E, Koopmanschap M (2001) Costing in economic evaluations. In: Drummond M, McGuire A (eds) Economic evaluation in health care: merging theory and practice, 1st edn. Oxford University Press, Oxford

Curtis L, Burns A (2018) Unit costs of health and social care. Personal Social Services Research Unit. University of Kent, Canterbury. https://kar.kent.ac.uk/70995/. Accessed 20 Aug 2018

Drummond MF, Sculpher MJ, Torrance GW, O'Brien BJ, Stoddart GL (eds) (2005) Methods for the economic evaluation of health care programmes. Oxford University Press, Oxford

Homer T, Maguire A, Douglas GVA, Innes NP, Clarkson JE, Wilson N et al (2020) Cost-effectiveness of child caries management: a randomised controlled trial (FiCTION trial). BMC Oral Health 20(1):45

Hunger T, Schnell-Inderst P, Sahakyan N, Siebert U (2016) Using expert opinion in health technology assessment: a guideline review. Int J Technol Assess Health Care 32(3):131–139

Husereau D, Drummond M, Petrou S, Carswell C, Moher D, Greenberg D et al (2013) Consolidated Health Economic Evaluation Reporting Standards (CHEERS) statement. Br Med J 346:f1049

Innes NP, Clarkson JE, Douglas GVA, Ryan V, Wilson N, Homer T et al (2020) Child caries management: a randomized controlled trial in dental practice. J Dent Res 99(1):36–43

National Institute for Health and Care Excellence (NICE) (2013) Guide to the methods of technology appraisal 2013. National Institute for Health and Care Excellence, London

Philips Z, Ginnelly L, Sculpher M, Claxton K, Golder S, Riemsma R et al (2004) Review of guidelines for good practice in decision-analytic modelling in health technology assessment. Health Technol Assess 8(36):1–158

Seirawan H, Faust S, Mulligan R (2012) The impact of oral health on the academic performance of disadvantaged children. Am J Public Health 102(9):1729–1734

Chapter 4
Measuring Effectiveness for Use in Economic Evaluations in Oral Health

Thomas Davidson

4.1 Outcome Measures Used in Economic Evaluation

Health economic evaluations analyse both costs and outcomes of health programs, often by means of a cost-effectiveness analysis. Such an analysis is intended to present a ratio between incremental costs and incremental outcomes with respect to alternative interventions. The outcome is generally presented as the denominator in the incremental cost-effectiveness ratio (ICER), so that the analysis discloses how much it costs to achieve one additional unit of outcome. A key issue is therefore the choice of outcome measure.

Health economic evaluations allow for any kind of outcome measure to be used, for example, the number of patients recovering or a value on a certain scale. However, it is important that the outcome measure is relevant to the issue in question – it should reflect the aims of the program under evaluation. For example, the outcome measure to be used when evaluating the effectiveness of a caries preventive program needs of course to be related to caries, but it might be broader than the number of DMFT (decayed, missing, or filled teeth). It could, for example, also include pain and aesthetics, but analysis of the patients' quality of life (QoL) would probably also be relevant. If QoL is to be applied as an outcome measure in the evaluation of a caries preventive program, it is necessary to use an instrument which has the potential to capture how caries is affecting QoL.

Three main types of outcome measure are applicable: clinical outcomes (including intermediate outcomes), measures of QoL, and monetary outcomes. All these outcomes are presented in this chapter, but the focus is on outcome measures related to QoL.

T. Davidson (✉)
Department of Health, Medicine and Caring Sciences, Linköping University, Linköping, Sweden
e-mail: thomas.davidson@liu.se

C. Zaror, R. Mariño (eds.), *Introduction to Economic Evaluation in Oral Health Care*, https://doi.org/10.1007/978-3-030-96289-0_4

The outcome measure of choice will depend on the purpose and perspective of the analysis. The purpose of the analysis may be to disclose the program which has maximum health effects or which program reduces inequality in oral health. The main perspectives are an oral healthcare sector or a societal perspective. The category of the decision-maker may also be important. For many programs, the decision-maker may be the single patient and/or the oral health professional. For more broadly based public programs, such as caries preventive programs in schools or a tax on sugar, the decision-maker may, however, be a politician or society.

4.2 Clinical Outcomes

When measuring effectiveness in oral health, it is often relevant to use clinical outcomes (natural units) as the outcome measure, for example, the number of DMFT if a caries preventive program is being evaluated or survival of a prosthetic construction if this is the question being evaluated. As a proxy for a final clinical measure, more intermediate measures could also be analysed, such as mm adjustment of brackets or the number of bacteria in the mouth, etc. Such clinical outcomes are often relevant and easy to estimate in the evaluation and therefore convenient to use. Furthermore, they can often be understood by all decision-makers, which may improve understanding of the results and facilitate acceptance of the decision.

However, the value of these outcomes may not be known nor how important they are assumed to be by patients in relation to other possible programs. Therefore, it might be difficult to use such outcomes for efficient priority setting or to reach an optimum of resources used. For example, if an analysis discloses that it would cost €500 per DMFT prevented in a caries preventive program, it is hard to tell whether that is cost-effective or not. Furthermore, if different outcome measures are being used, it is hard to compare the different analyses. For example, is €100 per mm adjustment better or worse than €1000 per prothesis year gained? Finally, using clinical outcomes may limit the evaluation to only one aspect of health, disregarding others. In general, if clinical outcome measures are used, it is of value to know how these measures relate to broader concepts, such as QoL.

4.3 Quality-of-Life Outcomes

The purpose of most health programs is to improve an individuals' quality of life (QoL). More specifically, with respect to oral health programs, the aim is to improve those aspects of QoL related to oral health – in other words, oral health-related QoL (OHRQoL) (Cunningham and Hunt 2001). For example, active caries may negatively affect OHRQoL but might have less effect on general QoL.

It is generally recommended that QoL be defined and valued by the patients, so that the outcome measure can determine whether the program delivers outcomes that matter to patients (Ni Riordain and Wiriyakijja 2017). The term patient-reported outcome measures (PROM) is often used for this purpose. As many dental conditions may have far-reaching consequences (biological, psychological, and social), the use of PROM is important.

When measuring QoL, health-related QoL (HRQoL), or OHRQoL, decisions have to be made as to what instruments to use for the measurements, the time point for measurement, and the frequency of measurement (Brown 1999). The instruments could roughly be divided into disease-specific and generic measures but also into oral health measures and generic health-related measures. An example of a disease-specific instrument is the Caries Impacts and Experiences Questionnaire for Children (CARIES-QC) (Gilchrist et al. 2018). Perhaps the most commonly used generic OHRQoL instrument is the Oral Health Impact Profile (OHIP) (Slade and Spencer 1994), which has been translated into many languages. The original version of OHIP comprised 49 items, in 7 domains, but shorter versions, of 14 and 5 items, respectively, are also available (John et al. 2006; Slade 1997). If OHIP is used as the outcome measure in the health economic evaluation, the result would be presented as the additional cost per improved OHIP score achieved by one program, compared with the best alternative. As in the case with the clinical outcomes, it may be difficult to know whether such a result reflects a cost-effective use of the resources. Other available OHRQoL instruments are, for example, the Geriatric Oral Health Assessment Index (GOHAI) (Atchison and Dolan 1990), the Child Oral Impacts on Daily Function (Child-OIDP) (Gherunpong et al. 2004), and the Child Perception Questionnaire (Jokovic et al. 2002; Jokovic et al. 2004). A systematic review of the responsiveness of validated OHRQoL questionnaires to dental caries interventions reported that the OHRQoL of children and adolescents improved following caries intervention procedures but that the quality of the supporting evidence was very low (Aimee et al. 2019).

Generic HRQoL, on the other hand, can be used to measure the effectiveness of any health program but is generally less specific than OHRQoL with respect to certain aspects of QoL that the program tries to affect. Examples of commonly used generic HRQoL instruments are the 36-item short-form health survey (SF-36) (Rand 2020) and EuroQol's five-dimension (EQ-5D) instruments (EuroQoL 2020). The latter is often used in health economic evaluations in general but not as frequently for oral health. The EQ-5D questionnaire addresses five dimensions of health: mobility, self-care, usual activities, pain/discomfort, and anxiety/depression. In the original version, the multiple choice response to each dimension offers three options: no problems (1), moderate problems (2), and extreme problems (3). A newer version offers five options in the multiple choice response. At the end of the questionnaire, the participants are asked to rate their individual health today on a VAS from 0 to 100, where 0 is the worst of health and 100 the best of health. The EQ-5D instrument is often used when quality-adjusted life years (QALYs) is used as the outcome measure (QALY is presented in Sect. 4.5).

Generic instruments measuring HRQoL may be less sensitive than disease-specific instruments, as exemplified by the EQ-5D instrument, which consists of only five general questions. OHIP has been found to be more sensitive than EQ-5D to differences in oral health, but the latter nonetheless exhibits discriminative validity and convergent validity in relation to oral health variables (Brennan 2013). As EQ-5D does not ask about oral health conditions, it may not capture the full consequences for patients with dental problems. It would therefore be relevant to find a path linking disease-specific or OHRQoL instruments to generic ones, in order to measure effectiveness in health economic evaluations of oral health. In one such attempt, OHIP-14 responses were linked to the value tariff on EQ-5D. One OHIP item in particular "painful aching in mouth" was related to the health state values (Brennan and Spencer 2006). To make oral healthcare more comparable with general healthcare and to prioritize different treatment strategies in dental care, it is essential to apply the same methods and outcomes used in healthcare in general to assess the cost-effectiveness of dental interventions.

4.4 Monetary Outcomes

Monetary units comprise the third type of outcome measure. This is often used in cost-benefit analyses (in which both costs and benefits are calculated and compared in monetary units). The monetary value of a program may be reflected by its market price, but only if there is a perfect market, no external effects, and perfect and symmetric information. Although oral healthcare is closer to fulfilling these criteria than healthcare in general, the market price rarely reflects the true value. Furthermore, many oral health programs do not have a market price, for example, broad caries preventive programs, or products which have a market price (such as brackets) but also require considerable clinical chairside time.

Two methods which may be used to estimate the monetary value are contingent valuation (measuring willingness to pay) and revealed preferences.

The willingness of individuals to pay for a procedure would theoretically represent their preferences for the treatment (and for the related health state), as it is assumed that their income is used to maximize their utility, and if more of the income is spent on one item, less will be available for other items which may give utility. Willingness to pay is often studied with the contingent valuation method, which involves the use of sample surveys to elicit respondents' willingness to pay for certain programs (Matthews et al. 1999). Typically, the survey asks how much money people would be willing to pay for a program or for the chance to achieve a certain health status. The method could also ask how much they would be willing to accept in compensation for deterioration of their health. The willingness-to-pay value can be compared directly with costs to determine whether the program has a positive net benefit (benefits exceed costs): if so, the program would be beneficial if implemented by society. The willingness-to-pay method is often, however, difficult to use. It has been applied in several studies in dentistry, undertaken in order to determine the strength of dental health preferences (Birch et al. 2004; Cunningham and Hunt 2000b; Oscarson et al. 2007), but all attempts have potential risks of bias when people are asked about one particular aspect (oral health) and do not actually have to pay.

For some topics, individual willingness to pay can also be studied by the revealed preferences method (Johannesson 2010). Revealed preferences models assume that consumers' preferences can be revealed by their habits or actions. In their daily life, individuals take actions which influence their potential to achieve or maintain good oral health. Using this method, it is possible to study how much individuals pay for preventive treatment and how much such treatment reduces the risk of oral disease.

When monetary outcome measures are based on individual willingness to pay or revealed preferences, their value is generally related to their ability to pay. This method may therefore conflict with ethical principles guiding decision-making. Moreover, there may be a difference between individual willingness to pay for a program and the decision-makers' willingness to pay: the latter may also take public aspects into account in their estimate. There may also be altruistic aspects: individuals may be willing to pay for programs of which they themselves have no need, in order to help those with greater needs (Johannesson 2010), and this altruistic willingness to pay may be overlooked.

4.5 Quality-Adjusted Life Years (QALYs)

In healthcare fields other than dentistry, the most common outcome measure in health economic evaluations is quality-adjusted life years (QALYs). A QALY combines the value of a health state with the time of being in that health state. It provides scores on a scale with common anchor points, which allow for broad comparisons of the effects of multiple healthcare programs, in terms of both morbidity and mortality. QALYs are also expected to represent individuals' preferences for health. Sometimes this is also referred to as representing utility, but the way in which QALY is measured in practice does not generally fulfil the criteria for a utility. To date QALYs have not been as extensively applied in dentistry as in other healthcare fields (Hettiarachchi et al. 2018). The concept of QALY is illustrated in Fig. 4.1.

In Fig. 4.1, program A provides a mean health state value of 0.8 during the first 3 years, thereafter a value of 0.6 for 1 year and 0.4 for the next year, a total of 3.4 QALY. Program B provides 1 year with a health state value of 0.6, 2 years with a value of 0.4, and finally 1 year with a value of 0.2, a total of 1.6 QALY. Thus, the QALY gain by implementing program A instead of program B is 1.8 QALY. In this simple example, discounting of future effects is not considered.

The health state value might be elicited either by patients valuing their own health states or, more commonly, by individuals valuing hypothetical health states. It has been shown that this distinction, using patients' own health states or using hypothetical health states, is of importance to the values.

There are several methods for eliciting health state values, as presented below and also as discussed in some systematic reviews of preference-based outcome measures in oral health (Matthews et al. 1999; Birch and Ismail 2002). Either direct or indirect methods may be used to estimate such values.

4.5.1 Direct Methods to Elicit Health State Values

Commonly used direct methods to elicit health state values are standard gamble (von Neuman and Morgenstern 1944), time trade-off (TTO) (Torrance et al. 1972), and the rating scale method. Discrete choice experiments (DCE) have also been used for this purpose (Ryan et al. 2006). The standard gamble approach estimates the value of a health state by finding a probability (P), in which an individual is indifferent to living in that health state or participating in a gamble with a P of living with full health, but with the risk (1-P) of immediate death (Fig. 4.2).

The standard gamble technique has been applied in some studies to estimate health state values in dentistry (Downer et al. 1997; Fyffe and Kay 1992; Ismail et al. 2004). Two of these (Fyffe and Kay 1992; Ismail et al. 2004) did not include risk of death in the gamble, and their values can therefore not be interpreted as true

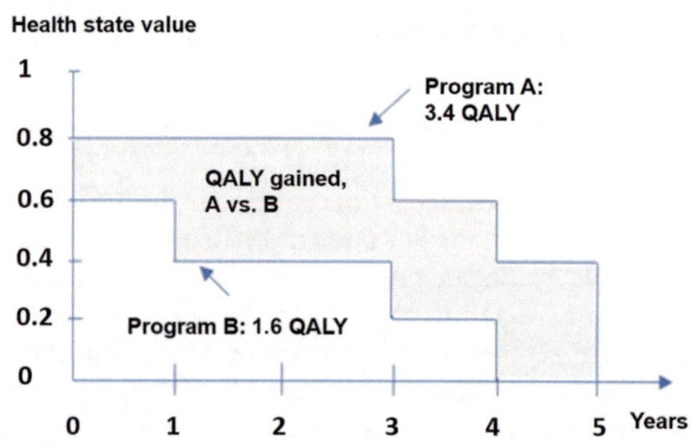

Fig. 4.1 Illustration of the QALY concept

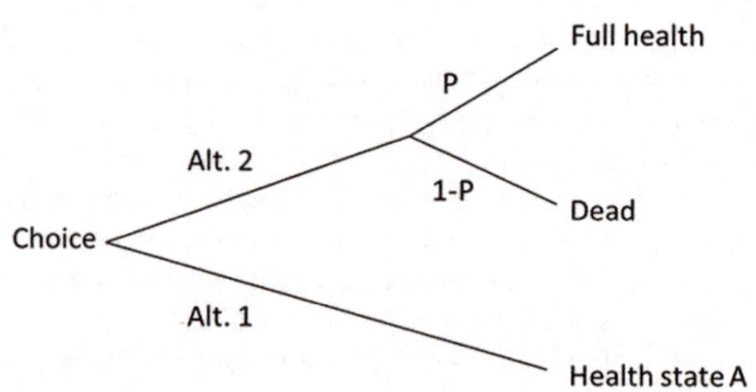

Fig. 4.2 Standard gamble. Davidson and Tranæus (2016). CC BY 4.0

preferences (as long as no transformation is undertaken). Instead, these values show preferences on another scale, and its value is uncertain. Another method of eliciting health state value is the TTO method. It is used to elicit the number of years in full health which makes an individual indifferent to living with full health and living in a certain state of less than full health, for a specific time (commonly 10 years). If the individual states that living 10 years in health state A is equal to living 5 years in full health, then the value of health state A is 0.5; see Fig. 4.3.

In some studies which apply TTO in dentistry (Fyffe et al. 1999; Karlsson 1991), the number of years has been replaced with sacrifice of free time or sacrifice of time with dental health before treatment, and, as in some of the examples presented above, this does not provide valid health state values. However, Cunningham et al. (2003) have conducted a study in which this method has been applied in a way that enables the calculation of QALYs. By using the TTO approach 5 times each for 21 patients undergoing orthognathic treatment, they found a decrease in health state values during the treatment procedure but an increase after completed treatment. Overall, the total QALY gain was found to be high (extending the analysis to a lifetime perspective).

Using a rating scale to estimate health state values is easier than the methods presented above, but the theoretical foundation of this method is weaker. Using the rating scale, individuals evaluate health states by ranking them on a cardinal scale, which is usually anchored between "best imaginable health" and "worst imaginable health" (see Fig. 4.4). The main theoretical problem is that when individuals do not have to choose between alternatives, their true preferences are not revealed.

Some studies have used the rating scale to assess outcomes in dentistry. For example, Nassani and Kay (2011) measured values in relation to tooth loss, Cunningham and Hunt (2000a, b) estimated values for dentofacial deformity, and Fukai et al. (2012) valued health states in order to compare the outcomes of an educational intervention in the field of dental health. They all concluded that this measure is feasible.

The use of discrete choice experiments has been tested to value health states. The method presents two or more profiles made up of levels of attributes. The

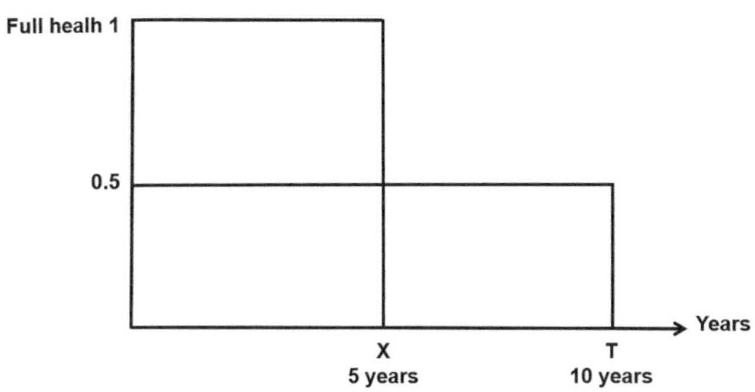

Fig. 4.3 Time trade-off (TTO). Davidson and Tranæus (2016). CC BY 4.0

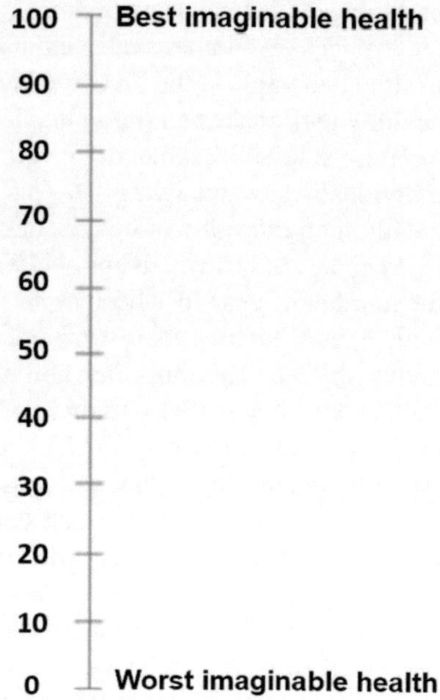

Fig. 4.4 Rating scale. Davidson and Tranæus (2016). CC BY 4.0

respondent is asked to choose which one he or she prefers, and by an iterative process, it is possible to define the preference for a certain attribute in the profile.

Cunningham and Hunt (2000a, b) also compared values for dentofacial deformity elicited by different direct methods and compared the values elicited by patients and the general public. All methods used in their study included "dead" as an anchoring point. They found no differences between the health state values for the two groups of respondents, but the various methods gave different results. The highest values for dentofacial deformity were found using standard gamble, 0.85, and the lowest using a rating scale, 0.57. This is a commonly found difference between the methods. The value elicited by TTO was 0.75. All the methods used were found to be acceptable to respondents.

4.5.2 *Indirect Methods to Elicit Health State Values*

Indirect methods to elicit health state values are based on questionnaires which can be scored using a pre-scored value set, derived by one or several of the direct methods (using a multi-attribute utility measure). For example, each combination of responses on the EQ-5D instrument can be assigned a health state value using specific value sets. A value set is found earlier with the use of a direct method. The British value set for EQ-5D, which is commonly used, has been developed by using TTO in a sample of the British general public (Dolan 1995). Moreover, several versions of the EQ-5D instrument have been developed. There is a version for children

(EQ-5D-Y) and a version with five levels of response to each question (EQ-5D-5L), which makes it more sensitive. However, values assessed by different versions or using different value sets are not directly comparable.

Other questionnaires which can be applied to elicit health state values indirectly include the short-form six dimensions (SF-6D) (Brazier et al. 2002), Health Utilities Index (HUI) (Feeny et al. 2002), and Child Health Utility Index 9 Dimensions (CHU9D) (Stevens 2012). The EQ-5D (Hulme et al. 2014) and CHU9D (Foster Page et al. 2015) have been used in oral health programs, but both lack some aspects of oral health (Foster Page et al. 2015; Kastenbom et al. 2019).

It would be valuable if health state values could be elicited from the OHIP, but to date no such value set has been developed. Some studies have however mapped results from the OHIP-14 to the EQ-5D in order to elicit health state values from OHIP and conclude that this enables health state values to be derived from OHIP-14 scores (Brennan and Spencer 2006; Hulme et al. 2016).

Below is a calculation showing conversion of an EQ-5D profile into a health state valuation. A predefined tariff is required. For example, if an individual's answers on the EQ-5D questionnaire state that he/she has some problems with mobility, no problem with self-care, some problems with performing usual activities, moderate pain or discomfort, and is extremely anxious or depressed, this would generate the health state described as 2, 1, 2, 2, 3. Using the British tariff from 1997 (Dolan 1997), the value of this health state would be 0.186 (Table 4.1).

In general, other tariffs assign a higher weight to the same health state, especially those using a tariff based on standard gamble rather than on time trade-off. Furthermore, tariffs using the individuals' own health states generally yield values higher than those based on hypothetical health states, at least for poor health states, which is often explained by the tendency of coping with poor health states.

Table 4.1 Example of QALY calculation from EQ-5D

Dimension	Coefficient
Constant (because of any problem)	−0.081
Mobility (some problems, 2)	−0.069
Self-care (no problem, 1)	0
Usual activity (some problem, 2)	−0.036
Pain/discomfort (some problems, 2)	−0.123
Anxiety/depression (extreme problem, 3)	−0.236
N3 (level 3 occurs within at least one dimension)	−0.269
Health state value	**0.186**

4.6 Quality-Adjusted Tooth Years (QATYs)

Quality-adjusted tooth years (QATYs) has also been proposed as an outcome measure of an individual's OHRQoL (Birch 1986). The measure was introduced in 1986 but has not been widely used. In short it gives each tooth the maximum value of 1 QATY for 1 year, and deductions in the value are made for injuries, treatments, etc. In the original version, it was proposed that a missing tooth should be weighted at 0.0, a filled tooth at 0.75, and a filled but carious tooth at 0.1. One study using weights derived from OHIP-14 to estimate QATY reported results consistent with improvements in clinical measures (Mohd-Dom 2014).

Perhaps the main advantage of using QATY is in modelling the long-term consequences of different programs, as this outcome measure enables modelling at a tooth level (rather than at an individual level). For example, a model analysis of 6-year-old children with high caries prevalence used QATY as the outcome measure for evaluating a school-based prevention program for the application of fissure sealants in molar teeth: compared with conventional dental care, QATY increased from 3.71 to 3.91 (Espinoza-Espinoza et al. 2019).

The main weakness with QATY to date has been to relate its value to individual preferences. Moreover, if it is not possible to link the measure to QALY, it will be difficult for decision-makers to use the analysis to compare different programs.

4.7 Discussion

This chapter presents various types of outcome measures applied in economic evaluation. Three main types of measures are outlined: clinical outcomes, quality-of-life measures, and monetary outcomes. All three may be relevant to measuring effectiveness in economic evaluation in the field of oral health. As QALY is the most commonly applied outcome in economic evaluations of healthcare programs in general, this should be the preferred outcome measure. The application of QALY allows comparison with outcomes of other studies, facilitating the effective prioritization of limited resources.

However, if QALY is to be used, it is important to be aware that the methods established to create QALY may capture OHRQoL aspects. One study which calculated and compared health state values (used for QALY calculations) of adults without caries and another group with high caries experience found no differences in health state values calculated by EQ-5D, indicating that EQ-5D may not be able to capture the impact of dental caries (Kastenbom et al. 2019). Another study which analysed the cost-effectiveness of silicone and alginate impressions for complete dentures found differences using OHIP-EDENT but not for EQ-5D (Hulme et al. 2014), which also suggests that EQ-5D might not be sensitive enough for oral health programs. The CHU9D could also be used for creating QALYs and may be useful in dental research in children, but more studies are needed.

The concepts of quality-adjusted tooth years (QATY) and willingness-to-pay outcomes have also been presented, and they may both be relevant to economic evaluations. Monetary outcomes may be especially relevant in dental care, as most people are used to paying most of the costs themselves, in contrast to other health-care fields where most of the cost is covered by society or by insurance companies. A study of patients undergoing orthognathic treatment found a correlation between willingness-to-pay values and health state values and concluded that willingness to pay may be used as a measure of strength of preference (Cunningham and Hunt 2000a, b).

There are also other outcome measures, which have not been discussed in this chapter. For example, use of healthy years equivalent (HYE) has been proposed instead of QALY to measure individuals' preferences. HYE assesses health profiles rather than health states (Johannesson 2010), and it has been tested on dental interventions, with positive results (Birch et al. 1998). HYE has however not been used for a long time as it is considered by many to complicate the valuation without providing any advantages. Another alternative to QALY is disability-adjusted life years (DALY), which calculates the loss of health attributable to a certain disease. Poor oral health has been shown to create many DALYs (Marcenes et al. 2013), but this is more an indication of the importance of oral health rather than an aid for decision-makers in priority setting. There have also been proposals to use quality-adjusted prothesis year (QAPY), etc. The extensive use of outcome measures leads back to the statement at the beginning of this chapter that health economic evaluations allow for any kind of outcome measure to be used but that it is important that the outcome measure selected is relevant to the issue in question – it should reflect the aims of the program under evaluation.

If the outcome measure is important for the implementation of a program, the decision-maker must be able to estimate the value of the outcome. If the applied outcome measure is of no relevance for a decision-maker, the analysis will not be of any use. Therefore, it is important to consider the decision-maker when choosing the outcome measure. Decisions can be approached from different perspectives, and an individual may not attribute the same value to outcomes as a decision-maker at government level. Health economic evaluations are used to inform the decision-makers about the cost-effectiveness of proposed programs, so the outcome measures need to be chosen carefully.

References

Aimee NR, Dame-Teixeira N, Alves LS, Borges GA, Foster Page L, Mestrinho HD et al (2019) Responsiveness of oral health-related quality of life questionnaires to dental caries interventions: systematic review and meta-analysis. Caries Res 53(6):585–598

Atchison KA, Dolan TA (1990) Development of the Geriatric Oral Health Assessment Index. J Dent Educ 54(11):680–687

Birch S (1986) Measuring dental health: improvements on the DMF index. Community Dent Health 3(4):303–311

Birch S, Ismail AI (2002) Patient preferences and the measurement of utilities in the evaluation of dental technologies. J Dent Res 81(7):446–450

Birch S, Gafni A, Markham B, Marriott M, Lewis D, Main P (1998) Health years equivalents as a measurement of preferences for dental interventions. Community Dent Health 15(4):233–242

Birch S, Sohn W, Ismail AI, Lepkowski JM, Belli RF (2004) Willingness to pay for dentin regeneration in a sample of dentate adults. Community Dent Oral Epidemiol 32(3):210–216

Brazier J, Roberts J, Deverill M (2002) The estimation of a preference-based measure of health from the SF-36. J Health Econ 21(2):271–292

Brennan DS (2013) Oral Health Impact Profile, EuroQol, and assessment of quality of life instruments as quality of life and health-utility measures of oral health. Eur J Oral Sci 121(3 Pt 1):188–193

Brennan DS, Spencer AJ (2006) Mapping oral health related quality of life to generic health state values. BMC Health Serv Res 6(96)

Brown R (1999) Strategies and pitfalls in quality of life research. Hepatology 29(Suppl 1):9S–12S

Cunningham SJ, Hunt NP (2000a) A comparison of health state utilities for dentofacial deformity as derived from patients and members of the general public. Eur J Orthod 22(3):335–342

Cunningham SJ, Hunt NP (2000b) Relationship between utility values and willingness to pay in patients undergoing orthognathic treatment. Community Dent Health 17(2):92–96

Cunningham SJ, Hunt NP (2001) Quality of life and its importance in orthodontics. J Orthod 28(2):152–158

Cunningham SJ, SculpherM SF, Manca A (2003) A cost-utility analysis of patients undergoing orthognathic treatment for the management of dentofacial disharmony. Br J Oral Maxillofac Surg 41(1):32–35

Davidson T, Tranæus S (2016) Time to assess cost-effectiveness of technologies in dentistry. Int J Dent Oral Health 2(5):1–5. https://doi.org/10.16966/2378-7090.200

Dolan P (1995) A social tariff for EuroQol: results from a UK general population survey. Centre for Health Economics, University of York, York

Dolan P (1997) Modeling valuations for EuroQol health states. Med Care 35(11):1095–1108

Downer MC, Jullien JA, Speight PM (1997) An interim determination of health gain from oral cancer and precancer screening: 1. Obtaining health state utilities. Community Dent Health 14(3):139–142

Espinoza-Espinoza G, Corsini G, Rojas R, Marino R, Zaror C (2019) The cost-utility of school-based first permanent molar sealants programs: a Markov model. BMC Oral Health 19(1):293

EuroQoL. EQ-5D 2020. https://euroqol.org. Accessed 15 June 2020.

Feeny D, Furlong W, Torrance GW, Goldsmith CH, Zhu Z, DePauw S et al (2002) Multiattribute and single-attribute utility functions for the health utilities index mark 3 system. Med Care 40(2):113–128

Foster Page LA, Beckett DM, Cameron CM, Thomson WM (2015) Can the Child Health Utility 9D measure be useful in oral health research? Int J Paediatr Dent 25(5):349–357

Fukai K, Yoshino K, OhyamaA TY (2012) Dental patient preferences and choice in clinical decision-making. Bull Tokyo Dent Coll 53(2):59–66

Fyffe HE, Kay EJ (1992) Assessment of dental health state utilities. Community Dent Oral Epidemiol 20(5):269–273

Fyffe HE, Deery C, Nugent Z, Nuttall NM, Pitts NB (1999) The reliability of two methods of utility assessment in dentistry. Community Dent Health 16(2):72–79

Gherunpong S, Tsakos G, Sheiham A (2004) Developing and evaluating an oral health-related quality of life index for children; the CHILD-OIDP. Community Dent Health 21(2):161–169

Gilchrist F, Rodd HD, Deery C, Marshman Z (2018) Development and evaluation of CARIES-QC: a caries-specific measure of quality of life for children. BMC Oral Health 18(1):202

Hettiarachchi RM, Kularatna S, Downes MJ, Byrnes J, Kroon J, Lalloo R et al (2018) The cost-effectiveness of oral health interventions: a systematic review of cost-utility analyses. Community Dent Oral Epidemiol 46(2):118–124

Hulme C, Yu G, Browne C, O'Dwyer J, Craddock H, Brown S et al (2014) Cost-effectiveness of silicone and alginate impressions for complete dentures. J Dent 42(8):902–907

Hulme C, Robinson P, Douglas G, Baxter P, Gibson B, Godson J et al (2016) The incentive study: a mixed-methods evaluation of an innovation in commissioning and delivery of primary dental care compared with traditional dental contracting, Southampton

Ismail AI, Birch S, Sohn W, Lepkowski JM, Belli RF (2004) Utilities of dentin regeneration among insured and uninsured adults. Community Dent Oral Epidemiol 32(1):55–66

Johannesson M (2010) Theory and methods of economic evaluation of health care. Kluwer Academic Publishers, Stockholm

John MT, Miglioretti DL, LeResche L, Koepsell TD, Hujoel P, Micheelis W (2006) German short forms of the Oral Health Impact Profile. Community Dent Oral Epidemiol 34(4):277–288

Jokovic A, Locker D, Stephens M, Kenny D, Tompson B, Guyatt G (2002) Validity and reliability of a questionnaire for measuring child oral-health-related quality of life. J Dent Res 81(7):459–463

Jokovic A, Locker D, Tompson B, Guyatt G (2004) Questionnaire for measuring oral health-related quality of life in eight- to ten-year-old children. Pediatr Dent 26(6):512–8Ni

Karlsson G (1991) Hälsoekonomisk analys av dentala implantat. Linköping University

Kastenbom L, Falsen A, Larsson P, Sunnegardh-Gronberg K, Davidson T (2019) Costs and health-related quality of life in relation to caries. BMC Oral Health 19(1):187

Marcenes W, Kassebaum NJ, Bernabe E, Flaxman A, Naghavi M, Lopez A et al (2013) Global burden of oral conditions in 1990-2010: a systematic analysis. J Dent Res 92(7):592–597

Matthews DC, Gafni A, Birch S (1999) Preference based measurements in dentistry: a review of the literature and recommendations for research. Community Dent Health 16(1):5–11

Mohd-Dom T (2014) Quality-adjusted tooth years (QATY) as an outcome measure of periodontal treatment. BMC Public Health 14(Suppl 1):P10

Nassani MZ, Kay EJ (2011) Tooth loss–an assessment of dental health state utility values. Community Dent Oral Epidemiol 39(1):53–60

Oscarson N, Lindholm L, Kallestal C (2007) The value of caries preventive care among 19-year olds using the contingent valuation method within a cost-benefit approach. Community Dent Oral Epidemiol 35(2):109–117

Rand Corporation (2020) 36-item Short Form Survey (SF-36). https://www.rand.org/health-care/surveys_tools/mos/36-item-short-form.html. Accessed 15 June 2020.

Riordain R, Wiriyakijja P (2017) Patient reported outcome and experience measures of oral disease in oral medicine. Br Dent J 223(9):713

Ryan M, Netten A, Skatun D, Smith P (2006) Using discrete choice experiments to estimate a preference-based measure of outcome–an application to social care for older people. J Health Econ 25(5):927–944

Slade GD (1997) Derivation and validation of a short-form Oral Health Impact Profile. Community Dent Oral Epidemiol 25(4):284–290

Slade GD, Spencer AJ (1994) Development and evaluation of the Oral Health Impact Profile. Community Dent Health 11(1):3–11

Stevens K (2012) Valuation of the Child Health Utility 9D Index. PharmacoEconomics 30(8):729–747

Torrance GW, Thomas WH, Sackett DL (1972) A utility maximization model for evaluation of health care programs. Health Serv Res 7(2):118–133

von Neuman J, Morgenstern O (1944) Theory of games and economic behaviour. Princeton University Press, Princeton

Chapter 5
Aspects of Decision Modelling for Economic Evaluation in Oral Health Care

Catherine De La Puente, Rodrigo Mariño, and Gerardo Espinoza-Espinoza

5.1 What Is a Model in the Context of Economic Evaluation?

A model is a representation of the real world using other elements to represent it, making it easier to understand. Oral health professionals work with models on a daily basis. The typical models used in dentistry are those three-dimensional representations (replica) of a patient's teeth, which is a reliable, transportable depiction of reality with the purpose of planning and making decisions about treatments. Scientific models can be visual (e.g., a diagram), mathematical (e.g., formulas), or computer models (e.g., algorithms). Although scientific models might be more complex than a dental model, they make a specific feature of reality easier to understand and manipulate. This chapter aims to describe how decision analytical modelling techniques can be used in economic evaluation and the relevance of each type of model when applied to oral health. The chapter introduces the types of decision models, the types of uncertainty (methodological, structural, and parameter), and the approaches to dealing with uncertainty.

Modelling in economic evaluations is a method to depict the complexities of decision-making and accurately captures costs and associated benefits (Hoang

C. De La Puente (✉)
Department of Health Technology Assessment and Evidence-Based Health, Ministry of Health Chile, Santiago, Chile
e-mail: catherine.delapuente@gmail.com; catherine.delapuente@ufrontera.cl

R. Mariño
Melbourne Dental School, The University of Melbourne, Melbourne, VIC, Australia
e-mail: r.marino@unimelb.edu.au

G. Espinoza-Espinoza
Department of Public Health, Universidad de La Frontera, Temuco, Chile

Center for Research in Epidemiology, Economics and Oral Public Health (CIEESPO), Faculty of Dentistry, Universidad de La Frontera, Temuco, Chile
e-mail: gerardo.espinoza@ufrontera.cl

C. Zaror, R. Mariño (eds.), *Introduction to Economic Evaluation in Oral Health Care*, https://doi.org/10.1007/978-3-030-96289-0_5

et al. 2016). As has been previously mentioned in this book, decisions about the perspectives of costs and benefits have a substantial impact on the model outcome. Economic evaluation models in health attempt to show all the phases of the health situation to be evaluated, in a simplified but understandable way. A model shows the consequences and difficulties of, for example, different therapeutic interventions and should correspond as closely as possible to the real health/disease situation (Nuijten and Starzewski 1998).

These models use a mathematical language (Rodríguez 2004) to infer results, both in terms of effectiveness and costs, by combining information from a variety of sources, and, by doing this, conduct simulations that will evaluate how an individual or the population of interest behaves with the different health intervention (e.g., health promotion, preventive services, etc.), diagnostic services, treatments, policy options, health technologies, etc., being compared. In this way, the model allows us to make decisions in the absence of hard data (Hoang et al. 2016).

5.2 Why Use Mathematical Models in an Economic Evaluation?

Because resources are limited, they should be invested in treatments/health interventions that provide maximum health benefits to the population within the available resources. Thus, to adopt a given health technology, decision-makers should have information on how much is to be invested and for how long. This is when modelling becomes relevant, since it infers health outcomes observed in a clinical trial for longer periods (Rodríguez 2004).

Models can be used to estimate the long-term effects and costs of a given treatment. For example, if the purpose is to evaluate two alternative treatments for bruxism, occlusal splints versus botulinum toxin (Botox), first we must make a chart identifying the stages of the health problem (i.e., bruxism) and, next, populate a model with all the variables that may influence the outcome. These include the probability of transition from one state of health to another; the probability of selecting one alternative over another; and the probability of adverse effects or any complication derived from the treatments. Subsequently, effectiveness data must be entered into the model (i.e., quality of life) for each alternative. In the last stage, the costs associated with each alternative must be entered, such as the costs of the occlusal splints and Botox, dental consultation costs, costs related to adverse events or complications, and all costs, both incurred and averted, per alternative treatment.

This example illustrates the data that must be available to be able to extrapolate the results within a temporal horizon defined by the time where the costs and consequences of the interventions can be observed. As demonstrated, there are several parameters that must be identified and included in the model. Some researchers argue that caution must be applied when using the results of an economic evaluation, due to the potential biased data introduced in the model. Because of this, it is encouraged, whenever possible, to use data from randomized clinical trials (RCT) for decision-making. However, RCTs also have limitations. Firstly, RCTs are designed to evaluate efficacy, that is, an intervention is evaluated under ideal conditions, with health professionals who are experts in treating the pathology under controlled situations. This does not always capture the complexity of real-world conditions (e.g., compliance with the treatment regime). RCTs do not always use an adequate comparison of health technologies, for example, comparing a certain drug with a placebo may not be the most appropriate comparator when making the decision to select a medicine for treatment. Lastly, RCTs often use intermediate clinical endpoints, rather than final outcomes (Brennan and Akehurst 2000), as they tend to have a relatively short follow-up period (Rodríguez et al. 2008).

Because of the reasons outlined earlier, it is not possible to know exactly the incremental cost-effectiveness of adopting a new treatment/intervention/healthcare technology, etc. This raises the question, if we do not design a mathematical model, what design could incorporate relevant economic aspects in order to make a decision?

Pragmatic RCTs might simulate what happens in clinical practice when new treatment/intervention/healthcare technology, etc., is introduced. This type of study should be carried out in a standard healthcare setting, similar to the environment in which the drug or healthcare intervention will be used once it is available in the market (Rubio-Terrés et al. 2004). The same applies for the participants in the study. Additionally, as the purpose is to evaluate the costs of the intervention, it is necessary to let the treatment be modified or changed, as well as to evaluate the masking and biases introduced by health workers and patients who are not blinded to the therapy (Buxton et al. 1997). This is because it is necessary to evaluate the advantages or disadvantages of the new therapy or the request for other tests that may have not been included in the protocol, as it might occur in real-world practice. Finally, the duration of this type of study should be long enough to capture all costs and benefits, for example, in the case of chronic disease treatments.

However, the limitation with this type of study is that it presents biases, given that patients and clinicians are not always blinded, and they are also very expensive, given that the follow-up time is long. That is why the best option is modelling.

5.3 Objective of Modelling in Economic Evaluations

The objectives of modelling in economic evaluations include the following:

- To extrapolate data over a period of time beyond a clinical trial (Rodríguez 2004), thus obtaining end results for the intervention and comparator being evaluated
- To deliver relevant information for coverage decisions in health
- To synthesize available evidence through a pictorial representation, delivering results with data coming from various sources
- To relate intermediate outcomes with end results
- To generalize results from one context to another

- To carry out simulations of the various parameters that affect long-term outcomes in terms of costs and effects, which contribute to making coverage decisions in health

5.4 Modelling Characteristics

Mathematical models are inexpensive analytical tools that extrapolate the effectiveness and economic consequences of an intervention. However, to ensure reliability, they must meet certain characteristic, including that they must be realistic and explicit, from their pictorial representation to the possible transitions between health states. Although they are able to summarize real-world situations, a model must reflect all the relevant information on the conditions in which the disease develops and the ways the health technology being evaluated behaves, as well as its comparators. It should be remembered that an economic evaluation must compare all interventions that are prescribed and available for the health situation under assessment.

Mathematical models must be transparent. The explanation of the model, both its graphic representation and the calculations and iterations that it carries out, is of utmost importance. In addition, the authors must indicate the sources of the data used to populate the model, that is, where the epidemiological data and effectiveness data were obtained, whether a systematic review was conducted, or data were obtained from clinical records. The model must also indicate the source of cost data, transition probabilities, and any other data that are incorporated into the model. The model must include sufficient information so as to be able to be reproduced by other researchers, obtaining similar results.

Every model must be validated by an interdisciplinary team, which includes experts in the health condition under study, health economists, statisticians, *pharmacists*, and other relevant health professionals, depending on the type of health technology being evaluated. An economic model must be built with the best available evidence. The use of a simple model that captures all relevant events is recommended. This is because it should always be considered that models should be populated with data that may not always be available. This may lead the researcher to either not be able to complete the economic evaluation, or insert wrong data in the model, or assume probabilities, all of which would bias the study.

Another feature to consider is assumptions. As mentioned above, the models synthesize complex processes occurring in the real world; although they represent a health state, this state is not exact, so it assumes the occurrence of only some situations. This does not mean that the model is invalid if these assumptions are justified and agreed as having a high probability of occurrence in the real world. For example, in a study of dental sealants in schoolchildren (Espinoza-Espinoza et al. 2019), the authors entered in the model the time and cost of that time that the assistant prepared the box before an intervention. For this purpose, as not data was available that measured this time, the assumption was included that all dental boxes had to be prepared before the intervention and that this time was on average 5 min.

It is essential to assess the uncertainties of a model that was generated by data that may be included in the model as a probability or data representing average values, etc. The sources for those uncertainties can be the following:

- Model. The structure of the model or its transitions did not capture the natural history of the disease. The structure of the model is generally determined by considering the relationship between the inputs (natural history of the disease, clinical pathways, evidence of the effectiveness of the interventions, utilities associated with health states, intervention, other costs, etc.) and the production measures required by the decision-maker (Brennan et al. 2006).
- Health Technology. An adequate calculation of treatment costs based on correct dosage was not conducted, or the health outcomes from the treatment were not incorporated. Health technology generates other situations, which may not have been added to the model.
- Population. The population being modelled could have different characteristics to the context population.
- Parameters. Uncertainty occurs when there are alternative sources of the data that are entered into the model. On the other hand, confidence in the model is lost when the author does not present the source of these data. In these cases, it may be suspected that the author might be manipulating the data to favor one intervention over another.

As mentioned in previous chapters, in the first stage of an economic evaluation, all the inputs which will populate the model, such as effectiveness, costs, and probabilities, must be considered. The sources from which these data were obtained should be indicated, whether primary or secondary sources. For that reason, it is relevant to corroborate with experts, in those cases where there is no national or domestic data available.

As mentioned, the model must resemble the real world, with any assumption justified by the disease's natural history and all the relevant clinical and economic parameters for what is to be evaluated. These must also be reviewed by relevant experts (e.g., clinicians). Finally, the results of an economic evaluation should always be subjected to a sensitivity analysis, where all the variables that influence outcomes can be evaluated.

5.5 Applying Models in Economic Evaluations

Mathematical models are useful for:

- Generation of health economic data that can be collected in a relatively short interval (Nuijten and Starzewski 1998). The effectiveness associated with the costs of a treatment can be projected within a certain time horizon, which might even be a lifetime.

- Negotiation of health technologies prices, since they allow for the evaluation of which ones generate greater effectiveness at a lower cost. However, this is not always feasible, since generally the decision-maker does not have the model used for the economic evaluation. Similarly, the models allow evaluation of different cost-effectiveness scenarios. For example, evaluating by subgroups of patients allows focusing the coverage in health decision-making on the subgroup where health technology is more cost-effective.
- Evidence for the inclusion of drugs in the national formulary.
- Evidence for the recommendations in the clinical practice guidelines.
- Evidence for budgetary impacts of health technologies. According to the health technology evaluation process, budgetary impacts are made of technologies whose effectiveness is demonstrated as well as their cost-effectiveness, since it provides us with evidence at the population level.

5.6 Classification of Models

Models can be classified according to their probabilistic nature as either deterministic and stochastic or probabilistic (Parada-Vargas and Taborda-Restrepo 2011).

- Deterministic models are those that use the average number of events in the population (Castillo-Riquelme 2010); they represent each of the model's parameters through point estimates (Darbà 2006).
- Probabilistic models consider the uncertainty within the calculation, so they use randomization techniques to simulate the probabilities of events that can be generated by chance (Rodríguez 2004).

Models can also be classified according to their structure. The most widely used models, including the oral health field, are decision trees and Markov models (Marshall et al. 2020).

5.6.1 Decision Trees

Decision trees are the most commonly used form of model in economic evaluation (Drummond et al. 2005). Decision tree used to represent available strategies and calculate the probability that an outcome will occur if a particular strategy is employed (Rodríguez-Pimentel et al. 2007) (see Fig. 5.1). They are used when the timeframe is short, the process is not complex, reoccurring of events are not important, or there is no interaction between individuals (Hoang et al. 2016).

Decision trees are made up of an action or decision node that is represented by a square. Branches emerge from these nodes that relate to a chance node. Chance

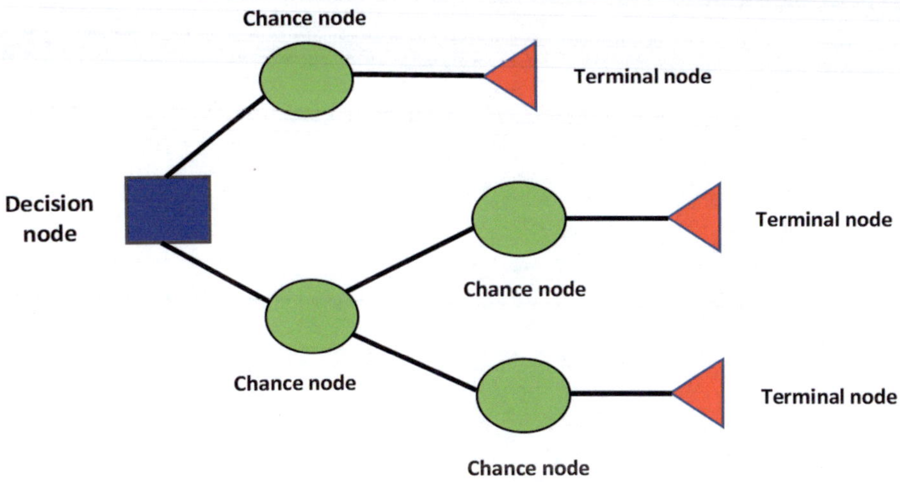

Fig. 5.1 Decision Tree
Original drawing

nodes are represented by a circle, and from these nodes the events emerge. Lastly, there are terminal/outcome nodes, represented by a triangle, and, as the name indicates, this node ends the events of each branch, so there is no branch associated with it. Each of the branches has associated probabilities of the event's occurrence, except the branches that arise from the decision node.

An example of a decision tree is shown in Fig. 5.2. For determined disease (Z), there are three alternatives, which begin at the decision node: "no treatment," "surgery," and "medical treatment." Each treatment alternative has events that are represented by the chance node. Each branch carries a probability of the event occurring.

- The alternative "no treatment" has only one event: "death."
- If "surgery" is chosen, the person may die or live.
- "Medical treatment" has more events. The numbers that are observed under each branch are the probabilities of occurrence for each of them.

It is important to note that the total probability for all branches leaving a node must be 1 or 100%. For example, in the "surgery" option, the probability that the patient dies is 0.5 and lives 0.5, both add up to 1. In the same way, for the alternative "medical treatment," the possibility that the patient dies is 0.4 and lives is 0.6, both add up to 1.

In this example, the effectiveness was measured in quality-adjusted life years (QALYs); at the end of each terminal node the QALYs and costs for each branch are reported. "No treatment" has 0.0 QALYs and a cost of USD$ 1,000. Those who undergo surgery and live have 0.8 QALYs and a cost of USD$ 3,500. To know the total effectiveness of each alternative, the probabilities that are in each branch must

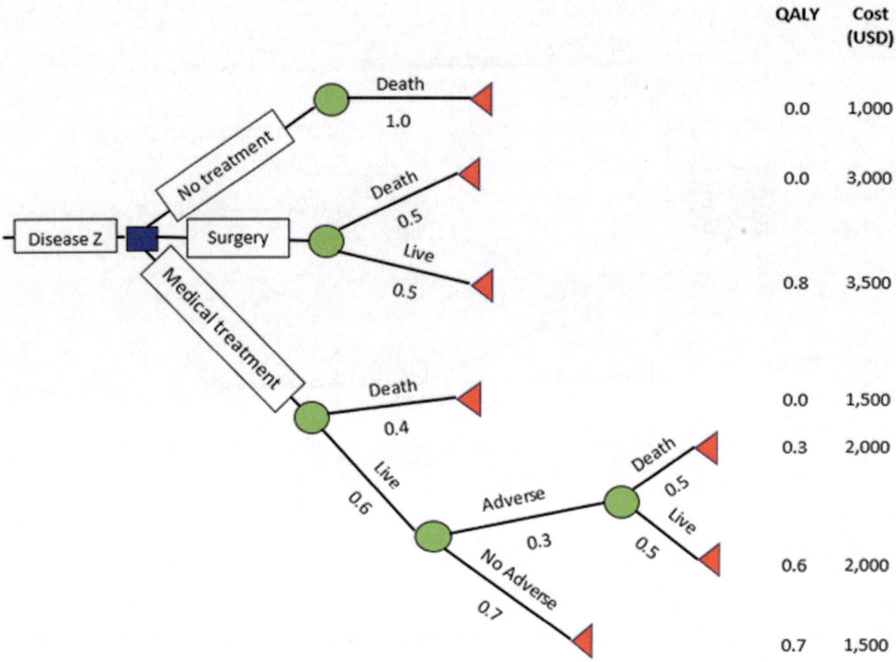

Fig. 5.2 Decision tree example

Table 5.1 ICER calculation

Alternatives	Effectiveness	Costs (USD)
No treatment	1 × 0.0 = 0.0	1 × 1,000 = 1000
Surgery	(0.5 × 0.0) + (0.5 × 0.8) = 0.4	(0.5 × 3,000) + (0.5 × 3,500) = 3,250
Medical treatment	(0.4 × 0.0) + (0.6 × 0.3 × 0,5 × 0.3) + (0.6 × 0.3 × 0.5 × 0.6) + (0.6 × 0.7 × 0.7) = 0.375	(0.4 × 1,500) + (0.6 × 0.3 × 0.5 × 2,000) + (0.6 × 0.3 × 0.5 × 2,000) + (0.6 × 0.7 × 1,500) = 1,590

be multiplied by the effectiveness measured in QALYs. When there is more than one option, the multiplication of each branch must be added, as shown in Table 5.1.

It is observed that the alternative "no treatment" is not effective, while "surgery" is the most effective alternative, although the most expensive. With the cost and effectiveness values we can calculate the incremental cost-effectiveness ratio (ICER) according to the following formula:

$$\text{ICER} \frac{\text{Cost Alternative B} - \text{Cost Alternative A}}{\text{Effectiveness Alternative B} - \text{Effectiveness Alternative B}}$$

If the cost and effectiveness values of the "surgery" and "medical treatment" alternatives are allocated, the ICER would be

$$\text{ICER} = \frac{3250\,\text{USD} - 1590\,\text{USD}}{0.4 - 0.375} = \frac{1660\,\text{USD}}{0.025} = 66{,}400\,\text{USD}\,/\,\text{QALY}$$

In other words, if the "surgery" alternative is chosen, you would have to invest USD$ 66,400 to earn 1 QALY.

Complex decision trees can be represented by subtrees (Rodríguez-Pimentel et al. 2007). These models are recommended only in the case of acute health conditions.

An example of a decision tree applied to oral health is given by Münzenmayer and her collaborators (2019) (see Fig. 5.3). The model was designed to compare the oral health professionals to provide oral hygiene services at residential aged care facilities (RACFs) in Victoria, Australia, compared to current practice. The principal outcome measured in this study is the cost per case of pneumonia averted. The first split is the decision node which determines alternatives of oral hygiene provision path (current practice vs. four possible scenarios). The probability of each branch is indicated as proportions, indicating how many residents followed each branch. The total proportion of the number leaving the chance node adds up to 1. For each outcome, the cost and effectiveness can be determined. These are weighted by the overall probability of the outcomes and add ed. to provide the expected cost and effectiveness of each option.

5.6.2 *Markov Model*

The Markov model is a type of probabilistic model, which assumes that the patient is always in one of a finite number of health states called Markov states (Sonnenberg and Beck 1993), which are characterized by being exhaustive, mutually exclusive, and amnesiac. The fact that the health states are exhaustive means that the model must present all the states of the disease being evaluated, since it must represent the natural history of the disease as closely as possible to reality. For example, dental caries is a preventable disease caused by complex interactions between bacteria that accumulate in dental biofilm (or plaque), diet, and other multiple factors. At its simplest level, the natural history of dental caries is delineated in Fig. 5.4.

The natural history of dental caries begins with a sound tooth surface that is colonized by cariogenic bacteria, establishing a biofilm over tooth structures. Some of the bacteria in dental biofilm live on sugars found in many foods. Sugar is metabolized by the oral bacteria, leading to the production of organic acids (acid formation). When organic acids are in sufficient concentration to lower the pH of the

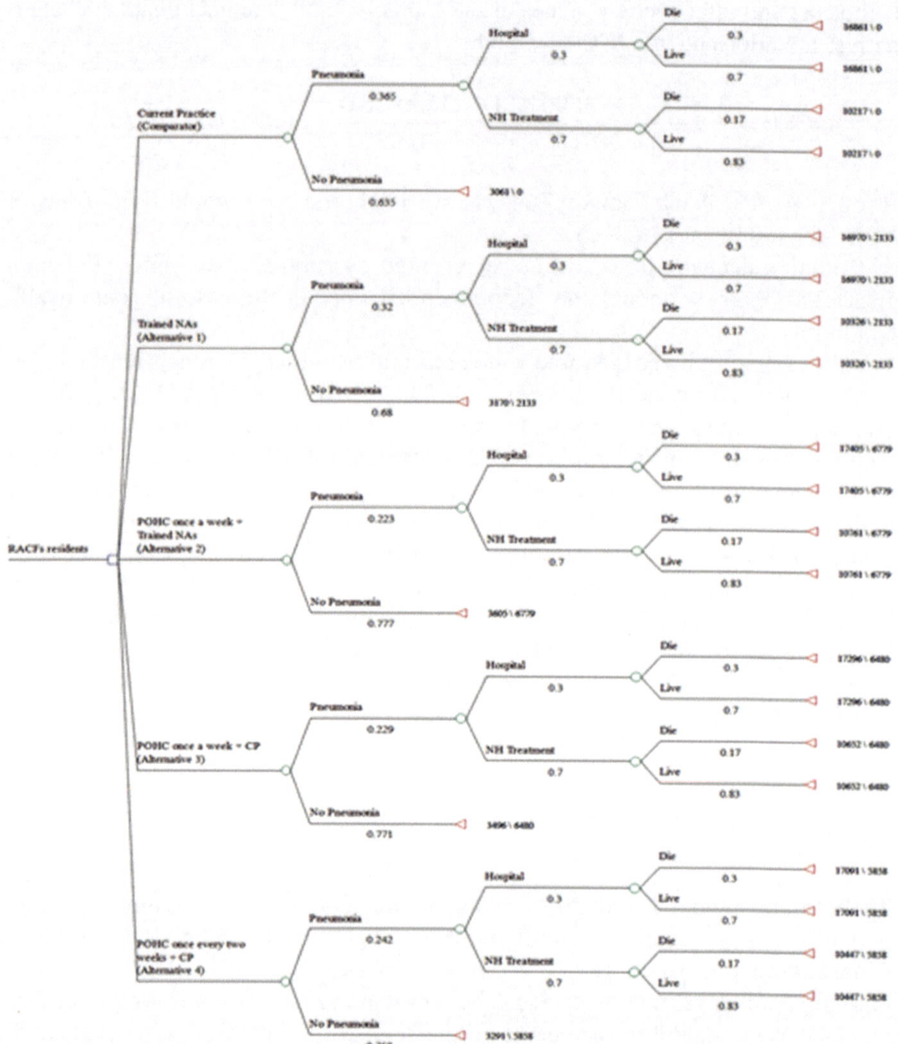

Fig. 5.3 Decision tree model to determine alternatives of oral health provision's cost-effectiveness. (Reprinted from Münzenmayer et al. 2019. © 2018 Gerodontology Association and John Wiley & Sons Ltd. with permission from John Wiley and Sons)

dental biofilm to the point where it will dissolve minerals (demineralization) in the hard structures of the tooth (enamel, dentine, cementum), a microscopic carious lesion occurs. When there is a well-balanced equilibrium, remineralization occurs; however, when the balance is lost, demineralization prevails and results in microscopically detectable carious lesions which will later merge, forming visible cavities (Zimmer et al. 2003). If left untreated, the process will continue to destroy the

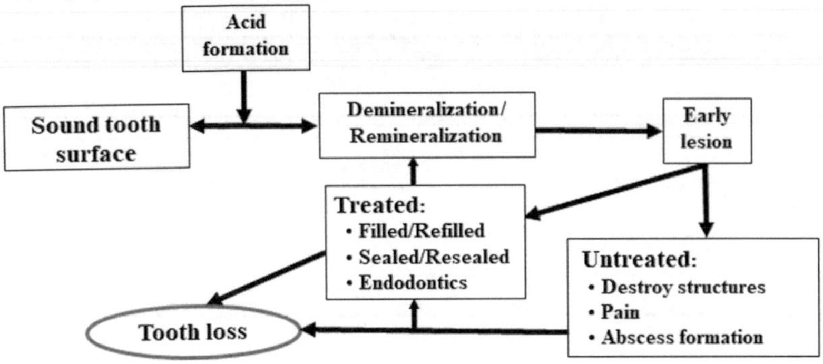

Fig. 5.4 The natural history of dental caries. (Modified from Mariño and Morgan 2016)

tooth and eventually result in pain, pulpal necrosis, tooth extraction, and loss of dental function, which may even progress to an acute systemic infection (Centers for Disease Control and Prevention 1999).

Markov states are mutually exclusive; a person is assumed to reside in one of a finite number of health states (Petrou and Gray 2011). A person cannot be in two states of health at the same time, for example, a person cannot be healthy and sick at the same time.

A limitation of the Markov model is that they are "amnesic," that is, they have no memory. This is known as the Markovian assumption, and it means that patients who are in a state of health have the same probability of having a particular prognosis, regardless of previous individual characteristics.

Health states can also be absorbent or nonabsorbent. The first refers to states of health in which patients who reach this one cannot go to another, for example, death. People who reach nonabsorbent states of health can revert to another state of health. For example, a person may be in the sick state and after being treated may transition to the healthy state.

Figure 5.5 presents a Markov diagram characterizing the natural history of a disease. Three states of health are observed: healthy, sick, and dead. The transitions of patients from one health state to another are represented by arrows, which are associated with probabilities and indicate the direction of the transition. Transitions from one state to another occur in regular periods of time, which can be months or years. This period is called the cycle, which is chosen according to the time in which these changes occur according to the natural history of the disease. For each cycle, costs and effectiveness results are added according to the time the patients are in each state of health. Table 5.2 presents the transition matrix of the health states with their probabilities. The sum of the transition probabilities of each cycle must equal 1. This is because there is only one state at each discrete moment of time (Sato and Zouain 2010).

It should be emphasized that all transitions that arise from the model must occur at the same time. For example, if patients transition from healthy to sick every

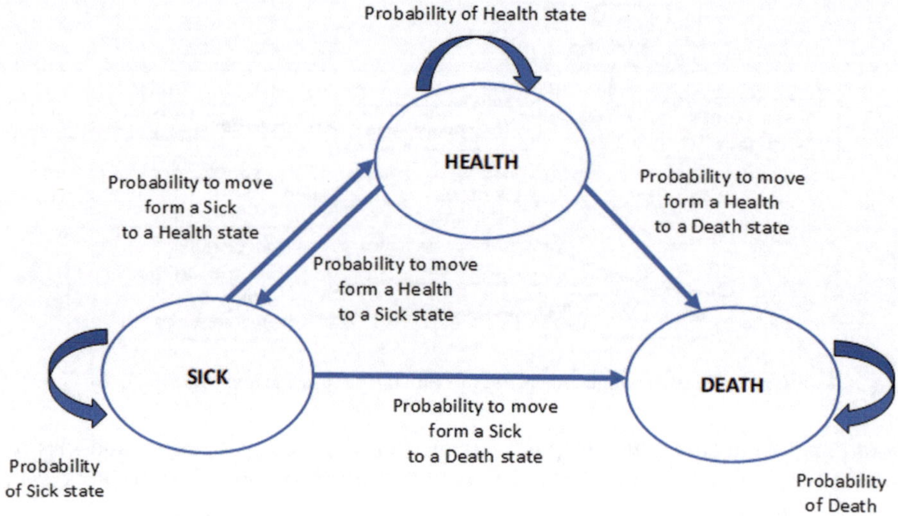

Fig. 5.5 Markov diagram

Table 5.2 Markov transition matrix

	Next states of health		
States of health	Health	Sick	Death
Health	0.3	0.6	0.1
Sick	0.4	0.2	0.4
Death	0.0	0.0	1.0

3 months, patients who are sick must transition to either healthy, dead, or remain in the sick state every 3 months, according to the probabilities of getting sick, staying sick, or dying.

A Markov model simulates hypothetical cohorts of patients, with the characteristics of an average patient. As previously mentioned, the model considers all patients who are in a state of health as being exposed to the same risks. Figure 5.6 presents the transition matrix of a Markov model, where the number of patients passing through each cycle can be observed. This hypothetical cohort begins in the healthy state with 10,000 patients. During the initial period there are no sick or dead patients; however, during cycle 1, defined by the period of 1 year, 3000 people go from healthy to sick, and 2000 to death, leaving 5000 people in the healthy state.

In cycle 2, 2,000 people go from *healthy* to *sick* and another 2,000 to *death*, so that 1,000 people continue to be healthy. From the sick state 2,000 people die, so that 1,000 people remain in that state and continue in that state plus the 2,000 who

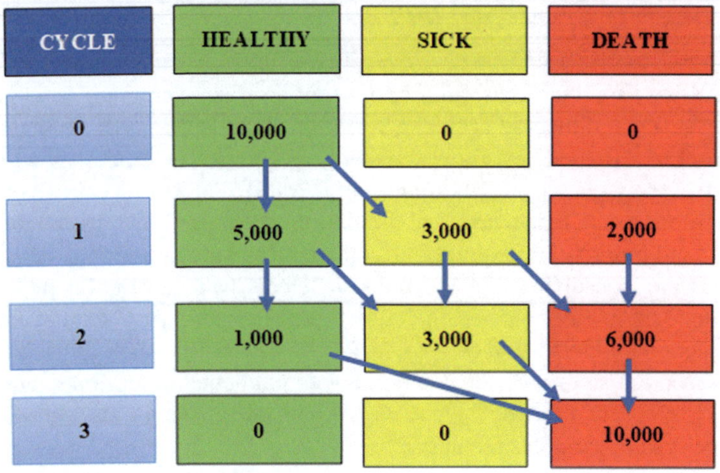

Fig. 5.6 Transition of a cohort in a Markov model

come from the healthy state. Then in cycle 3, the patients who were in the healthy and sick states die, finishing the projection of the model.

A good example of how a Markov model works in oral health is given by Espinoza-Espinoza and his collaborators (2019) who illustrated the progress in dental caries under a school-based prevention program for the application of sealants in molars of schoolchildren compared with nonintervention. A cost-utility analysis based on a Markov model was carried out using probability distribution. The utility was measured in quality-adjusted tooth years (QATY). At each point the patient was in one of a finite number of health states and made transitions over a series of discrete time intervals or cycles. For each health state, the patient may remain in that state or change to a different state. The final health state is represented by tooth extraction.

Once the model is run according to the time horizon of the economic evaluation, it results in the final total effectiveness and the final total costs of the health technologies or intervention that is being evaluated, and in this way the incremental cost-effectiveness ratio (ICER) can be calculated.

This type of model is useful when events can reoccur, or the risk of pathology is continuous over time, for example, chronic diseases such as high blood pressure, diabetes mellitus, chronic kidney disease, dental caries, etc. They are also used when a disease progresses from stage to stage like cancers. Criticisms of the Markov models point mainly to their lack of memory and inability to relate a patient's previous medical history with their current transition probability (Castillo-Riquelme 2010).

5.6.3 Discrete Event Simulation

This modelling technique is useful for representing processes at an individual level, where these can be subject to events, whether they are decisions or events over time (Marshall et al. 2020). They allow the study of systems or processes whose state changes discretely over time (Rodríguez et al. 2008).

These models are made up of a simulation clock, entities, attributes, events, resources, and queues. For example, if you want to evaluate the time of care in an oral healthcare consultation, the simulation clock will record the time of care elapsed since the patient entered the clinic, until he/she leaves. At the same time, relevant secondary clocks can be created for the evaluation, such as the exchanges with the receptionist, or with the examining general dental practitioner, who makes the diagnosis, before referring the patient to a specialist. Every time a relevant event occurs, the system variables are updated.

Entities are objects that have attributes, experience events, consume resources, and enter queues over time (Karnon et al. 2012). In this example, the entities are patients, who have attributes such as age, dental medical history, previous dental treatments, etc. These individuals may come and go until the model is completed. After that, everything that happens during the simulation are events, that is, interaction with the receptionist, with the dentist who performs the diagnosis, and with the specialist. Another event may be the adverse reaction of a patient to anesthesia.

This model, like the previous ones, must have variables, such as effectiveness or benefits, costs, discount rate, and time horizon, which are maintained throughout the simulation. Both human and physical resources that will be used for the simulation, such as number of dentists, dental assistants, secretaries, dental chair identification, etc., must also be included.

Once a patient uses a resource, another patient must wait to receive this resource. That is, while the patient is being treated by the dentist who makes the diagnosis, the practitioner would be generating queues in the consultation room, which creates delays in providing care to other patients.

Each time an event occurs, statistical data is collected, a report is generated, and it is evaluated until the next event.

For an example, let's evaluate the optimization of the resources of a dental chair. To do this, we need to know the rate of use of the chair, the number of dental treatments performed, the time taken for dental care, among other details. Then we need to identify what the entities will be, in this example the entities will be the patients. For each entity, that is, for each patient, the characteristics or attributes by which they differ must be identified, these are sex, age, comorbidities, presence of any oral disease or condition, such as periodontal disease, previous orthodontic treatment, oral hygiene habits, type of dental care required, whether it is urgent or not, etc. Another relevant attribute is quality of life, which can also be included in the model.

All entities must have the same attributes, but with different values. These attributes will influence the events that occur at a later stage.

On the other hand, resources must be identified, such as medical/dental supplies, and human resources such as the receptionist and other administrative staff, dental assistants, and other oral health professionals. These resources will generate an interaction with the entities, which we need to identify, that is, what will happen with these patients. This is what we must model; therefore, we must be clear about the events that could occur during this interaction. In the present example, the events begin with the admission of patients to the dental consultation, check-in with the receptionist, admission of the patient for initial evaluation by a dentist, and when required, admission of the patient for an evaluation by a dental specialist. For all these events, the time that elapses from when a patient enters the consultation until he/she receives care should be considered. In addition, any resources involved (e.g. time for each care action, time to discharge, etc.) should also be considered.

5.7 Final Remarks

Modelling in EE combines information from multiple sources into a decision analytical framework to inform decision-making. Modelling is a powerful tool to reproduce events and possible consequences. Models offer several advantages over other formats for economic evaluation. The most commonly used models are decision trees and Markov models, although other models can also be used. Different models are appropriate for different purposes.

In any case, when choosing a mathematical model, the target population must be considered, its characteristics, and the disease in which a health intervention, (e.g. health promotion, preventive program, screening program, diagnostic services, treatments, policy options, health technologies, etc.) is being compared. Also, it is necessary to describe all the relevant variables and events of the health condition and evaluate which model is most representative of the disease or condition's natural history. Decisions about perspectives of cost and benefits have a substantial impact on the model. The use of relevant basic evidence from several sources to inform the model is one of the strengths of this approach, but it can also lead to errors.

Although models must represent and reflect a real situation, it is advisable not to make them too complicated. At a minimum, models should be understandable for the target population to whom the evaluation will be presented, as well as decision-makers. Additionally, simplicity helps to make an evaluation feasible. If the model is too complex, it is likely that not all of the data needed to populate the model, may be available, and many unjustified assumptions might be made, leading to error.

Always keep in mind that all the inputs and outputs of the model must be transparent and straightforward, indicating the sources, presenting alternatives scenarios, and carrying out sensitivity analyses. Finally, the limitations of the study should be presented.

References

Brennan A, Akehurst R (2000) Modelling in health economic evaluation. What is its place? What is its value? PharmacoEconomics 17:445–459
Brennan A, Chick SE, Davies R (2006) A taxonomy of model structures for economic evaluation of health technologies. Health Econ 15:1295–1310
Buxton MJ, Drummond MF, Van Hout BA et al (1997) Modelling in economic evaluation: an unavoidable fact of life. Health Econ 6:217–227
Castillo-Riquelme M (2010) El uso de modelos matemáticos en evaluación económica de intervenciones de salud. Rev Med Chil 138(Suppl 2):98–102
Centers for Disease Control and Prevention (1999) Fluoridation of public drinking water to prevent dental caries. MMWR 48:933–990
Darbà J (2006) La utilización de métodos probabilísticos para la evaluación económica de tecnologías sanitarias. Gac Sanit 20:74–79
Drummond MF, Sculpher MJ, Torrance GW et al (2005) Methods for the economic evaluation of health care programmes, 3rd edn. Oxford University Press, Oxford
Espinoza-Espinoza G, Corsini G, Rojas R et al (2019) Cost-utility analysis of sealants applied to first permanent molars in schoolchildren at a community-level. A Markov model. BMC Oral Health 19:293
Hoang VP, Shanahan M, Shukla N et al (2016) A systematic review of modelling approaches in economic evaluations of health interventions for drug and alcohol problems. BMC Health Serv Res 16:1–14
Karnon J, Stahl J, Brennan A et al (2012) Modeling using discrete event simulation: a report of the ISPOR-SMDM Modeling Good Research Practices Task Force-4. Med Decis Mak 32:701–711
Mariño R, Morgan M (2016) Oral health in older adults. In: Pachana N (ed) Encyclopedia of geropsychology. Springer, Singapore
Marshall DA, Grazziotin LR, Regier DA et al (2020) Addressing challenges of economic evaluation in precision medicine using dynamic simulation modeling. Value Health 23:566–573
Münzenmayer M, Mariño R, Hsueh A (2019) Cost-effectiveness of professional oral health care in Australian nursing homes. Gerodontology 36:107–117
Nuijten MJ, Starzewski J (1998) Applications of modelling studies. PharmacoEconomics 13:289–291
Parada-Vargas LA, Taborda-Restrepo A (2011) Modelos de evaluación económica: su aplicación en las decisiones sanitarias. Rev Colomb Psiquiatr 40:352–362
Petrou S, Gray A (2011) Economic evaluation using decision analytical modelling: design, conduct, analysis, and reporting. BMJ 342:d1766
Rodríguez JM (2004) Papel de los modelos en las evaluaciones económicas en el campo sanitario. Farm Hosp 28:231–242
Rodríguez JM, Serrano D, Monleón T, Caro J (2008) Los modelos de simulación de eventos discretos en la evaluación económica de tecnologías y productos sanitarios. Gac Sanit 22:151–161
Rodríguez-Pimentel L, Silva-Romo R, Wacher-Rodarte N (2007) Estudios económicos y análisis de decisiones en la autogestión de recursos. Rev Med Inst Mex Seguro Soc 45:297–304

Rubio-Terrés C, Sacristán JA, Badia X et al (2004) Métodos utilizados para realizar evaluaciones económicas de intervenciones sanitarias. Med Clin (Barc) 122:578–583

Sato RC, Zouain DM (2010) Markov models in health care. Einstein (Sao Paulo) 8:376–379

Sonnenberg FA, Beck JR (1993) Markov models in medical decision making: a practical guide. Med Decis Mak 13:322–338

Zimmer S, Jahn K, Barthel CR (2003) Recommendations for the use of fluoride in caries prevention. Oral Health Prev Dent 1:45–51

Chapter 6
Interpreting Economic Evaluation in Oral Health

Marj Moodie, Utsana Tonmukayakul, and Lan Gao

6.1 Incremental Cost-Effectiveness Ratio

Scarcity of available resources means society needs to make choices and to be efficient with the limited resources available. Be it at the level of an individual, a household, a hospital, or a healthcare system, decisions are made to purchase some goods and services and to forego others. Economic evaluation plays an important role in such decision-making; it entails a comparison between two or more options in terms of their costs and outcomes. It helps the decision-maker to choose between competing options, by providing evidence of which will be the 'best buy'. Determination of an intervention's cost-effectiveness answers the question of whether the benefit to be gained from the intervention justifies the cost of implementing it.

Cost-effectiveness evaluations compare the incremental costs and effects of programs or the additional cost that one program imposes compared to the additional benefit it delivers (Drummond et al. 2015). The incremental cost-effectiveness ratio (ICER) provides a summary measure of an intervention's cost-effectiveness or 'value for money'. It is calculated by dividing the difference in total costs (incremental cost) by the difference in effect (incremental effect) between two programs or interventions.

$$\text{ICER} = \frac{\left(C_{\text{B}} - C_{\text{A}}\right)}{\left(E_{\text{B}} - E_{\text{A}}\right)} = \frac{\Delta C}{\Delta E}$$

M. Moodie (✉) · U. Tonmukayakul · L. Gao
Deakin Health Economics, Institute for Health Transformation, Deakin University, Geelong, VIC, Australia
e-mail: marj.moodie@deakin.edu.au; utsana.tonmukayakul@deakin.edu.au; lan.gao@deakin.edu.au

C. Zaror, R. Mariño (eds.), *Introduction to Economic Evaluation in Oral Health Care*, https://doi.org/10.1007/978-3-030-96289-0_6

where C_B and E_B are the cost and effect in the intervention group, C_A and E_A are the cost and effect in the comparator group, and ΔC and ΔE are the change in costs and benefits, respectively.

The ICER is essentially a ratio of the extra cost per extra unit of health effect provided by the intervention being evaluated compared to an alternative. It is most useful in a situation where a new intervention is more costly but provides for additional health gains. The ICER helps to determine whether those extra benefits are worth the additional cost.

Let us suppose that the standard treatment for prevention of gum disease costs \$300 and, on average, leads to 1.3 additional quality-adjusted life years (QALYs) for those patients receiving the treatment. A new alternative therapy is found that costs \$450 and, on average, results in 1.7 additional QALYs. The ICER for the new therapy would be \$375 per QALY gained, based on the calculation below:

$$\text{ICER for new therapy}\frac{\$450-\$300}{1.7\text{QALYs}-1.3\text{QALYs}}=\frac{\$150}{0.4\text{QALYs}}=\$375/\text{QALY gained}$$

In the dental field, cost-effectiveness analyses are the most common economic evaluation study design. The scoping review of economic evaluations in dentistry conducted by Eow et al. 2019 reported that 68 (or 75%) of the identified studies were cost-effectiveness analyses; these reported ICERs as costs per a wide range of diverse physical units such as costs per decay averted, cost per periodontal surgical procedure reduced, and cost per sealing treatment provided, etc. The heterogeneity of the outcome measures used in calculating the ICERs means that the results of such diverse interventions cannot be easily compared. On the other hand, 17(19%) of the identified studies were cost-utility analyses where the ICERs were expressed in terms of a more generic metric which allows for comparison between interventions. ICERs expressed in terms of units such as life years gained, QALYs, or disability-adjusted life years (DALYs) saved enable dental interventions to be compared to non-dental interventions. There have also been some attempts to develop specific measures of dental utility analogous to QALYs, such as quality-adjusted tooth years (QATYs) (Mohd-Dom 2014; Sischo and Broder 2011).

There are several important facts to note about ICERs. Firstly, the ICER captures the incremental cost per unit of effect, rather than the average cost (Hoch and Dewa 2008). The key issue when deciding whether to adopt a new therapy is whether what is gained at that point is worth more than what is given up. What is the extra cost? What is the extra effect or benefit for the patient, and is the trade-off worth it? So the ICER is closely linked to the economic concepts of opportunity cost (benefits foregone of the next best alternate use of resources) and marginal analysis (marginal costs and marginal benefits are the costs and benefits of any changes at the margin or of one more unit of output). Incremental analysis is different to average analysis where costs and benefits are equally spread across all units of production.

Secondly, negative ICERs are generally not reported given that they can be misleading. An intervention that is both less expensive and more effective will generate a negative ICER, but equally, so will an intervention that is more expensive and less effective. A negative ICER, in and of itself, does not convey which of these two opposing situations is being presented. Furthermore, the magnitude of negative ICERs is meaningless. To avoid confusion, ICERs are not reported in these situations and are replaced by the terms 'dominant' (where an intervention produces more health gains and costs less) and 'dominated' (where an intervention produces less health gains and costs more) (Drummond et al. 2015).

Thirdly, ICERs by themselves do not necessarily indicate whether an intervention is an efficient use of resources. They need to be compared to a benchmark of cost-effectiveness, referred to as a ceiling ratio or the cost-effectiveness threshold (see Sect. 6.4).

6.2 Cost-Effectiveness Plane

The results of cost-effectiveness analyses are usually presented in either tables or plotted on a cost-effectiveness plane. If reporting in table format, it is useful to present results in a disaggregated form showing changes in costs and changes in outcomes together with the ICER. The example below (Table 6.1) is drawn from the cost-effectiveness analysis of biannual fluoride varnish for preventing dental caries in permanent teeth conducted by Nguyen et al. (2020). For both arms of the trial, total costs, the number of decayed, missing and filled teeth (DMFT), and quality-adjusted life years (QALYs) gained were reported, plus the ICERs relating to both of these outcome measures.

A cost-effectiveness plane visually represents the difference in costs and outcomes between two alternative options plotted against each other on a four quadrant, two dimensional graph (Fig. 6.1). The incremental differences in costs (between the intervention of interest and the comparator) are plotted along the *y* (vertical) axis and the incremental differences in outcomes across the *x* (horizontal)

Table 6.1 The results of the base-case analysis including the 95% upper and lower limit clinical efficacy of biannual fluoride varnish, discounted

	Current practice		Intervention	
Outcomes	Number	Cost ($)	Number (95% CI)	Cost ($) (95% CI)
Total cost		2303		3600 (1117, 3483)
DMFT	15.52		13.99 (13.13, 14.57)	
QALY gained	14.74		15.44 (15.19, 15.77)	
ICER per prevented-DMFT			849 (494, 1453)	
ICER per QALY gained			1851 (1142, 3042)	

Reprinted from Nguyen et al. (2020, Table 2. CC BY 4.0)
CI confidence interval, *DMFT* decay, missing and filled teeth, *QALY* quality-adjusted life years, *ICER* incremental cost-effectiveness ratio

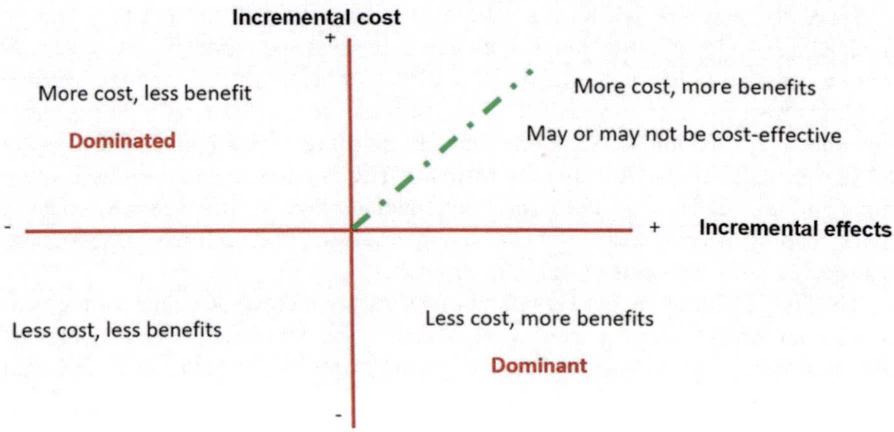

Fig. 6.1 Cost-effectiveness plane

axis. The further right you move on the *x* axis, the more effective is the intervention. The further you move up the *y* axis, the more costly is the intervention.

The four quadrants of the cost-effectiveness plane allow for all possible combinations of costs and benefits; compared with the comparator, the intervention can be more or less effective and more or less costly. The two quadrants on the positive (right-hand) side of the *y* axis indicate an increase in effect (health gains) (Fig. 6.1). Interventions falling in the lower right-hand quadrant are associated with both better health and a reduction in costs. These are termed ‘cost saving’ or ‘dominant’ and should be high on a decision-maker’s priority list for funding. Interventions in the upper right-hand quadrant also offer better health but at an increased cost; this is generally the most common scenario where a new initiative improves health but for additional costs. It may or may not be cost-effective, depending on the threshold of cost-effectiveness being employed (see Sect. 6.4).

The two quadrants on the negative (left-hand) side of the *y* axis indicate that an intervention is less effective. Interventions in the upper left quadrant are both less effective and more costly and are termed ‘dominated’; decision-makers should immediately dismiss them from consideration for funding. Interventions falling in the lower left quadrant provide for less health gain but at a lower cost; they may sometimes enter into funding consideration if the loss of health gain is relatively small, whilst there are significant savings in cost to be made.

Where an intervention results in higher health gains coupled with cost savings (i.e. lower right hand quadrant), the decision about whether to allocate funds to its implementation is clear-cut. Decision-makers should prioritise such dominant interventions for funding. However, when an intervention results in higher health gains but at a higher cost (i.e. in the upper right quadrant), the decision is not straightforward. Interventions falling in this quadrant may or may not be cost-effective; it will depend on the benchmark or threshold for cost-effectiveness that they are being measured against.

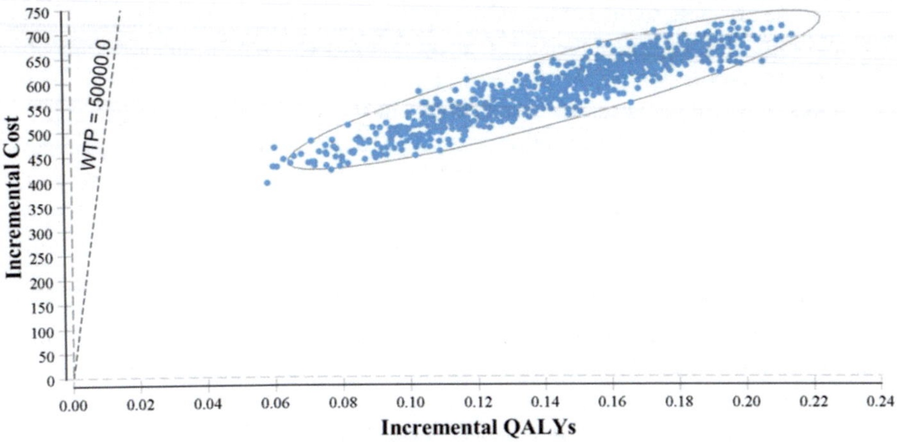

Fig. 6.2 Example of cost-effectiveness results, high value oral health care for a remote indigenous community. (Reprinted from Kularatna et al. 2020. CC BY 4.0)

The example below (Fig. 6.2) is taken from a study demonstrating the cost-effectiveness of high value care to improve the oral health of a remote indigenous community in Australia. The scatter plot on the cost-effectiveness plane shows that all iterations fell in the upper right-hand quadrant, resulting in higher QALY gains for higher costs.

6.3 Cost-Effectiveness Threshold

The cost-effectiveness threshold or ceiling ratio is the maximum amount that a decision-maker is willing to pay for a unit of health outcome. Where an intervention sits in relation to the threshold, will determine whether it is cost-effective, or, in other words, whether the increase in benefit gained is worth the extra cost. The threshold is used to develop a decision rule about funding or not funding an intervention (McFarlane and Bayoumi 2004; Brouwer et al. 2018). If the ICER for an intervention falls below the threshold, a decision-maker is likely to recommend the new intervention (depending on their available budget). On the other hand, if the ICER exceeds the threshold value, the intervention is regarded as not cost-effective and is likely to be rejected; it is considered too costly in the context of the additional benefit which it will provide. The hatched diagonal line on Fig. 6.2 represents the cost-effectiveness threshold.

The cost-effectiveness threshold is closely related to the concept of opportunity cost. The value of an intervention is considered to be the value of what is foregone when it is implemented. In other words, the threshold value equates to the health outcome that could have been achieved if the resources required to implement the intervention had been used elsewhere.

The issue arises as to the setting of the threshold value – how or who determines the maximum amount that a decision-maker is willing to a pay for an additional unit of outcome. Some countries including the UK, Ireland, and the USA have made the thresholds used for decision-making explicit. In the UK, the National Institute for Health and Clinical Excellence (NICE) currently uses a cost-effectiveness threshold in the range of £20,000–£30,000 per QALY (McCabe et al. 2008). Whilst it recommends against funding interventions with an ICER above these thresholds, it sometimes justifies the use of a much higher threshold in special circumstances (such as for life-extending treatments for small populations at the end of life or for patients with a short life expectancy) (Thokala et al. 2018). McCabe et al. (2008), in their analysis of the NICE thresholds, argue that it would preferable to have an explicit single threshold rather than a range and that the selected value should be regularly reviewed.

Many countries, including Australia, Canada, Brazil, New Zealand, and Scotland, do not specify an explicit threshold, despite using cost-effectiveness analyses for decision-making (McDougall et al. 2020). In some cases, researchers have implied a threshold value based on analysis of historical decisions and then have used it as a guide to interpret cost-effectiveness results. Whilst Australia has not formally specified a cost-effectiveness threshold, a value of $50,000/QALY is often cited as the commonly used benchmark of cost-effectiveness (George et al. 2001). Whilst the country's Pharmaceutical Benefits Advisory Committee employs no single maximum ICER when making funding decisions about new drugs, an analysis of its funding decisions by Paris and Belloni (2013) showed that new medicines were rarely recommended for listing with an ICER above $70,000/QALY, and those greater than $45,000 were recommended only in exceptional circumstances, such as a high clinical need and where there was no alternative treatment (Wang et al. 2018). Likewise, the Pharmaceutical Management Agency (PHARMAC) in New Zealand does not have an explicitly stated threshold. Whilst researchers have endeavoured to imply the threshold from previous decisions, PHARMAC argues that it is not possible to infer it as cost-effectiveness is only one of multiple decision criteria used to inform decision-making (Thokala et al. 2018).

The WHO Commission on Macro-Economics and Health (2001) recommended valuing DALYs at between one and three times a country's Gross Domestic Product per capita (Marseille et al. 2015). In recent years, a few countries have embarked on empirical studies to estimate cost-effectiveness thresholds specific to their setting. There is no consensus however around the most appropriate methods of determining threshold values (Claxton et al. 2015). An example of this is the work undertaken by Edney et al. (2018) to establish a reference ICER appropriate to the Australia health system; they estimated a value of $28,033/QALY as representing the average opportunity cost of decisions to fund new technologies (Edney et al. 2018). Another methodology which has been suggested for countries lacking a threshold is that employed by Huang et al. (2018) who used life satisfaction as an indicator of 'experienced utility' and estimated the dollar equivalent value of a QALY using a fixed effect model. Using a nationally representative longitudinal survey of 28,347 Australians followed in the period 2002–2015, they estimated individual willingness to pay for one QALY as between AUD42,000 and 67,000; this result is not dissimilar to the QALY threshold of AUD50,000 commonly used in decision-making in Australia.

Cost-effectiveness thresholds are specific not only to a particular jurisdiction but to the unit of health outcomes being measured. Most economic evaluations of preventive dental programs report cost-effectiveness in terms of incremental cost per the two standard measures of dental caries: DMFS (decayed, missing, and filled surfaces) or DMFT (decayed, missing, and filled teeth) avoided (Oscarson et al. 2003; Warren et al. 2010; Crowley et al. 2000; Mariño et al. 2012; Tonmukayakul et al. 2015). The issue here is that there are no defined thresholds for such ICERs, and cost-effectiveness can only be established by comparison with evaluations of other similar interventions, if any, which have used the same metrics. A review by Tan et al. (2017) identified 25 studies which attempted to elicit willingness to pay for oral health interventions; however, the usefulness of their results was limited by the lack of methodological rigor and the failure to account for bias.

6.4 Measuring Uncertainty in Cost-Effectiveness Analyses

The cost-effectiveness plane provides a visual snapshot of the likely spread of the cost-effectiveness results and so provides a measure of the uncertainty surrounding the ICER. Simulation modelling or bootstrapping is commonly used to facilitate the presentation of an uncertainty interval around the ICERs (and other parameters). A software and statistical package such as @RISK, TreeAge, R, or STATA can be used to conduct the probabilistic sensitivity analysis. Monte Carlo simulations allow multiple recalculations of the ICERs; each time, a value is randomly chosen from the specified distribution of each input variable in the model. The bootstrapping will result in a 'cloud' of results which may span across more than one quadrant of the cost-effectiveness plane. For this reason, it is important that the four quadrants of the cost-effectiveness plane represent all combinations of possible outcomes. The cost-effectiveness plane provides a visual summary of how costs and outcomes are likely to behave with respect to the particular intervention under evaluation.

In the example shown in Fig. 6.3, taken from the cost-effectiveness analysis by Tonmukayakul and Arrow (2017) of atraumatic restorative treatment as an approach to managing caries in early childhood, the ICER was AUD719 per referral to specialist care avoided. When probabilistic sensitivity analysis was conducted, all 1000 iterations of the model resulted in the ICERs falling on the right-hand side of the y axis. Most (63%) were located in the lower right-hand quadrant, meaning that the intervention results in more health gains at lower cost or is 'dominant'. The remainder of the iterations (37%) were located in the upper-right hand quadrant, which indicates that the additional benefits will be achieved with extra costs. However, the lack of an established cost-effectiveness benchmark for this outcome measure means that it is not possible to determine what proportion of this latter group can be classified as cost-effective.

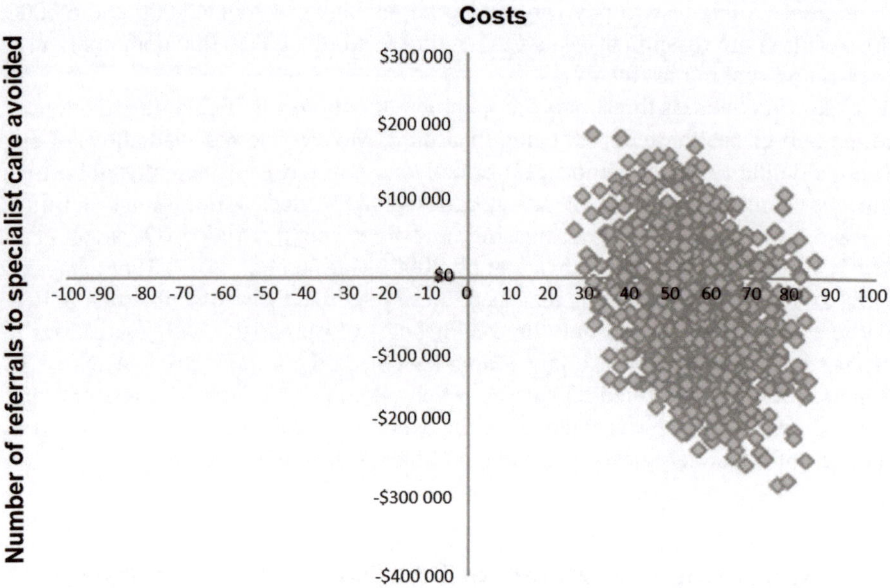

Fig. 6.3 Cost-effectiveness plane: incremental costs per referral to specialist care avoided. (Reprinted from Tonmukayakul and Arrow 2017 © with permission from John Wiley & Sons)

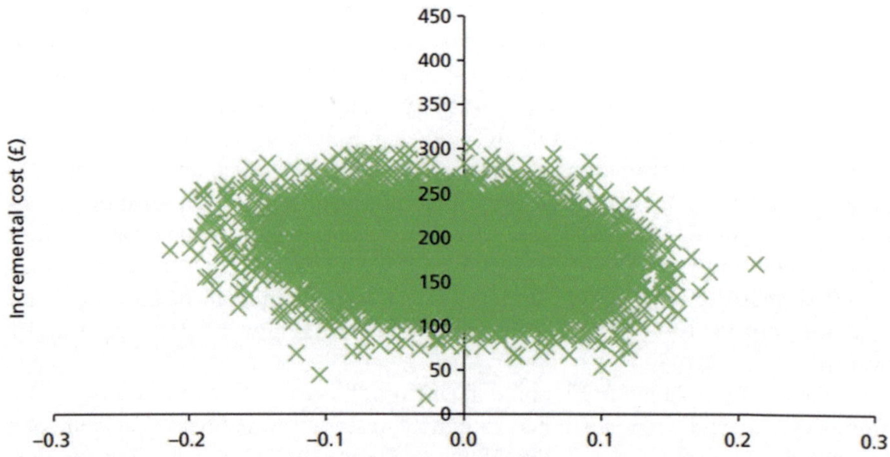

Fig. 6.4 Cost-effectiveness plane for incentive care practice compared with traditional care practice. (Reproduced with permission from Hulme et al. 2016. © Queen's Printer and Controller of HMSO 2016. www.journalslibrary.nihr.ac.uk)

The 2016 INCENTIVE study (Hulme et al. 2016) compared a blended/incentive-driven model of dental service provision compared with traditional dental contracting. Using QALYs as the outcome measure, Fig. 6.4 suggests that incentive care practice is unlikely to be cost-effective from the commissioner's perspective. The iteration results are spread roughly equally across the two upper quadrants, making it difficult to draw any conclusions on whether the intervention is cost-effective. What can be concluded from the cost-effectiveness plane is the wide range of uncertainty around the ICER results; a considerable proportion of the iterations indicate poorer health outcomes (fewer QALYs) at higher costs, whilst others indicate improved health outcomes for additional costs.

6.5 Cost-Effectiveness Acceptability Curves

The examples given in the previous section indicate that when multiple iterations of an intervention are simulated, the resultant ICERs may be distributed across more than one quadrant of the cost-effectiveness plane. This may mean that an intervention deemed cost-effective may not necessarily be so in some circumstances. Such uncertainty may give rise to the possibility that a funding decision made on the basis of it may prove to be incorrect. A decision-maker will be interested in the probability that a new technology is cost-effective compared to the existing alternative. That probability will depend on the proportion of the scatter plot points that fall below the cost-effectiveness threshold.

As an example, Cobiac and Vos (2012) found that extending the coverage of water supply fluoridation to all Australian communities of at least 1000 people would lead to improved population health (3700 DALYs averted) and have a 100% probability of being dominant or cost saving. On the other hand, extending the intervention to smaller communities would not be cost-effective, despite significant improvements in health. The median cost-effectiveness ratio for that scenario was AUD92,000 per DALY, with only a 10% probability of being under the AUD50,000 per DALY threshold.

Since the cost-effectiveness threshold will vary depending on the jurisdiction, the construction of cost-effectiveness acceptability curves has gained popularity amongst health economists as a way of visualising the information from the bootstrapping results. The concept of the cost-effectiveness acceptability curve was developed by van Hout et al. (1994) as a way of expressing the uncertainty inherent in cost-effectiveness calculations, in a statistically meaningful way. The probability that the intervention under study would be cost-effective is plotted on the *y* axis over a wide range of possible thresholds, depicted on the *x* axis (Cohen and Reynolds 2008). It shows the probability that an intervention is cost-effective for a range of different values that a decision-maker might be willing to pay for a unit change of outcome (Hoch and Dewa 2008). They were essentially developed as an alternative to the statistical challenge of determining confidence intervals around ICERs.

The cost-effectiveness acceptability curve is constructed by plotting from the scatter plot of results on the cost-effectiveness plane the proportion of cost and effect pairs that are cost-effective for a range of willingness to pay values. Returning to our earlier example from the INCENTIVE study (Sect. 6.5) (Hulme et al. 2016), the cost-effectiveness acceptability curve below (Fig. 6.5), based on 10,000 iterations, shows that the probability of incentive care practice being cost-effective for a

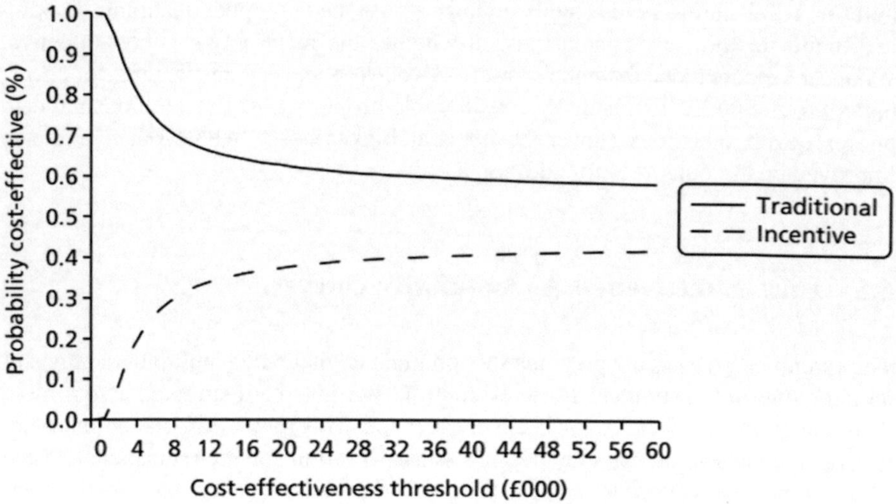

Fig. 6.5 Cost-effectiveness acceptability curve based on bootstrap replications for incentive compared with traditional practice care. (Reproduced with permission from Hulme et al. 2016. © Queen's Printer and Controller of HMSO 2016. www.journalslibrary.nihr.ac.uk)

range of threshold values between £0 and £60,000 per QALY. There is a 37% probability of the intervention being cost-effective against the threshold of £20,000 recommended by NICE, compared to a 63% probability for traditional care practice (Hulme et al. 2016).

6.6 League Tables

Much of the discussion in both this chapter and this book has centred on the economic evaluation of single stand-alone interventions in the dental field. However, often when allocating resources, decision-makers will need to compare interventions and to make choices and trade-offs. Health economists have traditionally used league tables, which rank interventions in order of their ICER, to provide information to decision-makers about the relative merits of different interventions. Too often, however, league tables are compiled by drawing on the results of single intervention studies in the published literature. The included studies are likely to differ quite markedly in terms of methodology and assumptions related to choice of comparator, reference year, target group, perspective, outcome measures, time horizon and discount rate, etc. Such methodological variations will influence the rankings produced by the league table and may potentially lead to questionable funding decisions (Mauskopf et al. 2012; Wilson et al. 2019).

The ACE (assessing cost-effectiveness) methodology was developed in Australia as an 'ideal' approach to priority setting (Carter et al. 2008). It was an attempt to address the reservations about league tables compiled from economic evaluations in the published literature with no regard to differences in methods, context, and setting. In the ACE approach, the economic evaluations of multiple interventions are undertaken as an integral part of the priority setting exercise, using standardised methods which are open to scrutiny and facilitate comparison of results. The setting, context, comparator, and outcome measures are common to all of the interventions, and country-specific data are used for costs and demographic and epidemiological inputs. The methodology entails a two-stage concept of benefit. For each intervention evaluated, the technical cost-effectiveness results are considered alongside a series of implementation filters or other factors which are important in the making of resource allocation decisions; these filters include equity, strength of evidence, feasibility of implementation, and acceptability of stakeholders.

Whilst there have been no ACE studies conducted specifically for oral health, the large ACE-Prevention study conducted in Australia evaluated 5 oral health interventions as part of its evaluation of 150 preventive and treatment interventions (Table 6.2) (Vos et al. 2010). Only one of the five oral health interventions – fluoridation of public water supply of all Australian towns with a population of at least 1000 – was cost-effective. It was dominant, resulting in both health gains and cost savings. It was one of 23 prevention interventions in the study which fell into the dominant category. The standard methodology employed across all intervention (both oral health and non-oral health) enabled this cost-effective intervention to be ranked against others in terms of different parameters such as ICERs, costs, health gains, cost offsets, etc.

The ACE-Obesity Policy study (Ananthapavan et al. 2020) provides a recent example of the use of the ACE dual concept of benefit process to rank and prioritise

Table 6.2 Oral health interventions evaluated as part of the ACE-Prevention study

	ICER (cost/DALY)	Lifetime DALYs	Lifetime intervention cost	Filter issues
1. Public water fluoridation for all towns >1000 people	Dominant	3700	$13M	Limited strength of evidence; public acceptability
2. Public water fluoridation for all towns in Australia	$92,000	5900	$680M	Limited strength of evidence; public acceptability
3. Annual dental check at ages 12–17; oral examination only	$54,000	590	$32M	No evidence
4. Annual dental check at ages 12–17; oral examination, X-ray and clean	$220,000	590	$130M	No evidence
5. Annual dental check at ages 12–17; oral examination, X-ray and clean and scale and sealant	$620,000	590	$370M	No evidence

Source: Compiled from Vos et al. (2010)

multiple interventions. For each of the 16 policy interventions targeting obesity prevention, each implementation filter was given a rating, high, medium, or low, based on the best available evidence. Eleven of the 16 interventions were classified as dominant and therefore could not be ranked in terms of their ICERs; alternatively, they were ranked in terms of health-adjusted life years (HALYs) gained or one of the other parameters. The study highlights how the ranking of interventions will vary substantially depending on the parameter being used as the basis of the ranking.

6.7 Net Benefit

This chapter has focused on the calculation and interpretation of ICERs, which have commonly been used by health economists for the past several decades as a summary measure of the results of economic evaluations. Yet ICERs are not without their critics; there have been some recent moves to encourage health economists to replace them by measures of net benefit.

Paulden (2020) specifies a number of arguments as to why the ICER should be abandoned. He argues that the ICERs are laborious to calculate, difficult to interpret, require a threshold to facilitate their interpretation, cannot be used to rank strategies or to consider relative cost-effectiveness, and cannot be easily used for sensitivity or scenario analysis, probabilistic analysis, or in the consideration of equity concerns. Paulden promotes the abandonment of ICERs in favour of net monetary benefit (NMB).

The net health benefit equates to the net of the health gain experienced by patients receiving the intervention under study minus the health loss experienced by other patients whose treatment has been forgone as a result. For example, if a dental health intervention results in 27 QALYs and $1.2 million cost, assuming a threshold of $50,000 per QALY, the health loss experienced by other patients equals $1.2 million/$50,000 or 24 QALYs. The net health benefit then equals 27 QALYs – 24 QALYs =3 QALYs.

To calculate the NMB for each intervention, the net health benefit is multiplied by the threshold, which reflects the monetary value of the unit of benefit. Assuming the intervention has a benefit of 27 QALYs, this equates to a monetary value of $1.35 million. The NMB is calculated by subtracting the cost of the intervention from this benefit ($1.35 million – $1.2 million = $150,000).

ICERs and NMB are both methodological tools which assist in determining whether an intervention is cost-effective, but they differ in a number of fundamental aspects. The ICER is a 'pairwise' measure that is based on incremental analysis of two options (usually an intervention and usual practice), regardless of the total number of strategies being evaluated. On the other hand, NMB can be calculated for each intervention individually. Secondly, the ICER is a ratio between incremental costs and incremental benefits of an intervention measured against a comparator, whereas measures of net benefit are not ratios. Thirdly, a threshold is required to calculate measures of net benefit but is not required to calculate ICERs; conversely, a threshold is required to interpret ICERs but is not required to interpret measures of net benefit. The ICER framework was specifically developed for use in the area of health, whereas other sectors such as transport and agriculture have traditionally used measures of net monetary benefit. To move beyond the ICER would probably require decision-makers to be explicit about the threshold value.

6.8 Reporting Cost-Effectiveness Analyses

Whilst there are no guidelines for measuring the quality of economic evaluations, there are established guidelines relating to their reporting. The Consolidated Health Economic Reporting Standards (CHEERS) statement (Husereau et al. 2013) was developed in 2013 in an attempt to consolidate and update previous health economic evaluation guidelines into one current, useful reporting template. The recommendations are contained in a user-friendly, 24-item checklist. The aim of the guidelines is to improve the reporting of economic evaluations by promoting completeness and transparency of reporting of both context, methods, and results. It is recommended that the checklist be routinely used in the preparation of all journal articles reporting on economic evaluations; some journals now require the checklist to be completed as a condition of article submission.

6.9 Summary

This chapter has laid the groundwork for understanding the concept of cost-effectiveness. It illustrates the different formats of presenting cost-effectiveness analysis results and discusses the issues associated with their interpretation. It introduces willingness to pay thresholds, which provide a necessary guide in assessing whether an intervention offers good value for money. The chapter also touches on the use of league tables in prioritising multiple interventions, the reporting of cost-effectiveness results, and the potential use of net monetary benefit as an alternative measure of an intervention's cost-effectiveness.

References

Ananthapavan J, Sacks G, Brown V, Moodie M, Nguyen P, Veerman L, Mantilla Herrera AM, Peeters A, Carter R (2020) Priority-setting for obesity prevention – the Assessing Cost-Effectiveness of obesity prevention policies in Australia (ACE-Obesity Policy) study. PLoS One 15(6):e0234804

Brouwer W, van Baal P, van Exel J, Versteegh M (2018) When is it too expensive? Cost-effectiveness thresholds and health care decision-making. Eur J Health Econ 20:175–180

Carter R, Vos T, Moodie M, Haby M, Magnus A, Mihalopoulos C (2008) Priority setting in health: origins, description and application of the Australian Assessing Cost-Effectiveness initiative. Expert Rev Pharmacoecon Outcomes Res 8(6):593–617

Claxton K, Martin S, Soares M, Rice N, Spackman E, Hinde S, Devlin N, Smith PC, Sculpher M (2015) Methods for the estimation of the National Institute for Health and Care Excellence cost-effectiveness threshold. Health Technol Assess 19(14):1–503

Cobiac LJ, Vos T (2012) Cost-effectiveness of extending the coverage of water supply fluoridation for the prevention of dental caries in Australia. Commun Dent Oral Epidemiol 40(4):369–376

Cohen DJ, Reynolds MR (2008) Interpreting the results of cost-effectiveness studies. J Am Coll Cardiol 52(25):2119–2126

Crowley SJ, Campain AC, Morgan MV (2000) An economic evaluation of a publicly funded dental prevention programme in regional and rural Victoria: an extrapolated analysis. Community Dent Health 17:145–151

Drummond MF, Sculpher MJ, Claxton K, Stoddart GL, Torrance GW (2015) Methods for the economic evaluation of health care programmes, 4th edn. Oxford University Press, Oxford

Edney LC, Afzali HHA, Cheng TC, Karnon J (2018) Estimating the reference incremental cost-effectiveness ratio for the Australian health system. PharmacoEconomics 36(2):239–252

Eow J, Duane B, Solaiman A, Hussain U, Lemasney N, Ang R, O'Kelly-Lynch N, Girgis G, Collazo L, Johnston B (2019) What evidence do economic evaluations in dental care provide? A scoping review. Community Dent Health 36:118–125

George B, Harris A, Mitchell A (2001) Cost-effectiveness analysis and the consistency of decision making: evidence from pharmaceutical reimbursement in Australia (1991 to 1996). PharmacoEconomics 19(11):1103–1109

Hoch JS, Dewa CS (2008) A clinician's guide to correct cost-effectiveness analysis: think incremental not average. Can J Psychiatr 53(4):267–274

Huang L, Frijters P, Dalziel K, Clarke P (2018) Life satisfaction, QALYs, and the monetary value of health. Soc Sci Med 211:131–136

Hulme C, Robinson P, Douglas G, Bacter P, Gibson B, Godson J, Vinall-Collier K, Saloniki E, Meads D, Brunton P, Pavitt S (2016) The INCENTIVE study: a mixed-methods evaluation of an innovation in commissioning and delivery of primary dental care compared with traditional dental contracting. Health Serv Deliv Res 4(18). https://doi.org/10.3310/hsdr04180. www.journalslibrary.nihr.ac.uk

Husereau D, Drummond M, Petrou S, Mauskopf J, Loder E (2013) Consolidated Health Economic Reporting Standards (CHEERS) – explanation and elaboration: a report of the ISPOR Health Economic Evaluation Publication Guidelines Good Reporting Practices Task Force. Value Health 16(2):231–250

Kularatna S, Lalloo R, Kroon J, Tadakamadla SKK, Scuffham PA, Johnson NW (2020) Demonstration of high value care to improve oral health of a remote Indigenous community in Australia. Health Qual Life Outcomes 18:43. https://doi.org/10.1186/s12955-020-01300-8

Mariño R, Fajardo J, Morgan M (2012) Cost-effectiveness model for dental caries prevention programmes among Chilean schoolchildren. Community Dent Health 29(4):302–308

Marseille E, Larson B, Kazi D, Kahn JG, Rosen S (2015) Thresholds for the cost-effectiveness of interventions: alternative approaches. Bull World Health Organ 93:118–124

Mauskopf J, Rutten F, Schonfeld W (2012) Cost-effectiveness league tables. PharmacoEconomics 21:991–1000

McCabe C, Claxton K, Culyer A (2008) The NICE cost-effectiveness threshold: what it is and what it means. PharmacoEconomics 26(9):733–744

McDougall JA, Furnback WE, Wang BCM, Mahlich J (2020) Understanding the global measurement of willingness to pay in health. J Mark Access Health Policy 8(1):1717030

McFarlane PA, Bayoumi AM (2004) Acceptance and rejection: cost-effectiveness and the working nephrologist. Kidney Int 66:1735–1741

Mohd-Dom T (2014) Quality-adjusted tooth years (QATY) as an outcome measure of periodontal treatment. BMC Public Health 14(Suppl 1):P10

Nguyen TM, Tonmukayakul U, Warren E, Cartwright S, Liew D (2020) A Markov cost-effective analysis of bi-annual fluoride varnish for preventing dental caries in permanent teeth over a 70-year time horizon. Health Promot J Aust 31:177–183

Oscarson N, Kallestal C, Fjelddhal A, Lindholm L (2003) Cost-effectiveness of different caries preventive measures in a high-risk population of Swedish adolescents. Community Dent Oral Epidemiol 31:169–178

Paris V, Belloni A (2013) Value in pharmaceutical pricing, OECD Health Working Papers, No. 63. OECD Publishing, Paris. https://doi.org/10.1787/5k43jc9v6knx-en

Paulden M (2020) Calculating and interpreting ICERs and net benefit. PharmacoEconomics 38(8):785–807

Sischo L, Broder HL (2011) Oral health-related quality of life. What, why, how, and future implications. J Dent Res 90(11):1264–1270

Tan SHX, Vernazza CR, Nair R (2017) Critical review of willingness to pay for clinical oral health interventions. J Dent 64:1–12

Thokala P, Ochalek J, Leech AA, Tong T (2018) Cost-effectiveness thresholds: the past, the present and the future. PharmacoEconomics 36:506–522

Tonmukayakul Y, Arrow P (2017) Cost-effectiveness analysis of the atraumatic restorative treatment-based approach to managing early childhood caries. Community Dent Oral Epidemiol 45:92–100

Tonmukayakul U, Calache H, Clark R, Wasiak J, Faggion CM (2015) Systematic review and quality appraisal of economic evaluation publications in dentistry. J Dent Res 94(10):1348–1354

Van Hout B, Al MJ, Gordon GS, Rutten FFH (1994) Costs, effects and C/E-ratios alongside a clinical trial. Health Econ 3(5):309–319

Vos T, Carter R, Barendregt J, Mihalopoulos C, Veerman JL, Magnus A, Cobiac L, Bertram MY, Wallace AL, ACE–Prevention Team (2010) Assessing cost-effectiveness in prevention (ACE–prevention): final report. University of Queensland/Deakin University, Brisbane/Melbourne. https://public-health.uq.edu.au/files/571/ACE-Prevention_final_report.pdf. Accessed 15 Aug 2020

Wang S, Gum D, Merlin T (2018) Comparing the ICERs in medicine reimbursement submissions to NICE and PBAC. Does the presence of an explicit threshold affect the ICER proposed? Value Health 21(8):938–943

Warren E, Pollicino C, Curtis B, Evans W, Sbaraini A, Schwarz E (2010) Modeling the long-term cost-effectiveness of the caries management system in an Australian population. Value Health 13(6):750–760

WHO Commission on Macroeconomics and Health (2001) Macroeconomics and health: investing in health for economic development: report of the Commission on Macroeconomics and Health. World Health Organization, Geneva. https://apps.who.int/iris/handle/10665/42435. Accessed 15 Aug 2020

Wilson N, Davies A, Brewer N, Nghien N, Cobiac L, Blakely T (2019) Can cost-effectiveness results be combined into a coherent league table? Case study from one high-income country. Popul Health Metr 17(1):10

Chapter 7
Worked Example in Cost-Effectiveness Analysis

Ann S. Goldman-Hawes

7.1 Step 1. Objective of the Economic Evaluation

This chapter presents the findings of an economic evaluation of a community randomized oral health prevention trial in a low-income, underserved population in Brasilia, Brazil. The trial compared two primary oral health strategic approaches to preventing the development of dentine carious lesions on permanent molars. It evaluated the comparative cost-effectiveness of a supervised toothbrushing (STB) education promotion program with that of a clinical intervention program, using two different sealant intervention strategies.

7.2 Step 2. Define the Economic Evaluation Framework

7.2.1 *Perspective of the Economic Analysis*

Brazil has sought to develop a national oral health policy and integrate oral health into its National Health System [Sistema Único de Saúde (SUS)] (Pucca Jr. et al. 2015; Goldman et al. 2017). The national program's policymakers and program developers, who are interested in identifying the most cost-effective approaches to achieving improved oral health outcomes, were the primary audience for the evaluation. Dental practitioners and other private oral health service providers are interested stakeholders.

A. S. Goldman-Hawes (✉)
Department of Epidemiology, The George Washington University Milken Institute of Public Health, Washington, DC, USA
e-mail: annieg@gwu.edu

C. Zaror, R. Mariño (eds.), *Introduction to Economic Evaluation in Oral Health Care*, https://doi.org/10.1007/978-3-030-96289-0_7

The study adopted a government oral health program perspective. Costs included were those incurred in delivering services such as sealant placement and supervision of toothbrushing in the schools; societal and patient costs were excluded.

7.2.2 *Alternatives Being Compared*

The approaches compared were two clinical intervention strategies: treatment with composite resin (CR) and atraumatic restorative treatment (ART) high viscosity glass-ionomer sealants (HVGIC) and one health education behavioral change strategy of supervised toothbrushing. Each clinical strategy applied different techniques and materials. The study evaluated the cost-effectiveness of the impact of these two strategies on the prevention of dentine carious lesions.

The study had three objectives: (1) to collect all relevant costs associated with each strategic approach adopted in the process of protecting the developing permanent molars; (2) to estimate the unit cost of each primary care strategy in terms of protecting molar development, e.g., placement of sealant intervention and the health education promotion of supervised toothbrushing; and (3) to evaluate the incremental cost-effectiveness for each prevention strategy in protecting the first permanent molars, given their rates of caries-free survival after 3 years.

7.2.3 *Time Horizon*

The study's 3-year time frame covers the period when the primary or deciduous teeth exfoliate, and the permanent teeth erupt. During this period it is important, for the normal development of the oral cavity, to protect the deciduous teeth until they are ready to exfoliate to ensure normal eruption of the permanent teeth, particularly the first and second molars. Currently, most cost-effectiveness research considers a minimum of 3–4 years.

7.3 Step 3. Determine Costs and Benefits of Alternatives

7.3.1 *Study Activities*

Full details of the study and its results, summarized here, were published in Caries Research in 2017 as "Treating High-Caries Risk Occlusal Surfaces in First Permanent Molars Through Sealants and Supervised Toothbrushing: A Three-Year Cost-Effective Analysis" (Goldman et al. 2017).

The effectiveness study was a cluster randomized controlled clinical trial of 6–7-year-old children (de Amorim et al. 2012); it used a parallel group design. The study was implemented in all six public primary schools of Paranoá, a low-income suburban area of Brasilia, Brazil, where the water system was artificially fluoridated (de Amorim et al. 2012). Children who participated were in good general health with at least two cavitated dentine carious lesions in vital, pain-free molars; erupted first permanent molars with the occlusal surface fully visible and accessible; high-caries risk occlusal surfaces in first permanent molars with medium or deep fissures and/or an enamel carious lesion; and a consent form signed by the child's parent or carer.

The study groups reviewed were divided into three categories; one supervised toothbrushing group and two sealant intervention groups, one, CR, for application with conventional methods and rotary equipment group, and the other, ART/HVGIC, for sealants applied with the minimal intervention atraumatic restorative treatment (ART) method and hand instruments group. A dmfs evaluation done at the initiation of the study showed no differences between the three study groups, with respect to dmfs (de Amorim et al. 2013).

Of the six primary schools in Paranoá, the CR intervention strategy group was allocated to the only two equipped with dental units; these had not been used in over 5 years. The remaining ART/HVGIC and STB strategy groups were randomly allocated among the remaining four schools.

In the two clinical intervention strategy groups, before the sealant treatment started, pits and fissures were cleaned with toothbrushes and toothpaste (Goldman et al. 2017), three trained and calibrated pedodontists, aided by trained dental assistants, placed the sealants between May and July 2009, on the school premises.

At the start of the study, and annually during the evaluation period, all children participating in the study group received an oral hygiene kit with a conventional toothbrush, a 1000-ppm fluoridated toothpaste, plaque-disclosing paste, and dental floss. The children were instructed on how to use these devices and encouraged to brush their teeth twice daily. Each month a dental assistant visited the four schools where the CR and ART/HVGIC sealants were performed to check if there were any complaints.

Toothbrushing supervision took place daily during the school year for the STB group, from May 2009 to December 2012. One dental assistant, trained in identifying plaque, supervised the toothbrushing sessions. When necessary, brushing instructions were repeated. The assistants encouraged the children to maintain the same hygiene practices at home and during school vacations (Goldman et al. 2017).

7.3.2 *Study Measurement*

Given the study's assumption of a government perspective, the study inputs costed were those that would best reflect a government-level program. These included salaries and per diem for the three pedodontists and their dental assistants, transportation costs to and from the schools, dental equipment, and instruments and supplies utilized in the study. Cost data were collected prospectively for all inputs, whether purchased or donated.

7.3.3 Cost Data Collection

The principal investigators used a Microsoft Excel instrument designed for the study to collect data prospectively from the University of Brasilia and the study participants. Salary data came from the university. Most purchases, especially of instruments and supplies, were made through the university.

Study data were collected prospectively during the community trial, estimating the cost per sealant and comparing the costs per additional outcome averted (cavitated dentine carious lesions) for each intervention group.

7.3.4 Calculate Costs

Costs of instruments and supplies were recorded by group. Transportation and equipment costs were apportioned by group, according to the number of interventions performed in each group. Personnel costs were apportioned by group, and data on dentists' and dental assistants' time was factored into the cost.

In this study, some instruments were donated or purchased outside of the country, and the HVGIC was donated. Two of the schools had dental chairs not acquired for the study; their replacement cost was researched in the local market and their annual cost calculated and attributed to the study. The costs of any instruments and supplies donated or purchased outside the country were also researched, and because they were purchased in a foreign currency, those costs were converted to the national currency and adjusted to the year of the study.

Other costs that might be factored into an analysis like this include facilities costs – the annualized cost of a building or office, annual rent, and/or utilities such as electricity and water. In this study, a decision was made not to collect that cost information since study implementation took place in schools that had similar facilities and costs.

7.3.5 Data Collection

Baseline data for the community randomized control trial were collected by the dental assistants during the intervention. Evaluation was performed by two independent evaluators at 6 months and 1, 2, and 3 years. An experienced epidemiologist trained and calibrated the evaluators before each session. Inter-evaluator consistency was measured; the kappa coefficient was 0.76 in assessing carious lesions at each of the four evaluations; percentage of agreement of scores was 86.7%.

Personnel time data, estimates of the time the pedodontists devoted to the sealants, were collected in two ways. Dental assistants recorded sealant placement times for all sealants on the study data form, "beginning with the moment the pedodontists lifted their instruments until the moment they put them down once finished" (Goldman et al. 2017). The second method, the activity sampling method (Ampt et al. 2007), enabled the evaluation of the reliability of the data collected in the study as well as the collection of data on the entirety of the implementation sessions, thus including treatment and other ancillary activities (Goldman et al. 2017).

A countdown timer was used to collect data sampled in 15-min intervals in approximately 30 4-h intervention sessions. In each session, the timer was set at a different time after the session began at 8:00 am to avoid the bias of sampling the same intervals each day (Goldman et al. 2017). The last digit in the ID number of the first participant determined the amount of time elapsed before the timer was set. Each time the timer went off, the assistant would record the activity the pedodontist engaged in on the session data collection sheet. Activities were categorized as clinical (e.g., performing an examination or a sealant), complementary (e.g., instrument preparation), or nonclinical (e.g., equipment failure, coffee break, patient absent) (Goldman et al. 2017).

7.3.6 Discounting, Adjustment, Annualization

The discount rate of 3% (WHO 2003) was applied to study outcomes, including effectiveness data, costs incurred in implementation, and adverse events costs. The value of capital equipment was annualized at a rate of 3%. All costs were recorded in the Brazilian currency, reais (BRL). The World Bank GDP inflation deflator was used to adjust costs to 2012 values (The World Bank 2016). For the purposes of reporting, the costs were later converted to 2012 USD values; this conversion did not account for purchasing power parity (Goldman et al. 2017).

7.3.7 Definition of Outcomes

The presence of cavitated dentine carious lesions on the first permanent molars after 3 years was the prevention effectiveness outcome measured.

The cost outcome evaluated was the net cost per cavitated dentine carious lesion prevented over 3 years; this included sealant placement costs, supervised toothbrushing costs, and adverse event costs. Adverse events costs were defined as the cost to restore cavitated dentine carious lesions on the first permanent molars that developed after the intervention. Adding adverse event costs to sealant placement costs or toothbrushing supervision costs results in net costs. The pedodontists restored the first permanent molars that developed dentine carious lesions in keeping with each protocol; the restoration costs were added to the costs of the corresponding program (Goldman et al. 2017).

7.3.8 Evaluation Design

An incremental cost-effectiveness ratio (ICER), which measures the additional cost associated with preventing an additional adverse outcome (in this study, cavitated dentine carious lesion) for each intervention strategy, was employed to analyze the cost-effectiveness of the three strategies. The reference group was the CR sealant group, chosen as the comparator because it is considered the standard of care for sealants (Goldman et al. 2017).

7.3.9 Data Analysis

With the ICER, the intervention strategy with the worst effectiveness outcome is used as the base against which the other strategies are compared (Haddix et al. 2003; Gold et al. 1996). Thus, the results are ranked by effectiveness outcome, starting with the worst outcome first. For example, to calculate the ICER calculation for the study sample, the difference in the costs between the 2 sealant methods was first obtained by subtracting the total cost of the CR (reference group) which had the largest number of cavitated dentine carious lesions, from the total cost of ART/HVGIC. Next, the number of cavitated dentine carious lesions that developed for ART/HVGIC was subtracted from those for CR. Finally, ART/HVGIC and CR were compared in a ratio where the difference in the costs of the interventions was divided by the difference in the effectiveness of the interventions. This process was repeated for the STB-ART/HVGIC comparison (Goldman et al. 2017)

Because of interest in how the parameters of the study findings would hold in a larger population, the study results were applied to a projection of 1000 sealants/high-risk molars per group. The projection was created by increasing project inputs (such as personnel time, instruments and supplies, and transportation) proportionally, at the same rate as they occurred in the study sample. In addition, the sizes of the groups were uneven, so creating the projection standardized all of the groups. Annualized equipment costs were applied according to the proportion of time it took to create the number of sealants in the sample (4.5% per year) and the projection (25% per year for 1000 sealants) (Goldman et al. 2017). The assumption here is that there will not be economies or diseconomies of scale.

7.4 Step 4. Relate Costs to Outcomes

7.4.1 Effectiveness Results

At baseline, a total of 169 sealants were performed on 70 children in the CR group, 69 sealants were performed in 37 children in the ART/HVGIC group (Table 7.1), and 71 permanent molars in 38 children were identified and kept under observation in the STB group. After 3 years, the cumulative effectiveness of preventing dentine carious lesions in the molars was 95.6% in the STB group, 91.4% in the CR group, and 90.2% for the ART/HVGIC group. The effectiveness of the interventions, in terms of the number of dentine carious lesions that developed in the molars over the 3 years in the CR group, was 12, 6 in the ART/HVGIC group, and 3 in the STB group (Hilgert et al. 2015; Goldman et al. 2017).

7.4.2 Cost Results

Treatment time for performing ART/HVGIC sealants in the sample and the activity sampling data was close to 50% more at 6 min and 9.58 min than CR at 4.50 min and 6.77 min. The cost (USD 7.22) and net cost (USD 8.02) of performing the ART/HVGIC sealant were almost twice as high as for the CR application (cost, USD 3.74; and net cost, USD 6.96) in the sample data. In the activity sampling data, the

Table 7.1 Characteristics for the sample of children for high risk molars at baseline and at year 3 after the intervention

		Intervention[a]	
	Composite resin (CR)	ART/ HVGIC	STB
Baseline			
Schools (n)	2	2	2
Children (n)	70	37	38
Sealants (n)	169	69	71
D_3MFT (SE)	0.27 (0.56)	0.27 (0.51)	0.23 (0.42)
$d_3$mft	6.11 (3.12)	5.78 (3.94)	5.18 (2.51)
Year 3			
Children (n)	47	27	28
Sealants (n)	120	51	50
Dentine carious lesion increment (n) [cumulative]	12	6	3
Effectiveness [cumulative] SE	**91.4% (2.9)**	**90.2% (5.0)**	**95.6% (2.5)**

Reprinted from Goldman et al. 2017, with permission from S. Karger AG, Basel.

[a] *CR* composite resin, *STB* supervised toothbrushing, *ART/HVGIC* a traumatic restorative treatment/high-viscosity glass-ionomer cement, *SE* standard error

differences in the costs between the two groups were slightly lower. As the number of sealant applications reached 1000, the differences continued to narrow. The cost for ART/HVGIC from USD 7.22 in the sample decreased to USD 4.86 in the projection, while the cost of placing CR sealants rose from USD 3.74 to USD 4.81. For the STB initiative, the costs of supervising the brushing of molars in the STB group (180 days per year for 3 years for the study sample) were USD 18.56, at least 2.5 times higher than the sealant application method in the sample and activity sampling data and USD 9.14 in the projection.

7.4.3 Inputs

The analysis of intervention inputs revealed personnel was the major cost driver, consuming the most resources for all groups; the STB group led with 95% of the intervention costs, followed by CR with 54% and ART/HVGIC with 42%. Materials and supplies consumed by the CR and ART/HVGIC groups represented 38% and 56% of the costs, respectively, while STB consumed only 5% (Goldman et al. 2017).

7.4.4 Incremental Cost-Effectiveness Ratio

When the outcomes were ranked for the sample data for calculating the incremental cost-effectiveness ratios, the first ratio compared the ART/HVGIC and CR approaches and the result was a savings of USD 37 per new cavitated dentine carious lesion prevented in favor of ART/ HVGIC (Table 7.2). When STB (180 STB visits took place each year over 3 years) was compared to ART/HVGIC, the outcome was a cost of USD 264 per cavitated dentine carious lesion prevented. ART/HVGIC was cost-effective for the sample data, and CR was cost-effective for the projection of 1000 sealants/molars treated. When evaluated against STB, both sealant methods were cost-effective (Goldman et al. 2017). CR had a better outcome than ART/HVGIC with cost savings of USD 17. In the ratio comparing CR and STB, the result was that STB cost USD 140 per cavitated dentine carious lesion prevented for every 1000 sealants/molars treated.

Table 7.2 Results of the incremental cost-effectiveness ratios for the sample and projection of 1000 sealants by treatment group at year 3 (USD 2012)

Treatment	Effectiveness[a], new cavitated dentine carious lesions	Cost	New cavitated dentine carious lesions prevented	Incremental cost	Cost per new cavitated dentine carious lesion prevented
Sample					
CR	11	738			DOMINATED
ART-HVGIC	6	553	6	−185	−37
STB[b]	3	1346	3	793	264
Projection, 1000 sealants/group					
ART-HVGIC	84	5506			DOMINATED
CR	69	5322	16	−184	−17
STB	41	9138	27	3816	140

[a] Effectiveness outcomes are discounted by 3%.
[b] For the STB study, the toothbrushing supervisor went to the schools 180 days per year to supervise the children. Reprinted from Goldman et al. 2017, with permission from S. Karger AG, Basel.
CR composite resin, *STB* supervised toothbrushing, *ART-HVGIC* atraumatic restorative treatment/high-viscosity glass-ionomer cement

7.5 Step 5. Adjust for Uncertainties

7.5.1 *Sensitivity Analysis*

Sensitivity analyses were conducted to evaluate how variations in the incidence of cavitated dentine lesions would affect the ICER. The impact of changes in the number of STB visits on the cost per lesion averted was explored. The daily supervision by dental assistants in the schools (180 days/year) was highly labor-intensive, and the expectation that the resulting cost might not be sustainable for a government program prompted the development of two alternative scenarios to evaluate the impact of fewer STB visits on costs.

In these scenarios the dental assistants would visit the children during the school year to ensure the habit of toothbrushing is adopted. The parameters for the first scenario were 36 visits per school year and an increase of 33% in the number of cavitated dentine carious lesions. In the second scenario, dental assistants visited the schools nine times a year, and caries increased by 52%. These analyses assumed that effectiveness in both scenarios over 3 years would be similar to that in the study. This assumption requires further investigation (Goldman et al. 2017).

7.5.2 *Sensitivity Analysis Results*

The sensitivity analysis focused on STB supervision because supervision costs accounted for 95% of the cost of the intervention. And, although STB was dominated by the sealant intervention approaches in the analysis, exploration of supervision in terms of the number of visits and the incidence of cavitated carious lesions would provide information about how the comparison of STB, and the sealant approaches might be affected.

The results of the sensitivity analysis, shown in Table 7.3, revealed that the net cost per STB molar decreased considerably as the number of days of supervision decreased. For Scenario 1, with 36 days the net cost ranged between USD 2.71 for the sample and USD 1.50 per caries free STB molar, while for Scenario 2 the range was USD 2.15 to USD 1.21 per caries free STB molar.

With respect to cost-effectiveness, Table 7.4 shows that despite increased incidence of cavitated dentine lesions in both scenarios, the cost of STB decreased markedly in comparison to both sealant interventions. STB produced savings of USD 180 in Scenario 1 and USD 395 in Scenario 2 compared to ART/HVGIC in the sample data. The comparison of STB to CR in the projection results showed savings of USD 273 and USD 686 for Scenarios 1 and 2, respectively, per 1000 STB molars.

7.6 Step 6. Summary and Interpretation

A major struggle in the field of successful primary care prevention efforts is demonstrating their true value in the act of preventing the occurrence of adverse health outcomes. Economic evaluation of primary oral healthcare curative and preventive services provides us the opportunity to attach a price to the prevention of one additional bad outcome – in this case a cavitated dental caries lesion in the study population. The two key contributory elements that enable the capacity to conduct

Table 7.3 Sensitivity analysis: costs and net costs per STB molar for the sample, activity sampling data, and a projection of 1000 STB caries free molars, by STB Scenario

Sensitivity analyses	STB S1 36d/yr	STB S2 9d/yr
Cost per STB molar		
Sample	2.17	0.77
Activity sampling	2.17	1.55
Projection of 1000 sealants	1.07	0.72
Net cost[a] STB molar		
Sample	2.71	2.15
Activity sampling	2.57	1.95
Projection of 1000 sealants	1.50	1.21

Table 7.4 Sensitivity analysis: incremental cost effectiveness results by STB Scenario for the sample and a projection of 1000 STB caries-free molars

	Effectiveness[b], new cavitated dentine carious lesions	Cost	New cavitated dentine carious lesions prevented	Incremental cost	Cost per new cavitated dentine carious lesion prevented
STB scenario 1					
Sample					
CR	11	738			DOMINATED
ART-HVGIC	6	553	5	−185	−37
STB	4	193	2	−361	−180
Projection, 1000 sealants/group					
ART-HVGIC	84	5506			DOMINATED
CR	69	5322	16	−184	−12
STB	55	1499	14	−3823	−273
STB scenario 2					
Sample					
CR	11	738			DOMINATED
ART-HVGIC	6	553	5	−185	−37
STB	5	159	1	−395	−395
Projection, 1000 sealants/group					
ART-HVGIC	84	5506			DOMINATED
CR	69	5322	16	- 184	−12
STB	63	1209	6	−4113	−686

STB S1, scenario where toothbrushing supervision takes place weekly or 36 days over one school year; STB S2, toothbrushing supervision takes place monthly or 9 days over one school year. CR, composite resin; STB, supervised toothbrushing; ART/HVGIC, atraumatic restorative treatment/high-viscosity glass-ionomer sealants.

[a] Net costs include the cost of STB supervision per molar and restoration if cavitated dentine carious lesions developed.

[b] Effectiveness outcomes are discounted by 3%. Reprinted from Goldman et al. 2017, with permission from S. Karger AG, Basel.

cost-effectiveness analyses of oral health intervention and promotion efforts are (i) the ability to cost all the inputs that went into achieving the strategic prevention outcome and (ii) the ability to generate the unit cost of the occurrence of an additional bad outcome per intervention strategy – its incremental cost effectiveness ratio (ICER) value which represents the incremental cost per adverse event prevented.

This project analyzes the cost of adopting a health education promotion effectiveness approach versus an early clinical intervention approach. The early intervention clinical approach involves the application of two kinds of sealants. The study presents and analyzes its findings, first, in terms of the costs per molar per group and a breakdown of the inputs that contributed to the interventions, providing information about basic costs and cost drivers. Next, the two sealant intervention methods are compared, and finally, the more cost-effective sealant intervention is compared to the STB education promotion program approach. It generates an ICER value that compares the cost of having to treat one additional bad outcome for each comparison.

The objective of this chapter is to present the cost-effectiveness outcome findings in a practical and applicable manner so that they may be of value to oral health policymakers, program developers, and dental care service providers. Adding the additional information on costing associated with one primary care intervention approach versus the other serves to further inform their decision-making process. Possessing this level of costing detail gives the decision-maker the power to use the information to implement effective primary care programs that best fit their available technical and administrative resources. In applying these methods, researchers, policymakers, program managers, and practitioners are able to determine the most cost-effective oral health primary care program in terms of protecting the pits and fissures in permanent molars to prevent the development of dentine carious lesions in children whose permanent teeth are beginning to erupt.

7.6.1 Report on the Study and Its Findings

The data used in the cost-effectiveness study presented here were collected prospectively. Costs of supplies, instruments, and equipment unique to each approach were allocated directly or according to the estimated amount used per intervention. Transportation was allocated similarly, since each time the pedodontists and their assistants went to a school all children were treated through the same approach. Other supplies used in common by all groups were allocated according to personnel time. Sampling of treatment sessions through activity sampling captured information about the amount of time it took to perform the interventions. The cost analysis included the oral hygiene kits given to each of the children in all six schools, the time devoted to teaching them how to take care of their teeth, as well as the time spent by the one assistant who visited the schools to supervise toothbrushing.

Cost data were evaluated using incremental cost-effectiveness ratios (ICER) to generate the additional cost associated with preventing an additional adverse outcome (in this study, the cost per additional cavitated dentine carious lesion) for each of the three primary care prevention strategies used. Study results showed both CR and ART/HVGIC sealants for the sample and the projection of 1000 sealants per group were more cost-effective than supervised toothbrushing. Nonetheless, although CR had the lowest cost, the difference between the two was minimal. Thus, the choice of sealant approach used might be related to other factors.

Although supervised toothbrushing promotion had the best outcome after 3 years, the two different clinical intervention strategies cost less and were therefore more cost-effective compared to STB promotion. The study results of the incremental cost-effectiveness analysis for the sample data and the projection show that STB, as administered for 180 days per year, had the highest costs and was too expensive to be viewed as affordable.

Consequently, policymakers and program managers might consider the lower costing CR as an alternative if costs are a priority. In efforts to reach larger segments of the population under conditions where dental clinics and equipment are scarce, ART/HVGIC, given its portability, might be the preferred alternative (Goldman et al. 2017).

7.6.2 Implications of Findings

A closer examination of the study data, specifically, the role of personnel as a major cost driver in the supervised toothbrushing intervention, prompted tests of the frequency of supervisory personnel in the intervention in the sensitivity analyses. The results of this analysis suggest an STB program in the schools could be cost-effective. The results from reducing supervisory personnel time point to the potential feasibility and affordability of STB. Further research could inform researchers, policymakers, and program managers in how such a program could be structured to function within Brazil's community-based oral healthcare policies. Key questions include: How much supervision will produce a good result? Who needs to do the supervision?

With such a program, in Brazil oral health professionals could examine children and provide them with oral health education in schools. These professionals could also train teachers and parents to replace the assistants and implement daily STB, developing a community-based preventive approach which would contribute to furthering national progress in oral health and lowering costs. If, in Brazil, teachers and parents could not perform STB, another option would be assigning the task to the country's national health program primary care family health team members, such as the oral health assistant or community health worker in areas where oral health teams are not available.

The effectiveness of STB and the sensitivity analysis, conducted on toothbrushing supervision, indicate there would be value in further research on the benefits of developing STB programs for school-age children in other countries, as well as in Brazil. Longitudinal research could investigate the conditions under which the children solidly adopt toothbrushing with fluoridated toothpaste – the number of annual visits by educators and supervisory personnel and the impact on the incidence of new cavitated dentine carious lesions – making the program cost-effective. Program managers could evaluate their administrative and technical resources and deploy them for country-appropriate programs.

This study demonstrates the basic elements of designing and implementing a cost-effective analysis. It highlights the importance of understanding the context of a cost-effectiveness analysis and who the principal audiences for this are likely to be. These techniques can be applied in other areas of oral health, covering both oral health promotion and clinical intervention programs.

Oral health policymakers, program managers, and practitioners can utilize the results of this and other cost-effectiveness studies to design programs that make the best use of the available resources and address the urgent need for effective oral health prevention strategies. In turn, this will help to address inequalities by adopting measures to increase health gain among the most vulnerable populations (Granham 2004; Moysés 2012; Goldman et al. 2017).

References

Ampt A, Westbrook J, Creswick N, Mallock N (2007) A comparison of self-reported and observational work sampling techniques for measuring time in nursing tasks. J Health Serv Res Policy 12:18–24

de Amorim RG, Figueiredo MJ, Leal SC, Mulder J, Frencken JE (2012) Caries experience in a child population in a deprived area of Brazil, using ICDAS II. Clin Oral Investig 16:513–520

de Amorim RG, Leal SC, Mulder J, Creugers NH, Frencken JE (2013) Amalgam and ART restorations in children: a controlled clinical trial. Clin Oral Investig 1:117–124

Gold MR, Siegel JE, Russel LB, Weinstein MC (eds) (1996) Cost-effectiveness in health and medicine. Oxford University Press, New York, p 425

Goldman AS, Leal SC, de Amorim RG, Frencken JE (2017) Treating high-caries risk occlusal surfaces in first permanent molars through sealants and supervised toothbrushing: A 3-year cost-effective analysis. Caries Res 51:489–499

Granham H (2004) Social determinants and their unequal distribution: clarifying policy understandings. Milbank Q 82:101–124

Haddix AC, Tatsch SM, Corso PS (eds) (2003) Prevention effectiveness: a guide to decision analysis and economic evaluation. Oxford University Press, New York, p 288

Hilgert LA, Leal SC, Mulder J, Creugers NHJ, Frencken JE (2015) Caries-preventive effect of supervised toothbrushing, composite resin and ART sealants: a cluster-randomized controlled clinical trial. J Dent Res 94:1218–1224

Moysés S (2012) Inequalities in oral health and oral health promotion. Braz Oral Res (Spec Iss) 26:86–93

Pucca GA Jr, Gabriel M, de Araújo ME, de Almeida FCS (2015) Ten years of a national oral health policy in Brazil: Innovation, boldness, and numerous challenges. J Dent res 94:1333–1337

The World Bank Group. World Development (2016) Indicators. http://databank.worldbank.org/Data/Home.aspx. Accessed 15 Aug 2020

World Health Organization (WHO) (2003) In: Tan-Torres Edejer T, Baltussen R, Adam T, Hutubessy R, Acharya A, Evans DB, CJL M (eds) Making choices in health: WHO Guide to cost-effectiveness analysis. World Health Organization, Geneva, p 318

Chapter 8
Worked Example in Cost-Benefit Analysis

Rodrigo Mariño

8.1 Cost-Benefit Analysis

As described in Chap. 1, there are different ways to conduct economic evaluations. These will depend on the perspective of the analyst and the evaluation method adopted. In general, the main difference is the way economic evaluations measure the results of the outcome, benefits, or consequences of the intervention or program. These can be measured in terms of effects (e.g., decayed, missing, filled tooth surfaces) in a cost-effectiveness analysis (CEA), or health states preferences as in a cost-utility analysis (CUA), or by willingness to pay as in a cost-benefit analysis (CBA).

Cost-benefit analysis is defined by Drummond as the type of economic evaluation which takes into account all costs and consequences of a program or intervention and expresses or values them in monetary terms (Drummond et al. 2015). Therefore, when the consequences of two or more programs are not the same or the outcome cannot be reduced to a common effect between alternatives, it is not possible to conduct CEA. In these situations, analysts assign an economic value to results and calculate, in monetary terms, the economic benefits from the intervention, in the form of a CBA. Thus, using CBA you can compare two completely dissimilar outcomes, while CEA and CUA are restricted to programs that produce similar units of outcome.

Government programs and interventions usually have multiple impacts, as well as short- and long-term effects, which may not all be under a common portfolio. Using CBA it is possible to answer questions about allocative efficiency (e.g., dental caries prevention program vs. construction of a highway), while CEA and CUA are more used for productive efficiency once it is decided in a program where strategy should be selected for that purpose (in the case of a dental caries prevention

R. Mariño (✉)
Melbourne Dental School, The University of Melbourne, Melbourne, VIC, Australia
e-mail: r.marino@unimelb.edu.au

C. Zaror, R. Mariño (eds.), *Introduction to Economic Evaluation in Oral Health Care*, https://doi.org/10.1007/978-3-030-96289-0_8

program, community water fluoridation, toothpaste, dental sealants, etc.). However, in order to use CBA, it is necessary to translate all effects to its benefits in monetary terms. Putting a value on benefits may look simple and straightforward, but it might not always be an easy task. For example, placing monetary values on attributes like human well-being for which no market price exists is often complicated, expensive, and controversial (Greenhalgh et al. 2017). CBA has been criticized for not producing ethically relevant information, as it might ignore immeasurable, intangible, or indirect benefits that are difficult to assess, even though they might be important (Greenhalgh et al. 2017).

8.1.1 Problems and Pitfalls in Cost-Benefit Analysis

The monetarization of all values creates limitations as there are some benefits that cannot be translated into money value or measured in monetary terms (Greenhalgh et al. 2017). For this reason, there are some debate about the validity of CBA (Greenhalgh et al. 2017). This is because while most costs can be quantified in monetary terms, many benefits cannot. This is a common case in oral health. For example, what should the value of losing a tooth be? How many dollars should be added to the effect of a preventive program because it leads to intact teeth, rather than to perfectly restored ones? (Horowitz 1986; Niessen and Douglass 1984). In those case, much of the value of an intervention or program can be lost (Greenhalgh et al. 2017). There is always debate on which costs and benefits to select for the analysis.

In oral health, it is difficult to measure the intangible values. For example, the preference for an early cure or for sound teeth is difficult to quantify in monetary terms, although there are attempts to do this by using a quality-of-life measure. Therefore, if we do not give adequate consideration to a lot of factors and we consider the saving only in cost of treatments of dental caries as the tangible benefit, the results, both the cost and benefits, of any dental preventive method will either be overestimated or underestimated.

Analysts often include in the cost of prevention some of the visible costs of the program and assume that if a program can reduce the cost of treatments, other benefits are assured in that way (Weinstein and Stasson 1977). Intangible benefits of preventive programs in dentistry include the following (Horowitz 1986; Niessen and Douglass 1984):

- Freedom from pain.
- A dentition free of dental caries.
- Improved social acceptability.
- Psychological value of retaining teeth: aesthetic, taste, speech.
- Less time missed from work or school.
- Reduction of prevalence of malocclusion.
- Prevention of future dental problems, extraction, and treatments.
- Reduction of anxiety and fear for oral heath treatments.
- Improved quality of life.

According to Drummond and his collaborators (2015), a basic principle of CBA is that it is the individual who assigns the monetary value for the outcome. There are generally three approaches to assigning value to health outcomes: human capital; revealed preference, and willingness to pay (not that people necessarily will pay for it). Human capital refers to the investment done in an individual in terms of individual production due to the intervention.

Revealed preference is an approach which assigns value to the wage rate required for an individual to accept that intervention, regime, treatment, etc. (Drummond et al. 2015).

Willingness to pay refers to the amount of money that an individual is prepared to sacrifice to obtain a given health benefit (Tan et al. 2017). Individuals are asked how much they would be prepared to pay to accrue a benefit or to avoid certain events, for example, individual willingness to pay to reduce the probably of oral diseases.

However, costs calculation puts limitations on CBAs in oral health. For that reason, other economic evaluations, particularly CEA and, to a lesser extent, CUA, are the preferred economic evaluations techniques in oral health (Mariño et al. 2020). Nonetheless, in the oral health literature, some studies described a cost-benefit analysis, for example, Wallace and her collaborators study (2019). However, the literature also indicates that there has been some confusion between CBA and the "benefits" from a study (Mariño et al. 2013). This is because of the imprecision of terms and language (Mariño et al. 2013). In economic evaluations "benefits" is a generic term that may indicate the outcome, which could be units of disease and therefore a CEA, or qualitative, and therefore a CUA, not a true CBA. Benefits are the services, capabilities, and qualities of each alternative system and can be viewed as the return on an investment. Benefits include direct costs being avoided, such as expenditure on oral health, and lost or reduced productivity. However, more recent reviews indicate improvements, as documented in detail by Mariño and his collaborators (Mariño et al. 2020).

8.2 Worked Example of Cost-Benefit Analysis

8.2.1 Step 1: Define the Objectives of the Economic Evaluation

8.2.1.1 Study Objectives

The objective is to model the potential economic benefits that might be achieved through the Senior Smiles program, from a societal viewpoint if the program is extended across the Australian state of New South Wales (NSW). "Senior Smiles" is a preventive model of oral healthcare for people living in residential aged care facilities (RACFs).

8.2.1.2 Background Information

This project targets older people living in RACF, an underserved, high-risk population and one with greater oral health needs. This project will promote affordable, timely oral healthcare by testing an oral health model in which qualified oral health practitioners (i.e., dentist oral health therapists) visit RACFs to provide preventative oral healthcare.

Older people living in RACFs have been identified as a significant risk group for dental diseases in Australia, and the changing demography and oral health needs of older Australians will present many challenges for the dental profession over the next 40 years. In 2020, there were more than 300,000 Australians living in high- or low-care residential facilities on a permanent basis in around 2,672 such facilities in Australia (Australian Institute of Health and Welfare 2021). These residents have poor oral health, and face significant barriers accessing dental services. They are often physically and cognitively impaired, medically compromised, and dependent on others to maintain their oral hygiene (Hopcraft 2015).

Oral health among residential aged care facility (RACF) residents has been identified as being in a state of crisis by Australia's National Oral Health Plan 2015–2024 (Council of Australian Governments 2015). Three out of ten adults have untreated tooth decay (Council of Australian Governments 2015). Dental plaque, or dental biofilm, is a significant factor in the development of tooth decay and gum disease as it contains bacteria which can destroy the enamel on the outer surface of teeth.

Improvements in oral health in Australia over the past 50 years have translated into more older adults retaining more teeth, increasing the risk of caries and periodontal disease. In the Australian state of Victoria, just over half of the residents are dentate, and dental treatment needs are high. Face-to-face patient's examinations are regarded as the most accurate method for correct oral health diagnosis. However, only 11% of residents have seen a dentist in the past 12 months, with few dentists available to provide dental care for residents of aged care facilities (Hopcraft et al. 2008). In fact, only half of Victoria's dentists reported providing care to residents of RACFs, and these spent only 1 h per month providing care (Hopcraft et al. 2008).

8.2.1.3 Define Patients (e.g., Inclusion/Exclusion Criteria)

Older people living in the 291 RACFs located in the Australian state of New South Wales.

8.2.1.4 Define Treatment Protocols (e.g., Duration of Treatments) and Scenarios

Under the Senior Smiles' model, a qualified oral health practitioner (i.e., dentist oral health therapists) is placed within the facility to:

- Provide the residents with oral health risk assessments and care plans.
- Establish referral pathways with private and public dentists, prosthetists, and specialists in geriatric dentistry to manage the more complex needs.

The practitioner also collaborates with other staff members in the facilities to ensure oral health becomes part of daily care needs and that a holistic approach to residents' care is established.

The program offers a preventive focus on oral care:

- It treats immediately simple oral health conditions such as xerostomia or ulcers.
- It initiates referral in a timely manner for more complex problems (periodontal disease, caries, or oral cancers).

8.2.1.5 Describe the Context of the Economic Evaluation

This evaluation models the roll out of Senior Smiles across all RACFs in New South Wales (NSW). Data used for the model came from the best data available from three scenarios:

(a) The pilot of the project in five RACFs.
(b) The rollout in 17 RACFs in New South Wales (NSW).
(c) Where data were not available, academic evidence and the literature were used. Therefore, the report corresponded to an evaluation based on secondary analysis of outcome data collected as part of the model.

8.2.1.6 Indicate Why You Are Doing the Economic Evaluation

An economic evaluation was conducted to understand the value impact achieved through the Senior Smiles program to understand the return on investment and opportunity for wider rollout. It may also help focus decision-making on the scale and decidedly which elements of the program are most suitable for replication.

8.2.1.7 State the Question Being Examined

The question being examined was "What would be the cost and outcome if residents of RACFs located on the NSW took part in the Senior Smiles prevention program?"

8.2.2 *Step 2: Define the Framework for the Economic Evaluation*

8.2.2.1 Identify the Type of Economic Evaluation to Be Conducted

The form of economic evaluation used in this study was cost-benefit analysis.

8.2.2.2 What Is the Perspective of the Economic Analysis? (Whose Resources Are at Stake?)

The evaluation used a societal perspective.

8.2.2.3 The Type of Program or Intervention Under Evaluation and Its Alternatives

The intervention group was the Senior Smiles program, and the comparator was no intervention (status quo).

8.2.2.4 Define the Time Horizon for Costs and Outcomes

The time horizon was 3 years.

8.2.3 *Step 3: Assessment of Costs and Benefits of Alternatives*

The study used diverse sources to identify cost and outcomes benefits. It included costs which fell on the public health system (i.e., the Australian government) but also captured the private costs of social care and costs falling on volunteers. The study also attempted to capture productivity costs. The Australian government uses standardized unit cost databases, which provided data for the CBA.

8.2.3.1 Determine and Calculate Costs

The study captured costs which fell on the public health system (i.e., the Australian government) but also captured the private costs of social care and costs falling on volunteers. The study also attempted to capture productivity costs.

8.2.3.2 The Costs Represented in the Study Were the Following (See Table 8.1)

- The dental hygienists' salaries.
- The cost of dental and GP referrals (when applicable).
- The healthcare costs generated by the decreased mortality, primarily additional length of stay resulting from patients who survive in hospital because mortality has fallen.
- The project management costs (salary of the project manager) when applicable.

8.2.3.3 Determine Consequences

Fourteen significant monetarised benefits of the program were identified, across the three benefit streams of cash-releasing and noncash- releasing healthcare system savings and societal benefits (See Table 8.2).

Health -system- related cash- releasing benefits were those benefits that produced immediate cashable savings to the provider. For example, the reduction of prescriptions following intervention. Health -system-related noncash- releasing benefits were those benefits resulting from a reduction in the demand of services. Noncash releasing included, for example, reduced hospital length of stay and reduced readmissions, etc. Social benefits were benefits to the public, For example, employment- related benefits, such as fewer sick days, improved health and wellbeing and quality of life, etc. QALY was given a financial following Huang et al.'s (2018) assessment.

8.2.3.4 Document Assumptions

Where data used were available, assumptions came from the results of a pilot implementation of the Senior Smiles program or from the actual implementation of the program. When data were not available for those two sources, it was based on the literature of experts' evidence.

Table 8.1 Overall costs ($,000, 2014 prices)

	Year 1 ($)	Year 2 ($)	Year 3 ($)	Total ($)
Dental hygienists' salary	4419.6	4166.2	3927.4	**12,513.2**
Project management costs	10,758.1	10,141.5	9560.2	**30,459.9**
Dental appointments (referral)	1413.5	1331.2	1253.7	**3998.3**
Healthcare costs (generated by decreased mortality)	14,839.9	13,849.3	13,164.0	**41,853.1**
Total	31,431.1	29,488.2	27,905.3	**88,824.6**

Table 8.2 Overall benefits ($,000, net present value, 2014 prices)

	Year 1 ($)	Year 2 ($)	Year 3 ($)	Total ($)
Healthcare system cash-releasing savings	1636.0	1540.7	1451.0	**4627.7**
Healthcare system noncash-releasing savings	73,626.0	69,334.6	65,299.8	**208,260.3**
Societal benefits	99,685.2	93,971.7	88,585.7	**282,242.7**
Total benefits	174,947.2	164,847.0	155,336.5	**495,130.7**

Table 8.3 Total costs, total benefits, and benefit to cost ratio for the overall Senior Smile program ($,000, 2014 prices)

	Year 1 ($)	Year 2 ($)	Year 3 ($)	Total ($)
Total benefits	174,947.2	164,847.0	155,336.5	**495,130.7**
Total costs	31,431.1	29,488.2	27,905.3	**88,824.6**
Net present value (benefits - costs)	143,516.1	135,358.8	127,431.2	**406,306.1**
Benefit to cost ratio	**5.57**	**5.59**	**5.57**	**5.57**

8.2.3.5 Discounting

Because the time horizon is more than 12 months, discounting is indicated. Costs and outcomes were discounted to their present value using an annual discount rate of 4% following Department of Treasury and Finance guidance (Government of Victoria 2014).

8.2.4 Step 4: Relating Outcomes to Costs for Cost-Benefit Analysis

For standard CBA, the benefit-cost ratio is simple:

$$\text{Cost} - \text{benefit ratio} = \text{benefits expected from the program / cost of the program}$$

The formula reflects the sum of all the benefits divided by the sum of all the costs. For the present example, those calculations are presented in Table 8.3.

8.2.5 Step 5: Adjusting for Risk and Uncertainty

8.2.5.1 Perform a Sensitivity Analysis

A sensitivity analysis using the Monte Carlo simulations technique was undertaken to test the robustness of the results to estimated parameter values (Drummond et al. 2015).

The sensitivity analysis showed that benefits could vary between \$0.390bn and \$0.706bn at the 90% confidence level. At the lower end of this range, the benefit-cost ratio was reduced to 4.55:1, assuming costs remained constant.

8.2.6 *Step 6: Interpret and Report the Findings*

The study, which looked to identify the costs and benefits of the Senior Smiles program, indicated that the program was estimated to deliver tangible value in the order of \$5.57 of benefit within the healthcare system for every \$1 invested in the project for its implementation through NSW. That is, present findings suggest that the Senior Smile program would lead to an improved oral health outcome and a reduction in total costs (i.e., savings).

In CBA a cost-benefit ratio greater than one indicates a positive outcome suggesting that it should be considered supporting such a program. Furthermore, in the present case, the cost-benefit ratio of the program remained positive even with more stringent and pessimistic assumptions than those projected for the base case. Thus, it is concluded that, considering the study assumptions and for situations equivalent to those prevailing in the Australian state of New South Wales, the implementation of a Senior Smile preventive program would represent an efficient use of community resources.

8.3 Discussion

Oral health among residential aged care facility (RACF) residents has been identified as in a state of crisis by Australia's National Oral Health Plan 2015–2024 (Council of Australian Governments 2015). Given that 200,000 Australians are living in high- or low-care residential facilities on a permanent basis in around 2,672 such facilities in Australia, it was considered important to evaluate the implementation of a model to provide prevention oral healthcare for these communities.

The CBA worked example examined both costs and consequences of the Seniors Smile program compared with no intervention (status quo) from a societal viewpoint. It could be argued that not all costs and benefits accruing to society were measured. For example, the reputational value and staff confidence and satisfaction levels were not included. In a CBA only monetary benefits, or those which can be converted into monetary benefits, are included. Also, the 3-year time framework maybe limiting, as benefits of the Seniors Smile program may extend for periods longer than 3 years.

The effectiveness of the program was established by data from pilot testing in five RACFs, which would reflect what would happen in regular practice. Potential biases from pilot studies were discussed. All the important and relevant costs and consequences for each alternative were identified in a range wide enough for the research question to be answered. Costs and consequences were measured accurately in appropriate physical units (e.g., hours of dental hygienist time, number of dentist visits, etc.) and using the original source data where possible to identify the most relevant and credible source (e.g., NSW Department of Health, Independent Hospital Pricing Authority, etc.). The year of reference was also provided.

Costs and consequences were "discounted" to their present values using a published discount rate. Also, allowances were made for uncertainty in the estimates of costs and consequences. A sensitivity analysis was included in the report.

Overall, conclusions of the analysis were based on an incremental cost-benefit ratio. The study also discussed the generalizability of the results to other settings and its limitations. Issues around implementation were discussed and addressed in the report.

8.4 Final Remarks

The use of economic evaluation of oral healthcare projects, intervention programs, or policies is being increasingly published in the literatures (Mariño et al. 2020). In this chapter, the structured review of a CBA study provided a practical demonstration of the elements of designing and implementing this type of economic analysis in oral health. It highlighted the importance of understanding the assessment of costs and benefits in a CBA. CBA techniques can be applied in any area of oral health, from oral health promotion and oral disease prevention to clinical intervention.

The use of a monetary terms, particularly in the assessment of benefits, may facilitate allocative efficiency decisions to either endorse or reject a particular program. However, some methodological and ethical issues may limit its uses. It has to be emphasized that CBA studies deal with health economics, not with their human aspects. Additionally, oral health policymakers, program managers, practitioners, and any type of consumers of economic evaluations should be cautious about studies labelled as CBA in oral health, without carefully assessing their methodology. Mislabeling of economic evaluations could be problematic. Still, economic evaluations can provide useful information to decision-makers to help make allocative decisions regarding the use of available resources.

References

Australian Institute of Health and Welfare (AIHW) (2021) Services and places in aged care. https://www.gen-agedcaredata.gov.au/Topics/Services-and-places-in-aged-care. Accessed 26 May 2021

Council of Australian Governments (2015) Oral health monitoring group. Healthy Mouths, Healthy Lives: Australia's National Oral Health Plan 2015–2024. http://www.coaghealthcoun-

cil.gov.au/Portals/0/Australia%27s%20National%20Oral%20Health%20Plan%202015-2024_uploaded%20170216.pdf. Accessed 26 May 2021
Drummond MF, Sculpher M, Torrance GW, Claxton K, Stoddart GL (2015) Methods for the economic evaluation of health care Programmes, 4th edn. Oxford University Press, New York
Government of Victoria (2014) Victorian guide to regulation, Department of Treasury and Finance, Melbourne. https://www.dtf.vic.gov.au › funds-programs-and-policies. Accessed 26 May 2021
Greenhalgh S, Samarasinghe O, Curran-Cournane F et al (2017) Using ecosystem services to underpin cost-benefit analysis: Is it a way to protect finite soil resources? Ecosyst Serv 27(PartA):1–14
Haung L, Frijters P, Dalziel K, Clarke P (2018) Life satisfaction, QALYs, and the monetary value of health. Soc Sci Med 211:131–136
Hopcraft M (2015) Dental demographics and metrics of oral diseases in the ageing Australian population. Aust Dent J 60(Suppl 1):213
Hopcraft M, Morgan M, Satur J, Wright FAC (2008) Dental service provision in Victorian residential aged care facilities. Aust Dent J 53:239–245
Horowitz H (1986) Cost value analysis in dentistry. J Public Health Dent 41:281–286
Mariño R, Khan AR, Morgan M (2013) Systematic review of publications on economic evaluations of caries prevention programs. Caries Res 47:265–272
Mariño R, Ravisankar G, Zaror C (2020) Quality appraisal of economic evaluations done on Oral health preventive programs-a systematic review. J Public Health Dent 80:194–207
Niessen LC, Douglass C (1984) Theoretical considerations in applying benefit-cost and cost-effectiveness analyses to preventive dental programs. J Public Health Dent 44:156–168
Splett P (1996) The practitioner's guide to cost-effectiveness analysis of nutrition interventions. https://www.ncemch.org/NCEMCH-publications/NtrnCstEff_Anl.pdf. Accessed 26 May 2021
Tan SHX, Vernazza CR, Nair R (2017) Critical review of willingness to pay for clinical oral health interventions. J Dent 64:1–12
Wallace J, Mohammadi J, Wallace LG, Taylor JA (2019) Cost benefits analysis of the Senior Smiles pilot. https://www.seniorsmiles.org.au/research/publication-9. Accessed 26 May 2021
Weinstein MC, Stasson WB (1977) Foundations of cost-effectiveness analysis for health and medical practice. NEJM 296:716–721

Chapter 9
Worked Example in Cost-Utility Analysis

Gerardo Espinoza-Espinoza and Carlos Zaror

9.1 Background

Cost-utility analyses allow for the evaluation of the success or failure of an intervention in a way that approaches real-life situations (Listl et al. 2019; Zarate 2010). In dentistry, when the effectiveness of a preventive intervention is analyzed, success is measured by a dental caries process being avoided (Bertrand et al. 2011; Chi et al. 2014), and that outcome is assigned a maximum value (i.e., value = 1), and failure is understood as a dental caries process which was not avoided, with the minimum value assigned (i.e., value = 0). However, clinically there are several intermediate values between 1 and zero (Mohd-Dom 2014). That is, if the value of a sound tooth is 1, and a tooth lost due to caries is valued at 0, intermediate values would depend on at what point the caries diagnosis was made and the treatment options available at that point. Thus, failure would be very different when we perform a minimally invasive restoration with an excellent prognosis, compared to when we have a large restoration with a high risk of fracture, or when the pulp is compromised at a level that could be solved only with endodontic treatment, or would require an extraction.

Although clinicians may use assessments based on biological criteria to decide that a minimally invasive restoration is very close to 1, a large restoration will be

G. Espinoza-Espinoza (✉)
Department of Public Health, Universidad de La Frontera, Temuco, Chile

Center for Research in Epidemiology, Economics and Oral Public Health (CIEESPO), Faculty of Dentistry, Universidad de La Frontera, Temuco, Chile
e-mail: gerardo.espinoza@ufrontera.cl

C. Zaror
Department of Paediatric Dentistry and Orthodontics, Faculty of Dentistry, Universidad de La Frontera, Temuco, Chile

Center for Research in Epidemiology, Economics and Oral Public Health (CIEESPO), Faculty of Dentistry, Universidad de La Frontera, Temuco, Chile
e-mail: carlos.zaror@ufrontera.cl

C. Zaror, R. Mariño (eds.), *Introduction to Economic Evaluation in Oral Health Care*, https://doi.org/10.1007/978-3-030-96289-0_9

assessed with a score between 1 and 0 and the extraction with 0. However, it is also necessary to be aware of patients' options and preferences in this assessment (Listl et al. 2019). If 1 is a sound tooth and 0 a tooth loss, how does a patient assess the possibility of having a restoration that improves aesthetics and function to their tooth and where no one notices that they had dental caries? Most likely, the assessment made by the patient would be much better than that made by the clinician, since the patient may not look long term and may not see the future consequences of the loss of the obturation and the successive retreatments throughout life. Under this perspective, measuring the effectiveness in terms of health utility could provide us with a broader spectrum of the different health states considering the preferences of the patients, especially if we consider that the objective of any dental program is to improve oral health-related quality of life of the people (Zaror et al. 2019).

Any model of economic evaluation is a simplification of reality (Ney et al. 2014), but when measuring effectiveness in terms such as caries either avoided or not avoided, it is an even greater simplification than allowing for intermediate values adjusted for success and failure weighted by the quality assessment that clinicians and patients give to the different outcomes which result in not avoiding dental caries.

In dentistry a cost-utility analysis (CUA) allows including patient preferences in the economic evaluations, approximating the model to a scenario that is more similar to how we value success or failure in reality.

9.2 Step 1. Objective of the Economic Evaluation

The objectives statement is very important in any scientific inquiry (Hernandez-Sampieri and Mendoza 2018), and it also gives the case for a cost-utility evaluation. The objective determines what is to be assessed. This chapter analyzes the study entitled "The Cost-Utility of School-Based First Permanent Molar Sealants Programs: A Markov Model"(Espinoza-Espinoza et al. 2019). That study presents the results of a hypothetical model that allows for the analysis of the cost-utility of an intervention to apply dental sealants on all first permanent molars (FPM) within a school-based prevention program, compared to a no-sealing strategy.

A Markov model, which contains all possible health states, from a sound molar to extraction, considering their intermediate states, is proposed. Within the school-based prevention program, children receive care once every 2 years from 6 to 12 years of age. The aim of this study was to determine the incremental cost-utility ratio (ICUR) of a school-based dental caries prevention program, applying dental sealants on first permanent molars in school children, compared with nonintervention, from the payer's perspective and after 6 years in the conditions prevailing in Chile.

9.3 Step 2. Define the Economic Evaluation Framework

9.3.1 Perspective of the Economic Analysis

To decide the perspective of the analysis, it was taken into consideration that the model aimed to replicate the care for a hypothetical cohort of children in the school-based prevention program that provides the dental sealants. The program is currently funded by the local government (i.e., municipality). For that reason, the most appropriate perspective for this analysis is that of the payer, that is, the body who finances the intervention.

9.3.2 Alternatives Being Compared

Ideally, an economic evaluation considers all possible alternatives for treatment (Bertrand et al., 2011); however, since the purpose of the economic information was to contribute to decision-making in the specific context where the study was carried out, only two alternatives were considered: (a) seal all first permanent molars of a hypothetical cohort of children who are under the school-based sealant program, and (b) do not provide a dental sealant intervention.

The literature reports a third alternative, the application of sealants with a caries risk approach (Akinlotan et al. 2018; Chi et al. 2014), but caries risk screening is not currently a realistic alternative within the specific school-based program's jurisdiction, since such program in Chile considers intervening all children regardless of their caries risk. Thus, its inclusion would introduce a variable to the model that would not fully reflect the local situation for the purposes of this analysis.

9.3.3 Time Horizon

The study's time horizon simulates the healthcare protocol as it takes place in the local school-based program. Under those protocols, school-age children aged from 6 to 12 years receive an oral health checkup and care as appropriate, once every 2 years (JUNAEB 2014). Thus, the time horizon extends for 6 years, and the Markov cycles correspond to 2-year cycles, since the information we want to reproduce in the model is that children receive care at 6, 8, 10, and 12 years of age. The model considers that the changes in dental status are reflected at the moment of the biannual controls.

9.4 Step 3. Determine Costs and Benefits of Alternative

9.4.1 Define Interventions

An economic evaluation can be based on a clinical trial or on a theoretical model that allows for the simulation of the reality of the study, using the best available evidence (Petrou and Gray 2011). The example we are working on is the latter, a study based on a model, specifically on a Markov model (Espinoza-Espinoza et al. 2019).

The model reproduces the follow-up of two cohorts of children: one covered by the school-based dental sealant program and another cohort which is not. Both cohorts have equivalent sociodemographic characteristics: 6-year-old children of low socioeconomic status, with fully erupted, sound first permanent molars, who are at high dental caries risk. The model assumes that, apart from exposure to the dental sealants program, these children are similar in other characteristics.

The intervention was modeled to reflect what would have happened if the program was carried out in urban public primary schools with access to community water that contains optimal levels of fluorides.

The "Seal all" intervention included in the theoretical model consisted of the application of dental sealant on all sound first permanent molars, regardless of the risk of caries. All estimates incorporated in the model, both for effectiveness and for costs and probabilities of transitions, considered that the intervention had the following characteristics: the resin-based sealants were applied to all erupted FPM in a fully equipped dental clinic, with cotton roll isolation and saliva suction, by dentists working in the public healthcare system, with clinical experience of between 1 and 10 years and with the help of a dental assistant.

Interproximal caries lesions were not assessed due to low X-ray coverage. The model simulates a 6-year follow-up of children, with controls every 2 years, in which hypothetical checkup examinations were carried out. Teeth with cavitated caries were filled, partially or completely fractured sealants and restorations were repaired or replaced, and any tooth with no treatment options was removed. The school-based oral healthcare program does not include endodontic care. Although it allows for referral to a service network for treatment, the reality is that the network has very low coverage, and children from 6 to 12 years old are not prioritized (at least at the date of the study); therefore, this procedure was not included in the model.

The comparison strategy was "Not to seal," that is, no intervention with dental sealants. This alternative is comparable to children left without coverage from the school-based sealant program. A 6-year follow-up with 2-year cycles was set in both groups. However, it was assumed that when the patient had a cavitated caries, he/she would go to the public oral healthcare center for conventional treatment or for emergency care. These local healthcare centers do not include endodontic care, being referred to the same health network as school-based care, therefore not affecting the model.

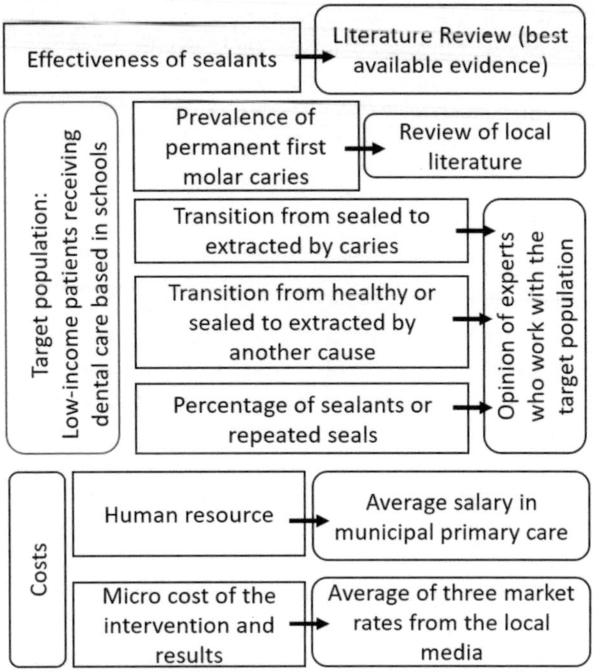

Fig. 9.1 Diagram with the inputs used in the model. (Reprinted from Espinoza-Espinoza et al. 2019. CC BY 4.0)

9.4.2 *Specify Measurements*

Since this example is model based, no direct measurements were made. But the model was built with the best available evidence of (a) effectiveness of the dental sealants (Ahovuo-Saloranta and Forss 2013); (b) quality-adjusted teeth years (QATY) (Bhuridej et al. 2007); (c) increases in dental caries prevalence in FMP every 2 years; (d) probability of FMP extraction; (e) probability of resealing in case of total or complete loss of dental sealants; and (f) probability of repeat of restoration in cases where it is partially or completely fractured (Fig. 9.1).

9.4.3 *Collect Cost Data*

The cost of a preventive strategy, as is the case in this analysis, considers the costs of implementing the strategy, as well as the costs of the consequences that could not be avoided (Ney et al. 2014). Therefore, this study (Espinoza-Espinoza et al. 2019) included data on costs for the initial placement of a dental sealants, which is the same for cases in which it is necessary to repeat a partially or totally fractured sealant. It also included the cost of treatments when caries was not avoided. This included the cost of restoring cavitated dental caries, as well as the cost of extractions. The costs of a root canal were not considered since the probability of this population having access to a molar root canal is very low. Since this study's perspective was the payer, it only included direct costs such as the costs of equipment, instruments, and supplies necessary for each intervention and the cost of the human resources necessary for each procedure.

9.4.4 Calculate Costs

Data costs were collected through either micro costing technique or by quoting the cost of supplies from three local dental suppliers; human resource data were collected from the local municipality salary table available online.

Estimates of the cost of instruments and supplies were obtained from quotes from three different dental providers, and the average of the three quotes was included in the model. Additionally, the highest and lowest values were considered in the sensitivity analysis. The equipment's lifetime span was considered to be 10 years, which is the average time determined by the municipalities to renew equipment.

To calculate human resources costs, the salary of a dentist and his/her dental assistant was taken from the salary table of the local municipality (Municipalidad de Temuco 2013). The average salary of professionals with between 1 and 10 years of experience was obtained. This was used to calculate the cost per minute worked placing dental sealants, which was determined by the time assigned for each intervention according to the school-based oral healthcare services guideline, which standardizes procedures for school dental clinics (JUANEB 2012). This corresponds to 15 min for the placement of dental sealants, another 15 min for an oral examination, and 30 min for dental restorations (i.e., fillings).

It is recommended that the cost models be carried out in local currency (Husereau et al. 2013); therefore, calculations were made in Chilean pesos as for May 7, 2019, and adjusted with the consumer price index (Instituto Nacional de Estadistica de Chile 2020). However, for the purposes of this chapter and other publications, the values were expressed in US dollars using the Central Bank of Chile exchange (exchange rate 1 USD = CLP 681.09) (Banco Central de Chile 2019).

9.4.5 Discount

The discount rate allows for the expression in present value, costs that will be spent in the future. It is important to follow the guidelines that each country has regarding the discount rate; in the case of Chile, the Methodological Guide for the Economic Evaluation of Health Interventions establishes a discount rate of 3% with a range of 0–5% to be used in sensitivity analysis (MINSAL 2013).

9.4.6 Define Outcomes

The study was planned as a cost-utility analysis; therefore, when defining the consequences, the outcome must be expressed as utility. Classic utility indicators such as quality-adjusted life years or disability-adjusted life years are difficult to equate with the health-related loss of quality of life of a FPM. For this reason, it was necessary to identify an indicator of a tooth's own quality; thus, quality-adjusted tooth years (QATY) were used (Fyffe and Nuttall 1995; Mohd-Dom 2014). QATY is a measure of dental health analogous to quality-adjusted life year that provides an outcome measure which could be compared across dental treatment. The assumption underlying QATY is that teeth with any health status (painful, poor aesthetic, filled, missing, etc.) are not equivalent to sound teeth without that health conditions (e.g., sound); thus it provides an adjustment to account for this difference (Fyffe and Nutall 1995). Therefore, QATY is an indicator that better reflects the reality of a tooth affected by caries. Nonetheless, to express its success or failure as a dichotomic outcome is impractical as we know that between the healthy tooth and the extraction there are several intermediate states that can be assessed and expressed in terms of the quality of the tooth. A filled tooth is superior to an extraction but inferior to a sound tooth.

In this example, a value of QATY = 1 was assigned to a sound or sealed sound tooth with no evidence of dental caries after a 6-year follow-up; a value of QATY = 0.81 was assigned to teeth that required restoration and a value of QATY = 0 for extracted teeth (Bhuridej et al. 2007).

9.4.7 Select Evaluation Design

Information on the cost-utility of the dental sealants applied to the first molars at the age of 6 years was needed in the school-based model of oral healthcare. For these purposes, a cost-utility analysis was designed, using a Markov model, which allows for modeling the natural course of events that represent different states of health. The Markov model assumed that, at any time, patients existed in one of a finite number of health states and transitioned between these health states during a series of cycles (Siebert et al. 2012) (three cycles of 2 years each).

A probabilistic model was chosen because it allowed for a better simulation of the current reality, considering the range of values that the variables can assume in each of the cases. It also allowed for the examination of how this variability can affect the cost-utility ratio and, at the same time, allowed for a multivariate sensitivity analysis. The design of the model was validated by a pediatric dentist and a health economist, both with extensive training in health technology assessment. Figure 9.2 shows a diagram of the model for each of the strategies.

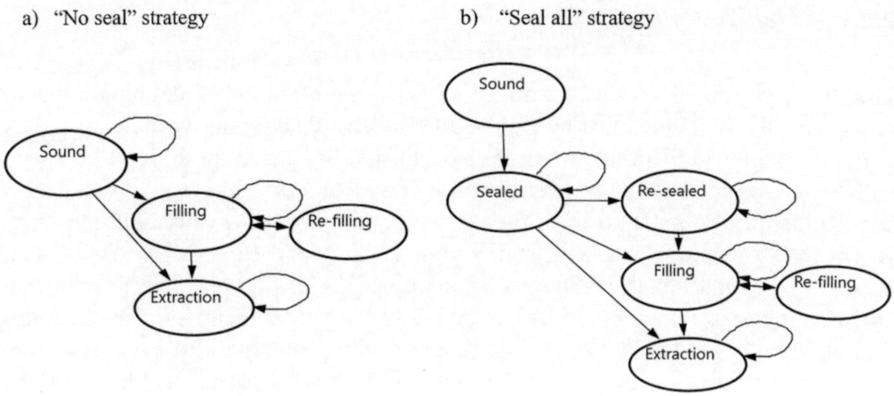

Fig. 9.2 Markov models for each strategy. (Reprinted from Espinoza-Espinoza et al. 2019. CC BY 4.0)

9.4.8 Data Collection

A systematic review of the literature was carried out to obtain the effectiveness of the dental sealants at 2, 4, and 6 years after application. The review determined effectiveness of 78% (CI 95%: 66–85%) after 24 months and 60% (CI 95%: 49–69%) after 48 months (Ahovuo-Saloranta et al. 2017). To determine effectiveness of the resin-based sealants after 72 months, a variation of 6% per year in adolescents was considered, as reported in the literature (48%; CI 95%: 37–57%) (Heyduck et al. 2006).

A review of local literature and of similar geographical areas allowed for the calculation of increases in the prevalence of dental caries every 2 years. Therefore, the prevalence studied in the untreated population was estimated at 25% in children aged 6 years, while prevalence for the other ages was determined under the assumption that the increase in caries (percentage increase of prevalence in each Markov cycle) was continuous over time. The increase in the prevalence of caries in the untreated population was 10.3% during each 2-year cycle. The prevalence values used in the models were 25% at 6 years, 35.3% at 8 years, 45.6% at 10 years, and 55.9% at 12 years (see Table 9.1).

A survey of dentists working in school-based oral healthcare allowed for the estimation of transition probabilities that were not found in the literature, such as tooth loss due to caries, resealing, and replace-restoration rates for each 2-year cycle (see Table 9.1).

Table 9.1 Parameters, probabilities, and distributions used in the model

Items	Seal everyone or Seal all (%)	No seal (%)	Type of distribution used
Effectiveness of sealants (CI 95%)[a]	2 Y: 78 (66–85)	–	A probability table was used
	4 Y: 60 (49–69)	–	
	6 Y: 48 (37–57)	–	
Prevalence of caries in first permanent molars (range for sensitivity analysis)[b]	6 YO: 0	6 YO: 25	Normal
	8 YO: 8 (± 2)	8 YO: 35.3 (± 2)	Normal
	10 YO: 18 (± 2)	10 YO: 45.6 (± 2)	Normal
	12 YO: 29 (± 2)	12 YO: 55.9 (± 2)	Normal
First permanent molars lost in each 2-year cycle[c]			
Cavities	1 in 1000	1 in 1000	Beta
Other causes	1 in 10,000	1 in 10,000	Beta
Reseal rate per cycle (range for sensitivity analysis)[c]	3 (0–13)	–	Beta
Refilling rate per cycle (range for sensitivity analysis)[d]	1 (0–14)	1 (0–14)	Beta

[a] Cochrane systematic review
[b] Local evidence from Chile and Latin America
[c] Survey of ten experts working in school-based dental clinics
[d] Survey of ten experts working in school-based dental clinics and literature review for the variability
Y years since application, *YO* years old

9.4.9 Data Analysis

Analysis for a base case scenario and sensitivity analyses were carried out. Firstly, the cost-utility analysis was performed: the incremental cost-utility ratio (ICUR) was computed, as incremental costs divided by incremental effects, to obtain the cost per additional QATY increased. An issue that was difficult to resolve was deciding on a payment threshold. The payment threshold for QALYs has a long history, and there are clear guidelines for countries to weigh the cost utility of interventions, but for QATYs this is not yet the case. Consequently, in the absence of a willingness to pay per QATY threshold, this study used a threshold of USD 29.36 (CLP 20,000). This figure represents the cost of a dental restoration in the Chilean public oral healthcare system in March 2018 (MINSAL 2010) and seemed reasonable and appropriate.

9.4.10 Types of Sensitivity Analysis Performed

The objective of the sensitivity analysis is to scrutinize changes in the results of the cost-utility ratio under the effects of possible variations in the base values of the model parameters, due to uncertainties. In this analysis, a two-stage sensitivity analysis was conducted.

- Deterministic sensitivity analysis. This is a type of one-way sensitivity analysis. The average value of each variable is taken as the base case, and different parameters are used for the sensitivity ranges depending on parameter. For effectiveness data, confidence intervals were considered (Anneli Ahovuo-Saloranta et al. 2017); for the incidence of caries, a variation of ±2% was used; for the repetition of sealant rate, a range of 13% was considered to take into account the clinicians' variability (Quiñonez et al. 2005). For the rest of the parameters, a variation of ±20% of the base value was considered. Finally, the results were ranked from highest to lowest and plotted on a tornado diagram.
- Probabilistic sensitivity analysis. This type of sensitivity analysis explores the simultaneous variation in the values of one or more variables. The probability distributions were assigned to each of the parameters (Table 9.1). Through a Monte Carlo simulation, 1000 iterations were performed, considering a random value within each distribution and generating an incremental cost-utility ratio (ICUR) result. This allowed us to estimate how the simultaneous variation of the parameters would affect the cost-utility estimator.

9.5 Step 4. Relate Cost to Outcomes

Table 9.2 shows details of the costs considered for each intervention and its consequences. The average cost of sealants was USD 5.4 (CLP 3682), ranging from USD 4.68 to USD 6.39. The average value used for composite restoration was USD 11.13 (CLP 7580), ranging from USD 9.63 to USD 13.08. The mean value used for dental extractions was USD 3.98 (CLP 2717), ranging from USD 3.46 to USD 4.66. The average value for a dental examination was USD 0.19 (CLP 131), ranging between USD 0.173 and USD 0.236.

Considering the effectiveness of the dental sealants in preventing dental caries, and the prevalence of caries in FPM in the control population, the prevalence of caries in FPM for the population under study was estimated. This corresponded to 8% 2 years after the placement of a sealant, 18% 4 years after placement, and 29% 6 years after the intervention (Table 9.1).

Table 9.2 Direct costs used in the model

Intervention	Item	Time required	Value per minute	Cost per molar intervened (cost range
Sealants	Dentist	15 min	USD 0.236	USD 3.546 (3.039–4.142)
	Assistant	15 min	USD 0.066	USD 0.991 (0.846–1.269)
	Supplies			USD 0.473 (0.433–0.532)
	Clinical site preparation	5 min	USD 0.066	USD 0.33 (0.305–0.374)
	Equipment and instruments	15 min	USD 0.004	USD 0.066 (0.059–0.079)
Total				USD 5.406 (4.682–6.394)
Filling (composite	Dentist	30 min	USD 0.236	USD 7.092 (6.089–8.274)
	Assistant	30 min	USD 0.066	USD 1.982 (1.691–2.539)
	Supplies			USD 1.593 (1.436–1.752)
	Clinical site preparation	5 min	USD 0.066	USD 0.33 (0.305–0.374)
	Equipment and instruments	30 min	USD 0.004	USD 0.132 (0.117–0.147)
Total				USD 11.129 (9.639–13.083)
Extraction	Dentist	10 min	USD 0.236	USD 2.364 (2.405–2.754)
	Assistant	10 min	USD 0.066	USD 0.661 (0.561–0.846)
	Supplies			USD 0.59 (0.532–0.639)
	Clinical site preparation	5 min	USD 0.066	USD 0.33 (0.305–0.374)
	Equipment and instruments	10 min	USD 0.004	USD 0.044 (0.04–0.048)
Total				USD 3.989 (3.462–4.663)
Oral exam	Dentist	15 min	USD 0.236	USD 3.546 (3.039–4.142)
	Assistant	15 min	USD 0.066	USD 0.991 (0.846–1.269)
	Supplies			USD 0.216 (0.197–0.226)
	Equipment and instruments	15 min	USD 0.004	USD 0.066 (0.059–0.079)
Total oral exam				USD 4.603 (4.142–5.72)
Total molar exam	Divided by 24 teeth			USD 0.192 (0.173–0.236)

Table 9.3 Incremental cost-utility ratio applying a Monte Carlo simulation

Strategies	Costs (USD)	Incremental cost (USD)	Utility (QATY)	Incremental utility	Incremental utility cost ratio
No seal	10.77		3.71		
Seal all	12.06	1.28	3.91	0.2	6.48

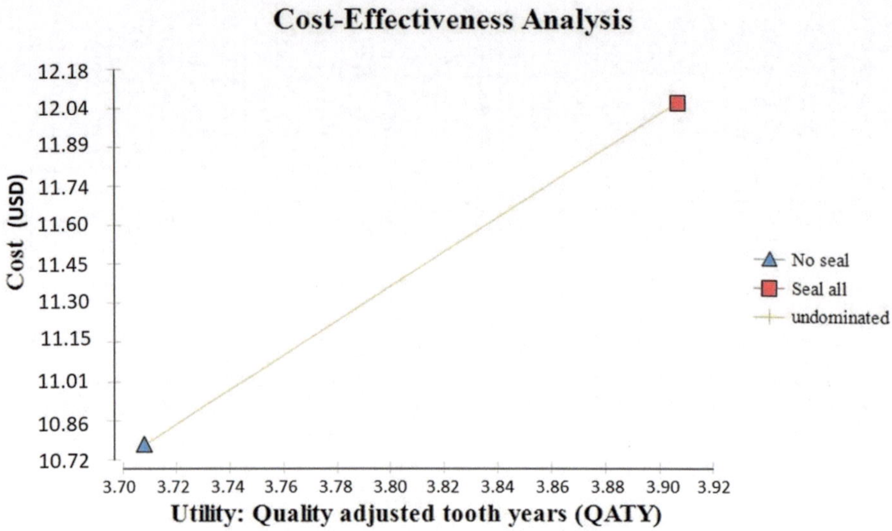

Fig. 9.3 Cost-utility plane. (Reprinted from Espinoza-Espinoza et al. 2019. CC BY 4.0)

9.5.1 Ratio

The "Seal all" strategy was more favorable, with a positive difference of 0.2 QATY. The ICUR for the "Seal all" strategy, compared to no-intervention, was USD 6.48 (CLP 4412) per QATY gained (Table 9.3; Fig. 9.3).

9.6 Step 5. Adjust for Uncertainties

The deterministic sensitivity analysis is summarized in the tornado diagram (Fig. 9.4). The parameter that most influenced ICUR was the increase in the prevalence of caries in FPM in the control group. The base case was calculated by estimating this increase in the prevalence of caries in FPM at 10.3% in each 2-year cycle. In populations where this increase in caries prevalence was greater than 17%, the "Seal all" strategy dominated, while in populations where the increase in caries was less than 5%, the ICUR doubles.

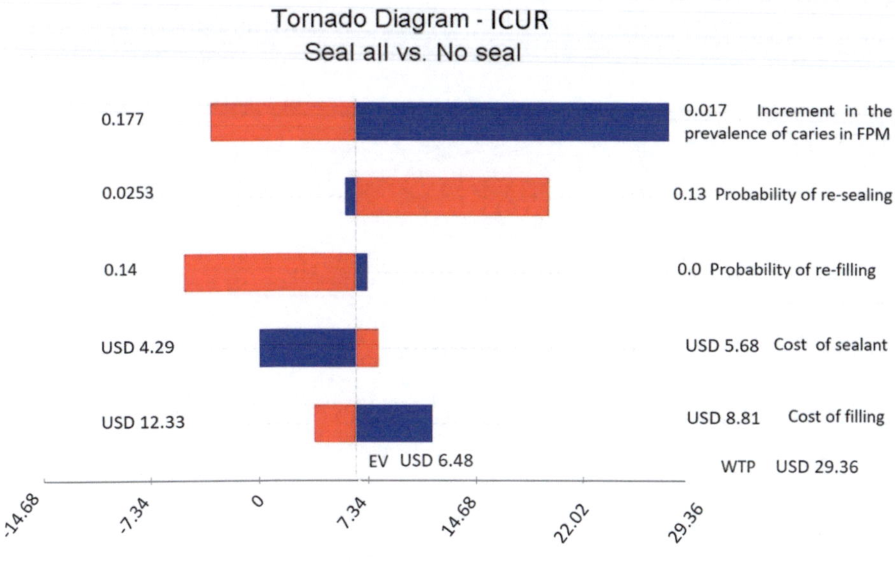

Fig. 9.4 Tornado diagram for univariate sensitivity analysis. (Reprinted from Espinoza-Espinoza et al. 2019. CC BY 4.0)

It must be noted that if the increase is 2% or less in each 2-year cycle, the ICUR is four times higher. If caries in FPM is less prevalent, this favors the "Do not seal" alternative. This is because, although there is no intervention, the number of cavitated caries will be lower. Therefore, the costs of restoring dental caries that were cavitated decrease, which means that in the "Seal all" strategy, the cost of each QATY gained becomes higher. On the other hand, if dental caries in FPM is more prevalent (i.e., both strategies would have more caries), this greatly affects the "Do not seal" arm, because the increment is completely transferred, while in the "Seal all" arm the increment will be reduced by the sealant's effectiveness.

Other variables that generated ICUR uncertainty were the probability of repeating either sealants or restorations. In relation to sealants, the assumption is that a percentage of them had to be completely or partially repaired/repeated in each cycle. According to experts' opinion, the average proportion of sealants that needed to be repaired/repeated in each 2-year cycle would be 3% with an uncertainty range of between 2.5% and 13.0%. This resulted in a variation in the ICUR range from USD 5.85 (CLP 3988) to USD 19.71 (CLP 13.430). Variations in this parameter only affected the "Seal all" arm; thus, when the percentage of sealants that had to be repaired or replaced was as high as 13.0%, this increased the base case ICUR in about three times but remaining within the payment threshold.

The repetition/repairing of restorations affected both arms of the study; however, it affected more the "Do not seal" than the "Seal all" strategy. This is because in that arm there would be more restorations, so there is also a greater probability of having to repair or replace a restoration. For this reason, the "Seal all" strategy becomes dominant (more effective and cheaper) when the probability of redoing restorations reached 14% in each cycle.

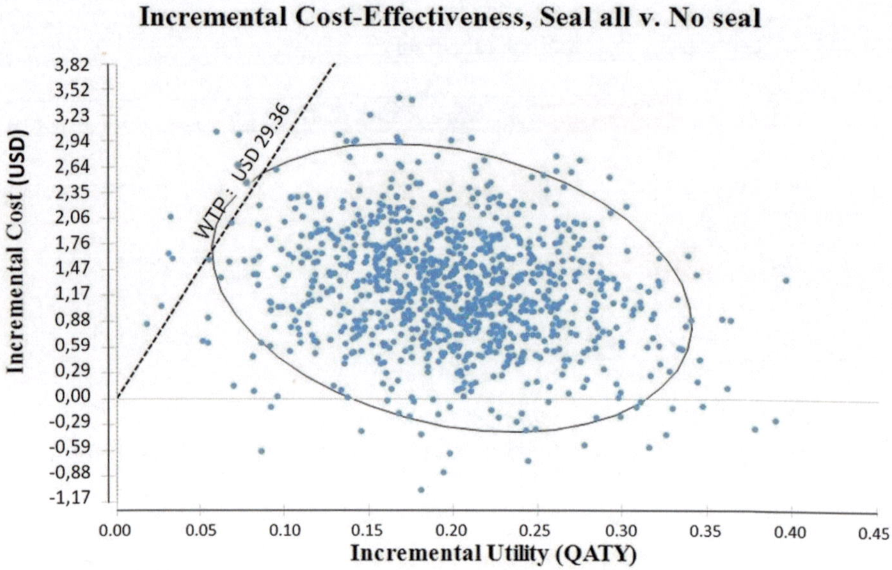

Fig. 9.5 Probabilistic sensitivity analysis. (Reprinted from Espinoza-Espinoza et al. 2019. CC BY 4.0)

Other parameters had little influence on the ICUR. The "Do not seal" strategy was not dominant in any scenario, which reflects the robustness of the results.

To assess the joint influence of all the parameters included in the model, a Monte Carlo simulation was conducted. As explained previously, this type of analysis considers 1000 hypothetical patients who assume some random value within the uncertainty range and according to a type of distribution. The type of distribution used is found in Table 9.1. With the data of these 1000 hypothetical patients, 1000 ICUR values are obtained, and using a payment threshold of USD 29.36 (CLP 20,000), in 0.9% of cases, the "Seal all" strategy did not produce a utility, it was dominant in 3.3% of the cases, and in 95.8% of the cases that strategy showed different levels of cost utility, mainly concentrated around the average profit of 0.2 QATY (Fig. 9.5).

9.7 Step 6. Summarize, Interpret, and Report Findings

The present analysis model (Espinoza-Espinoza et al. 2019) showing that the application of resin sealants to all the first permanent molars in 6-year-old children, in the context of a school-based dental healthcare system, is a cost-utility measure, especially in populations where the prevalence of caries in FPM had an increase of 10.3% or more every 2 years. This is consistent with Bertrand et al.'s (2011) findings who, using a model with the mouth as the unit of analysis and considering indirect costs, reached similar conclusions regarding the cost utility of dental sealants in school settings. In fact, the authors noted that, compared to other dental sealing strategies, school-based dental care is the best cost-utility option.

The sensitivity analysis highlights the fact that the parameter with the greatest influence on the ICUR was the increase in the prevalence of caries in the first permanent molars. The "Seal all" strategy became dominant when the increased prevalence of caries in the FPM was greater than in the base case, by at least 3%. This finding agrees with reports by Griffin et al. (2016) in their economic evaluation of pits and fissure sealant in the context of school-based dental care serving low-income children in the United States. They assumed a similar increase in caries to the present scenario and concluded that this parameter was also the most influential in the cost-effectiveness ratio. They also concluded that the program saved societal resources and remained profitable over a wide range of realistic values. Several other studies also confirmed that sealants have better utility than restorations, when applied to children with high caries prevalence (Bhuridej et al. 2007; Leskinen et al. 2008).

Another variable that generated uncertainty is the proportion of sealants that need to repeat/repair in each cycle. When a sealed molar comes to the next checkup with the sealant partially or fully fractured, there are additional costs to consider. In circumstances where the repetition rate of the sealant is high, the ICUR increases considerably. This was also reported by Chi et al., who analyzed the reverse situation. They observed that when the retention rate was 10% higher than the base case, the cost reduced to less than half, per obturation avoided (Chi et al. 2014).

A strength of the study presented was the use of a probabilistic analysis that assessed the joint effect of all of the parameters considered. This produced a model that best resembles the real-life scenario, including willingness to pay as reference, and uses a Monte Carlo simulation, which considers a thousand iterations. That analysis indicated that in more than 95% of the cases the "Seal all" strategy would be considered cost utility, and only 0.9% would be above the defined threshold, indicating that in less than 1% of the cases the strategy would not be cost-effective.

This model simulated the chance for children to repeat the sealant treatment in their 2-yearly checkups when a sealant was partially or completely lost. This increases the benefit of the sealant, since the effectiveness is calculated starting from when the sealant is repeated but also translates into an increase in cost in this strategy. For this reason, a resealing rate of 13% can triple the cost per QATY.

When considering the findings of the study, it is important to bear in mind that it is a theoretical model, in which both costs and effectiveness are estimated, some from the literature and others from general market conditions. To minimize this limitation, the literature was reviewed to include the best available evidence on the effectiveness of resin-based sealants. Local costs and conversions were used to facilitate the understanding of results.

This study simulated a dental sealant program within a school-based dental healthcare context, in which all permanent first molars were sealed without any caries risk analysis. This was because in the context in which the study was conducted, caries risk analysis is not part of the protocol. However, deciding whether to consider a risk analysis or not would depend on the prevalence of dental caries in the first permanent molars. Available evidence shows that the cost-effectiveness of the strategies depends on that prevalence. On the one hand, some studies have found that in populations where the prevalence of caries in the FPM is high, the "Seal all" strategy becomes more favorable compared to sealing only patients with high caries risk (Griffin et al. 2002; Quiñonez et al. 2005). Other authors have concluded that sealants have higher cost utility when placed on high-risk patients only (Bertrand et al. 2011; Gooch et al. 2010; Weintraub 2001). These conclusions depend on two factors" when sealing all FPM, there are higher costs because some of them, due to their risk analysis, might not need sealants, and secondly, because they are programs with limited coverage, they might leave high-risk children, who would benefit from the sealant, out of the program (Leskinen et al. 2008).

Another aspect to consider is that some of the probabilities were not obtained from the literature but from a panel of experts. These included the percentage of sealants and restorations that would fail in each cycle and the number of tooth extractions due to caries or due to other causes. However, although it is advisable that the likelihoods used in an economic evaluation should be based on clinical data, when this information is not available, expert opinion can ensure that the model reflects real-life practice (Simoens 2006).

Future studies should include long-term costs and expenses, benefits shown by determinants of quality of life, risk subgroup analyses, and patients' point of view. This would allow a better understanding of the social utility of dental sealants as a preventive measure, as proposed by Kitchens (2005). Additionally, in Chile the public and private costs are very different, so it may also be interesting to consider these differences in future analyses.

Despite these limitations, the study (Espinoza-Espinoza et al. 2019) provided evidence of the cost utility of dental sealant programs in schoolchildren with a high prevalence of caries, under the conditions prevailing in Chile. Considering that caries has an important social gradient, this evidence supports public policies for the targeting of state resources to finance comprehensive oral healthcare.

9.8 Final Remark

As reported in Chap. 11, there are an increasing number of publications describing CUA in oral health in the last few years (Mariño and Zaror 2020). This highlights the need to make future studies in oral health more in accordance with commonly used CUA in the health field. This chapter examined the use of CUA in the oral health context, its structure, and purpose together with the steps necessary for its development. Now we will summarize some key aspects to take into consideration when designing a CUA.

A comparative advantage of CUAs over other types of economic evaluation is that it considers the preferences of patients when evaluating the cost-effectiveness of competing interventions. This is particularly relevant when the purpose is to evaluate the cost-effectiveness of oral healthcare programs. Oral healthcare treatments often fail to resolve the condition completely (e.g., tooth loss) or require complex long-term treatments, impacting the quality of life of those who suffer from them. Within this context, a CUA is able to provide us with a more comprehensive evaluation of the worth of the various treatments and programs by considering the perspective of the users.

A second advantage is that CUAs allow us to compare interventions with different consequences by summarizing the effects in a single value, supporting the efficient allocation of resources. However, the main difficulty when deciding on a CUA is choosing the utility outcome measure that best represents the different health states in the oral health field. In this regard, although QALYs have not been widely used in dentistry, it appears to be the best measure of utility as it would allow a better relationship between oral and general health.

As already mentioned, models are simplifications of reality, but a model that considers utility would be a better representation of reality. For that reason, in the design of CUA it is important that the information on which this model is based must be of the best available quality, according to the technology evaluated, population studied, and perspective.

To conclude, please bear in mind that using probability distributions is better than using point values or averages. This is because the distribution of the values of a variable better simulates all the dispersion options of the values that the variable can assume. Also, consider that local costing is a necessary requirement to support local decision-making, but it can limit the transfer of conclusions to other contexts or jurisdictions; therefore, it is always advisable to carry out a sensitivity analysis that covers different cost scenarios.

References

Ahovuo-Saloranta A, Forss H, Walsh T, Hiiri A, Nordblad A, Mäkelä M, Worthington HV (2013) Sealants for preventing dental decay in the permanent teeth. Cochrane Database of Systematic Reviews, 2013(3). https://doi.org/10.1002/14651858.CD001830.PUB4/ABSTRACT

Ahovuo-Saloranta A, Forss H, Walsh T et al (2017) Pit and fissure sealants for preventing dental decay in permanent teeth. Cochrane Database Syst Rev 2017(7). https://doi.org/10.1002/14651858.CD001830.pub5

Akinlotan M, Chen B, Fontanilla TM et al (2018) Economic evaluation of dental sealants: a systematic literature review. Community Dent Oral Epidemiol 46(1):38–46

Banco Central de Chile (2019). https://www.bcentral.cl/. https://www.bcentral.cl/. Accessed 15 Nov 2019

Bertrand É, Mallis M, Bui NM, Reinharz D (2011) Cost-effectiveness simulation of a universal publicly funded sealants application program. J Public Health Dent 71:38–45

Bhuridej P, Kuthy RA, Flach SD et al (2007) Four-year cost-utility analyses of sealed and non-sealed first permanent molars in Iowa Medicaid-enrolled children. J Public Health Dent 67(4):191–198

Chi DL, Van der Goes DN, Ney JP (2014) Cost-effectiveness of pit-and-fissure sealants on primary molars in Medicaid-enrolled children. Am J Public Health 104(3):555–561

Espinoza-Espinoza G, Corsini G, Rojas R, Mariño R, Zaror C (2019) The cost-utility of school-based first permanent molar sealants programs: a Markov model. BMC Oral Health 19(1):1–11
Fyffe HE, Nuttall NM (1995) Decision processes in the management of dental disease. Part 1: QALYs, QATYs and dental health state utilities. Dental Update 22(2):67–71
Gooch BF, Griffin SO, Gray K et al (2010) Preventing dental caries through school-based sealant programs. 140:1356–1365
Griffin SO, Griffin PM, Gooch BF (2002) Comparing the costs of three sealant delivery strategies. J Dent Res 81(9):641–645
Griffin SO, Naavaal S, Scherrer C et al (2016) School-based dental sealant programs prevent cavities and are cost-effective. Health Aff 35(12):2233–2240
Hernandez-Sampieri R, Mendoza CP (2018) Metodología de la investigación. Las rutas cuantitativa, cualitativa y mixta. Mc Graw Hill. Ciudad de México
Heyduck C, Meller C, Schwahn C, Splieth CH (2006) Effectiveness of sealants in adolescents with high and low caries experience. Caries Res 40:375–381
Husereau D, Drummond M, Petrou S et al (2013) Consolidated health economic evaluation reporting standards (CHEERS)-explanation and elaboration: a report of the ISPOR health economic evaluation publication guidelines good reporting practices task force. Value Health 16(2):231–250
Instituto Nacional de Estadistica de Chile (2020) Índice de Precios al Consumidor. https://www.ine.cl/estadisticas/economia/indices-de-precio-e-inflacion/indice-de-precios-al-consumidor. Accessed 15 Nov 2019
Junta Nacional de Auxilio Escolar y Becas (JUNAEB) (2012) Normas y procedimientos de la atención en módulos dentales JUNAEB. http://anfitrion.cl/GobiernoTransparente/junaeb/2018/otras/153.pdf. Accessed 15 Nov 2019
Junta Nacional de Auxilio Escolar y Becas (JUNAEB) (2014) Manual de salud Odontologica
Kitchens DH (2005) The economics of pit and fissure sealants in preventive dentistry: a review. J Contemp Dent Pract 6(3):95–103
Leskinen K, Salo S, Suni J, Larmas M (2008) Practice-based study of the cost-effectiveness of fissure sealants in Finland. J Dent 36(12):1074–1079
Listl S, Grytten JI, Birch S (2019) What is health economics? Community Dent Health 36(4):263–275
Mariño R, Zaror C (2020) Economic evaluations in water-fluoridation: a scoping review. BMC Oral Health 20:115
Ministerio de Salud de Chile (MINSAL) (2010) Estudio Costo-efectividad de Intervenciones en Salud. https://desal.minsal.cl/wp-content/uploads/2013/09/01CostoEfectividad.pdf. Accessed 30 May 2019
Ministerio de Salud de Chile (MINSAL) (2013) Guía metodológica para la evaluación económica de intervenciones de salud en Chile. http://desal.minsal.cl/wp-content/uploads/2013/09/EE_FINAL_web.pdf. Accessed 30 May 2019
Mohd-Dom T (2014) Quality-adjusted tooth years (QATY) as an outcome measure of periodontal treatment. BMC Public Health 14(S1):2458
Municipalidad de Temuco (2013) Tabla de remuneraciones Municipalidad de Temuco. http://www.temucochile.com/newtransparencia/d_personal/2013/TablaRemuneracionesSalud2013.pdf. Accessed 30 May 2019
Ney J, van der Goes DN, Chi DL (2014) Economic modeling of sealing primary molars using a " value of information " approach. J Dent Res 93(9):876–882
Petrou S, Gray A (2011) Economic evaluation using decision analytical modelling: design, conduct, analysis, and reporting. BMJ 342:1766
Quiñonez RB, Downs SM, Shugars D et al (2005) Assessing cost-effectiveness of sealant placement in children. J Public Health Dent 65(2):82–89
Siebert U, Alagoz O, Bayoumi AM et al (2012) State-transition modeling: a report of the ISPOR-SMDM modeling good research practices task force-3. Med Decis Mak 32(5):690–700

Simoens S (2006) Using the Delphi technique in economic evaluation: time to revisit the oracle? J Clin Pharm Ther 31(6):519–522

Weintraub JA (2001) Pit and fissure sealants in high-caries-risk individuals. J Dent Educ 65(10):1084–1090

Zarate V (2010) Evaluaciones económicas en salud: Conceptos básicos y clasificación. Rev Med Chil 138(138):93–97

Zaror C, Pardo Y, Espinoza-Espinoza G, Pont A et al (2019) Assessing oral health-related quality of life in children and adolescents: a systematic review and standardized comparison of available instruments. Clin Oral Invest 23(1):65–79

Chapter 10
What Is the Literature Telling Us About Economic Evaluation in Oral Health

Rodrigo Mariño and Carlos Zaror

10.1 Economic Evaluations for Decision-Making in Dentistry

Oral health is about ensuring that people's lives are not affected by a range of conditions. Two major threats to oral health are dental caries and periodontal disease. However, there is a number of other oral health conditions such as dento-facial anomalies, diseases of the oral mucosa, oral cancer and precancerous lesions, and maxillofacial trauma and other less common conditions such as temporo-mandibular joint disorders, which also have an impact in at the individual, the healthcare services, and society levels. In many countries, the cost of providing oral healthcare represents a considerable proportion of the nation's health resources. For example, in Australia oral healthcare represents 6% ($10.2 billion) of the nation's health expenditure (Australian Institute for Health and Welfare 2019). In the EU the year expense in oral health is 5% of the total health expenditure (Platform for Better Oral Health in Europe 2020). It has been reported that in many countries, this is between 5% and 10% (Masood et al. 2015). However, this expenditure in oral healthcare does not include the cost of acute oral conditions in terms of restricted the participation of adults in the workforce, including restricted duties and lost workdays due to oral health-related illness.

To put this into perspective, oral healthcare expenditure exceeds that for other chronic diseases, including cancer, heart disease, stroke, and dementia in Australia

R. Mariño (✉)
Melbourne Dental School, The University of Melbourne, Melbourne, VIC, Australia
e-mail: r.marino@unimelb.edu.au

C. Zaror
Department of Paediatric Dentistry and Orthodontics, Faculty of Dentistry, Universidad de La Frontera, Temuco, Chile

Center for Research in Epidemiology, Economics and Oral Public Health (CIEESPO), Faculty of Dentistry, Universidad de La Frontera, Temuco, Chile
e-mail: carlos.zaror@ufrontera.cl

C. Zaror, R. Mariño (eds.), *Introduction to Economic Evaluation in Oral Health Care*, https://doi.org/10.1007/978-3-030-96289-0_10

and Europe (Platform for Better Oral Health in Europe 2020). Furthermore, the global burden of oral diseases is estimated to affect more than half of the world population (i.e. 3.58 billion people), with oral disease and conditions being in the top five most prevalent conditions (World Health Organisation 2020).

Based on cost and outcome, those responsible for policy making and planning public health programs must prioritize health interventions and select the option that offers the most advantages (Morgan and Mariño 2012). They must determine the most appropriate programs for using resources that could otherwise be employed in delivering a range of other types of services (Christell et al. 2014). The issue of how to best allocate scarce resources between competing health interventions is not uncommon in this field. At a basic level, decision-makers compare the value of competing alternative interventions that may have or may not have different health outcomes, and its benefits and its cost of an intervention must be considered. Based on that information, they select the interventions that offer the most financial benefit (Morgan and Mariño 2012).

Economic evaluations are useful in a situation of diminishing public resources for healthcare and increasingly sophisticated treatment options and demands and hard trade-offs about what services to choose. In this context healthcare planners and programmers rely on evidence from different sources, including economic evaluations, to allocate resources for different health interventions (Morgan and Mariño 2012). For that, they need to have the correct information and evidence to identify the economic impact of resources used for most interventions in oral health. That information must be sound in quality. Furthermore, to best allocate resources among competing alternative, healthcare planners and programmers are required to combine different sources of evidence and a full range of methods and skills to assure these resources are properly used.

Different strategies have been developed to help healthcare planners, programmers, and decision-makers in this process. It is in this framework that economic evaluations (EE) are relevant, as they are part of this process providing information that managers weigh, alongside other evidence. Nonetheless, although there are examples in the literature of EE in oral health, comparatively until recently reports on economic evaluations conducted in oral health were limited. More recent reviews indicate that this is changing (Mariño et al. 2013; Mariño and Zaror 2020).

Chapter 1 describes different types of methodological frameworks that exist to conduct EE, each of them aimed at addressing specific questions. This includes cost-effectiveness analysis (CEA), cost-utility analysis (CUA), and cost-benefit analysis (CBA). Nonetheless, although the first EE in oral health was published in 1976 (Higson 1976) and the interest in EE in oral health tends to increase in the last few years, still it is an under-used element in oral health evaluation. Reports indicate that not only the quantity has increased, but also their quality has been improving compared to EE published earlier (Mariño et al. 2020). This is important because if, as health professionals, we want to be able to provide evidence about what would be the most efficient use of scarce health resources for the benefit of the population, we must be prepared to understand and utilize the basic principles and types of EE to monitor their quality and influence policies (Mariño et al. 2020).

Some authors claim that systematic reviews of economic evaluation studies are of limited relevance, because of the issue of transferability of results (Anderson 2010). Furthermore, systematic review of economic evaluations of oral healthcare has been described as more difficult than that of other interventions in health, due to the lack of standardization in the choice of oral health outcome measure, which makes difficult comparisons of the cost-effectiveness ratio (Akinlotan et al. 2018). Thus, it was not the purpose of this chapter to conduct a proper scoping review of the literature, rather an umbrella review, as defined by Grant and Booth (2009). This approach was used to review and compile evidence from multiple reviews into document to assist in the provision of recommendations for practice and provide in recommendations for future research. The foundation for applying economic evaluation principles in the oral healthcare. This chapter is focused on the methodological quality of EE in oral health, hoping that this effort would guide program and better inform the priority setting in oral healthcare for policy makers. We hope to have clearer guidance for programmers and decision-makers, as to provide adequate information to promote shared informed decision-making.

10.2 Description of the Literature in EE in Oral Health

A systematic search in Medline was conducted to identify EE in oral health, particularly, for systematic and scoping reviews, from 2000 to 2020. In addition, references for all included articles were also reviewed to identify missing reviews. Details about the search are presented in Appendix 1. The reviews identified that there has been a gradually increased number of reviews in EE with 20 published since 1999, with 14 in the last 5 years. Topics varied from community water fluoridation (CWF), orthodontics, dental sealant, preventive interventions, etc. Table 10.1 provides a summary of the included reviews.

There is no gold standard evaluation tool to assess the quality of economic evaluations, instead there are several evaluation tools available that can be used to support reviewers and interested parties in assessing the quality of EE (Anderson 2010), for example, the Critical Appraisal Skills Programme (CASP) (Critical Appraisal Skills Programme 2017), the Consolidated Health Economic Evaluation Reporting Standards (CHEERS) (Husereau et al. 2013) checklist, the University of York checklist (Centre for Reviews and Dissemination 2009), and the Drummond et al. checklist (Drummond et al. 2015), to name a few. These tools capture elements of perspective, time horizon, discounting, outcome, etc. However, depending on which one of those is used, it may provide different review results. The CHEERS is now the most widely used in the medical literature (Listl and Weyant 2019). Nonetheless, in the present review, the Drummond checklist was one of the most used, followed by CHEERS.

Table 10.1 Characteristics of included studies by publication date

Study	Type of EE included	Tools	Core topic	Age group	Number reviewed	Years covered	Comments
Amilani et al. (2020)	CEA	CHEERS	School-based dental caries prevention	5–18	15	Up to June 2019	English only
Anopa and Conway (2020)	All + partial EE	CHEERS	Primary dentition dental caries prevention	2–5	39	No restrictions	No restrictions
Mariño and Zaror (2020)	All	Joanna Briggs Institute	Community water fluoridation	All	24	Up to 2019	English, Spanish, Portuguese
Mariño et al. (2020)	All	U of York	Oral health preventive programs	All	33	1975–2018	English, Spanish, Portuguese, Italian, French
Murthy and Fareed (2020)	All + partial EE	CHEERS	School-based dental caries prevention	6–15	32	Up to March 2019	English only
Eow et al. (2019)	All	Drummond's checklist	Oral health interventions, involving both prevention and treatment	All	91	1980–2017	English only
Fraihat et al. (2019)	All	Drummond	Child oral health promotion programs	0–12	8	N/A	English only
Tan et al. (2017)	N/A	N/A	Willingness to pay for clinical oral health	Adults	26	Up to 2016	Language N/A
Qu et al. (2019)	All	Phillips' checklist	Analytic models of dental caries interventions	All	25	Up to 2018	English
Rogers et al. (2019)		Drummond's checklist, CHEERS	Child oral health programs, involving both prevention and treatment	18 and under	46	1997–2017	Mostly preventive Language N/A
Akinlotan et al. (2018)	CEA	Drummond	Dental sealants	3–18	13	1996–2015	Language N/A

Study	Type of EE included	Tools	Core topic	Age group	Number reviewed	Years covered	Comments
Hettiarachchi et al. (2018)	CUA	CHEERS	Oral cancer, dental caries, prosthodontics, dento-facial anomalies, service provision	All	23	2000–2016	Language N/A
Leo et al. (2016)	All	Drummond (modified LaTorre)	Dental sealants	N/A	15	N/A	Language N/A
Sollenius et al. (2016)	All	Drummond's checklist	Ortho	2.5–19	26	1966–2014	Only RCT, CCT Language N/A
York Health Economics Consortium (2016)	All	NICE	Oral health promotion intervention	0–5 years	5	2012 onwards	English and OECD only
Tonmukayakul et al. (2015)	All + partial EE	Drummond's checklist	Oral health programs, involving both prevention and treatment	All	114	1975–2013	English only
Christell et al. (2014)	All	U of York	Diagnostic methods	N/A	12	Up to 2013	Language N/A
Coffin et al. (2013)	All	NICE	Dental caries	All	17	1993 onwards	English and OECD only
Mariño et al. (2013)	All	U of York	Dental caries	All		1975–2012	English, Spanish, Portuguese, Italian, French
Källestål et al. (2003)	All	N/A	Dental caries prevention	0–16	17	1966–2003	English, German, Spanish, Italian, French Scandinavian languages
Deery (1999)	All	N/A	Dental sealants	N/A	9		Language N/A

N/A not available, *OECD* Organization for Economic Cooperation and Development, *RCT* randomized clinical trial, *CCT* controlled clinical trial

10.2.1 Topic of the EE

These reviews indicate that there is a concentration of the economic evidence on certain interventions, with dental caries preventative interventions most common studies. Fissure sealants and fluoride treatment (e.g., community water-F) were the predominant intervention of interest of the studies published, followed by restorative interventions, prosthodontics interventions and periodontics interventions. In fact, community water-F dominated EE in oral health prevention (Mariño and Zaror 2020).

This might be an indication that EE are also influenced by the trends and interest of oral health disciplines, rather than whether more research is needed (Eow et al. 2019). Restorative, prosthodontic, and periodontal interventions were of interest to researchers as these are the most common treatments provided by general dental practitioners as compared to other interventions such as oral surgery, orthodontics, and special care.

While dental caries is the most common disease affecting humankind, other oral health conditions also have some serious financial consequences to individuals, oral healthcare providers, and society. For example, dental caries, together with periodontal disease and tooth loss, are on the top five most prevalent conditions (National Advisory Committee on Oral Health, 2004); however, these oral health conditions are less common than the matters of EE, which highlights that research into certain oral health conditions is in need of economic assessment. Additionally, there were few EE studies on oral cancer, and no studies assessed the cost-effectiveness of interventions for *molar-incisor hypomineralization (MIH)* or dental and *orofacial injuries*, which present larger societal impact (Rogers et al. 2019).

10.2.2 Type of EE

Reviews indicate that most studies have been conducted using predominantly cost-effectiveness analysis (CEA), although some cost-utility analysis (CUA) and cost-benefit analysis (CBA) have also been included. This could be related to the relatively easy way to conduct this CEA analysis, but it may also be because the priority has been in allocate efficiency, rather than other types of considerations (Eow et al., 2019). CUA is increasing, in particular, in treatment evaluations. As with other types of EE, there is increasing number of publications describing CUA in the last few years (Hettiarachchi et al. 2018; Mariño et al., 2020). CUA expresses effectiveness measuring of what an intervention means to patients (mostly quality-adjusted life years (QALY) or disability-adjusted life years (DALY)).

The use of quality of life allows for the comparisons of cost-effectiveness across interventions and health conditions. We strongly believe that oral health interventions can improve quality of life of the population. However, CUA is less used in EE or oral health interventions but is an area of expansion in oral health research. In fact, a review by Hettiarachchi (2018) found 23 studies for 2000–2016 using CUA. The majority of those studies used QALY and to a much lesser extent DALY, quality-adjusted tooth years (QATY), quality-adjusted prosthesis years (QAPY), and one study used quality of tooth years (QLTY) as qualitative outcome developed for oral health. But again, this type of studies requires the conversion of data to a common unit of quality (Hettiarachchi et al. 2018). However, QATY does not take into consideration the relationship between oral health and general health, as sometimes it is difficult to assess QATY, and it is only useful when DMFT/S is used as outcome (Rogers et al. 2019, Qu et al. 2019). Highlighting the need to develop an oral health measure for oral health outcomes that facilitates the use of QALY in future EE in oral health (Rogers et al. 2019).

10.2.3 *Time Period of an Analysis*

The time periods covered by oral health evaluations were usually short and sometime not sufficient to allow for the full effects of the programs on costs and outcomes. Because of the nature of analyses required to inform decisions, prospective epidemiological data for all the lifespan of a population, or at least from early childhood to old age, are needed (Mariño and Zaror 2020). Demand for evidence-supported decision-makers will require longitudinal studies, which now are lacking.

One study was found using synthetic cohorts. Campain and her collaborators (2010) modelled the cost-effectiveness of community water fluoridation (CWF) including the influences of an ageing population, lower rates of edentulism, and consequently higher rates of periodontal treatment need and replacement of restorations. They found that CWF continued to be a cost-effective measure. However, the study also suggested that CWF might stop being cost-effective due to the additional costs of treatment of periodontal disease and retreatment and replacement of broken or dislodged crowns and restorations, etc., highlighting the need to organize preventive interventions for other oral health problems (i.e., periodontal disease), not just interventions to prevent dental caries.

10.2.4 *Location of the Studies*

The review would indicate that most of the EE studies have been conducted in the USA, the UK, Germany and Australia, Sweden, and several other countries. There was a general lack of EE in African countries and to a lesser extent in Asian countries. In Latin America, apart from Brazil and Chile, there is also a general lack of EE. This would indicate that there are no EEs available to support the prioritization of oral health program. However, it is possible that studies in those countries are not included in systematic review due to language limitations from the research teams, who commonly exclude non-English publications.

EEs are very context specific and most likely reflect the local conditions only, and conclusions from one jurisdiction may not be readily applicable to other populations and jurisdictions (Murray et al. 2000). Thus, care must be exerted when generalizing results, as it remains difficult to compare economic results from one country to another (Mariño and Zaror 2020) or even within a jurisdiction from a given year to another, and the cost of a technology may also vary after its initial introduction (Laupacis et al. 1992).

There are a number of reasons for this, which support the contention that EE should be constantly reviewed and locally based (Anderson 2010; Mariño and Zaror 2020), among them: (i) differences in price for resources; (ii) variability in willingness to pay for health and healthcare; (iii) variations in prices of health consequences (O'Brien et al. 1997); (iv) variation in approaches to treatment and resource use; and (v) risk behaviours of the population, healthcare infrastructure, and a society's ideological and ethical norms could also differ (Mariño and Zaror 2020). Furthermore, the prevalence of a condition has a high level of influence in determining whether health interventions are cost-effective or not (Källestål et al. 2003, Amilani et al. 2020). For example, a reduced prevalence of caries may render earlier model assessment of an intervention's cost-effectiveness outdated (Källestål et al. 2003). Also, the cost of a technology at the points of its introduction may be different from its cost at a different point in time (Laupacis et al. 1992; Hutubessy et al. 2002).

10.3 Quality of EE Gaps in Knowledge in the Field

Several reviews of EE in oral have suggested that although there has been an increase in the number of economic evaluations conducted in oral health over the last few years, existing economic evaluations may not provide strong evidence to draw conclusions from. This would be mainly because their standards still needed improvement to increase the robustness of the EE in oral health (Mariño et al. 2020; Källestål et al. 2003; Mariño et al. 2013; Tonmukayakul et al. 2015). These conclusions were reached by reviewing EE done on wide area of oral health programs, comprising both prevention and treatment. Moreover, a recent systematic review of decision analytic models for the prevention and treatment of dental caries also concluded that the methodological quality still leaves room for improvements and suggested that future EEs should adhere to good practice guidelines, especially with respect to data quality evaluation and handling of uncertainty analysis (Qu et al. 2019; Mariño et al. 2020).

Reviews of economic evaluation in dentistry, as well as in other health areas, indicate that there is also some confusion in what constitutes a true economic evaluation, the appropriate labels of different types of economic evaluation, the correct methodology to be used, etc. (Hawe et al. 1990; Walker and Fox-Rushby 2000). These reviews also suggested several other areas where further improvements could be achieved. Areas in need of improvements include:

- Insufficient consideration given to the reporting of time horizon of the study. The time horizon is the relevant period for the normal course of the intervention (Splett 1996). The time period to be covered by an evaluation must be sufficient to allow for the full effects of the program on costs and outcomes (Drummond et al. 2015). For example, for preventive interventions, benefits are often achieved in the future. Therefore, if the time horizon does not allow for these benefits to be achieved, they might be not included or appear to be worth very little.
- The incorporation of additional information on discounting, including information about the choice of discount rate, as well as information to warrant the credibility of cost and cost discounting.
- Accounting for uncertainties is central when using models modelling. The inclusion of sensitivity analyses is essential in any economic evaluation. Therefore, detailed information about chosen variables and range used to conducting sensitivity analysis must be declared. This should also include evidence of the validity of the data used in the sensitivity analysis, particularly when working with assumptions.
- Lack of inclusion of productivity costs and intangible costs. Additionally, several authors (Kroon and Wyk 2012a, b; Mariño et al. 2014, 2020) emphasized the difficulties in measuring indirect or intangible outcomes in oral health (e.g., sound teeth, or less pain, or disability), since they are difficult to quantify in monetary terms. This is because oral health EE do not usually capture all the cost involved or fail to recognize the full economic benefits of interventions in oral health beyond immediate benefits within an oral health scope (Akinlotan et al. 2018). This has implications for decision-making, because if an intervention is not cost-effective, resources might be employed in delivering other types of services.
- Failing to report on the perspective of the EE. This is important because the perspective determines the input parameters and measurement of costs in an EE. Depending on the perspective of the study (e.g., health sector, patient, societal), costs and consequences are seen differently from different points of view. For example, whether costs for productivity lost due to the time spent in oral healthcare, costs of transportation to and from the health centre, are to be included or not (Mariño et al. 2020).
- Improvements in the reporting incremental cost-effectiveness analysis. The ICER informs how much more we must pay to obtain an additional effectiveness unit of the new intervention in relation to its comparator. It is essential that the studies report the ICER or at least the basic information to calculate it to facilitate the interpretation of the results by health decision-makers.
- Failure to choose the model used and the key parameters on which it was based. One study reviewed the decision analytical model in EE in the field or dental caries (Qu et al. 2019). They found that even though the quality of the models used is comparable to those used in other areas of health, they were still unsatisfactory. The quality and availability of effectiveness data are key element in modelling studies; however, it is not always based on systematic reviews. In any case, the selection of models should be based on the natural history of the disease

under study and the characteristics of the different alternatives of intervention. The quality of the data should also be reviewed, particularly when using models. Some reviews reported lack of data, or of sound, recent data on which to base models on as a major limitation in their evaluation (Mariño et al. 2020). For example, in the absence of updated data it would be problematic to estimate the real prevalence of dental caries (Mariño and Zaror 2020). Furthermore, Anopa and her colleagues indicated that some of the studies include in the different reviews were underpowered or pilot studies (i.e., using small sample sizes), which makes it difficult to draw conclusion (Anopa and Conway 2020).

On the other hand, there is evidence that the methodological quality and the reporting of EE in oral health have improved in the last few years (Mariño et al. 2013, 2020; Anopa and Conway 2020). Among the most notable progress in reporting has been seen in stating the type of economic evaluation utilized and its justification, in the provision of more comprehensive information about the sensitivity analyses, and in declaring the perspective and comparators (Mariño et al. 2020). Additionally, Anopa and her collaborators (2020) did not find mismatch in the study descriptor in the EE studies included in their review.

Although there are studies in oral health analysing willingness to pay (Srivastava et al. 2020), willingness to pay has not been widely explored in oral healthcare (Listl and Weyant 2019). Willingness to pay (WTP) assigns a market value to health benefits by eliciting individual preferences according on the amount society is willing to pay for health. WTP is an important measure of valuation that is applicable and available to dentistry that allows for economic evaluations that enable meaningful comparisons across various healthcare provision scenarios (Tan et al. 2017). The main difficulty is that there is no accepted payment threshold to establish the WTP of interventions when health outcomes are expressed in natural measures (e.g., caries avoided or child free from caries). Although attempts have been made to establish an acceptable WTP in the dental field, its usefulness is limited due to the deficient methodological rigor used (Tan et al. 2017).

10.4 Direction to Better Guide Future Economic Evaluations in Oral Health

To improve the quality of future EE studies, there seem to be a clear need for both health economists and oral health researchers to work together on EE studies that achieve increased internal, as well as external validity (Morgan and Mariño 2012). This will increase the chances of decision-makers in selecting the most appropriate program to save future costs and provide better benefits to a wider population. However, oral healthcare has not received the same attention than other areas of healthcare (Listl and Weyant 2019) among decision-makers. This is not consistent with the burden of oral health disease and conditions affecting humankind with several health and financial consequences, to the individual, oral healthcare providers, and the society at large.

We have pooled together the main conclusions of several reviews of economic evaluation in oral healthcare, but caution is needed when comparing one study to another. A major limitation of these reviews (and of individual economic evaluations) is that the studies varied considerably in methodology, choice of outcome measures (e.g., tooth surfaces with dental caries history averted, dental visits, QATY averted, number of cavitation due to caries averted, QALY, individuals free from dental caries, etc.), assumptions used in the evaluation, setting, timeframe of the analysis, and so on. All this makes the cost-effectiveness ratios from the studies not exactly comparable to other studies because of the diversity in oral health indicators. This lack of standardization of oral health outcome measured has been indicated as one of the main limitations to the direct comparison of EE results (Akinlotan et al. 2018). Furthermore, oral heath EE varies a lot in terms of methodology outcome measure, assumptions, and perspective which makes comparisons difficult (Akinlotan et al. 2018).

While the volume of published economic evaluations in oral health has increased in the last few years, there is still a general lack of EE in African countries and to a lesser extent in Asian countries and Latin America, where apart from Brazil and Chile, there is also a lack of EE. However, it is possible that studies in those countries are not included in systematic review due to language limitations from the research teams, who commonly exclude publications in languages other than English (Hettiarachchi et al. 2018).

Call for more studies in high-, medium-, and low-income countries with follow-up programs to analyse clinical and financial efficacy is also necessary. As previously explained, EE is so context specific, and conclusions from one jurisdiction to another may be directly applicable. This would indicate that EE might not be available to prioritize health programs.

In particular, future studies should aim to identify the full benefits of oral healthcare interventions (i.e., prevention and early treatment). Risk-based delivery of intervention delivers better EE outcome as opposed to interventions that are given to the whole community/pop under study, leading to increased savings (Akinlotan et al. 2018). Therefore, it is relevant that EE evaluate the cost-effectiveness in different subgroups of populations, for example, according to cariogenic risk, age group, severity of the condition, etc.

Although, as with other types of EE, there is increasing number of publications describing CUA in the last few years (Hettiarachchi et al. 2018; Mariño et al., 2020), the need to increase of studies using CUA is worth to mention (Hettiarachchi et al. 2018). CUA allows for comparisons of the CEA across interventions and health conditions. However, CUA is less used in EE of oral health interventions. Some studies used QATY, however. As mentioned, QATY does not consider the strong interconnection between oral health and general health (Rogers et al. 2019). This indicates the need to develop an oral health measure for oral health outcomes that facilitate the use of QALY in future EE in oral health (Rogers et al. 2019). Thus, to make studies more in accordance to commonly used CUA in the health field, future studies in oral health should include QALY (Rogers et al. 2019, Hettiarachchi et al. 2018).

10.5 Final Remarks

Economic evaluations are commonly used in decision-making processes about health programs; however, comparatively, less examples exist in oral health. Furthermore, significant limitations have been highlighted in the quality of reporting economic evaluations done on oral health interventions. The literature also shows an increased awareness about the need to include EE in oral healthcare, with indications that this type of evaluations will only increase in the future (Buck 2000; Cunningham 2001). Despite this, there have also been increases in the quality of the reporting of economic evaluations. However, economic evaluation in oral health has not been extensive, and the majority have been targeted toward clinical interventions and dental caries preventive interventions, such as CWF and sealants. This suggests that the available research in EE in oral health has been somewhat narrowly focused, and other important interventions have not been investigated, for example, assessing the economic value of disease prevention, in particular, regarding the impacts on older people.

Accordingly, current information may not be fully appropriate to provide evidence on other oral health conditions which also have some serious financial consequences to individuals, oral healthcare providers, and society. As a consequence, in a context of diminishing public resources for oral healthcare and increasingly sophisticated treatment options (Morgan and Mariño 2012), users of these reviews (e.g., decision-makers) may not have enough information to identify the financial benefit per monetary unit of resources used for most interventions in dentistry.

To understand economic evaluation, let alone conducting one, requires a degree of expertise, and interested parties are encouraged to expand their current knowledge and efforts to include an economic evaluation in future efforts, thus contributing to a solid body of economic information about oral healthcare in both prevention and treatment. The effective use and conduction of economic evaluations will in turn make important research information accessible to a broad audience of policy makers, community leaders, practitioners, and researchers (Morgan and Mariño 2012). Evidence of sound quality will assist policy and decision-makers (Mariño et al. 2014; Salkeld et al. 1995).

Despite the limitations highlighted in this chapter, oral health researchers and health economists continue to conduct EE. It was an attempt to summarize what the literature is telling us about the scope and quality of economic evaluation reporting done on oral health interventions. The present chapter also aims to provide the foundation and encouragement for more economic evaluations, as well as quality appraisals in order to maintain and improve the standard of economic evaluations conducted and published in the future.

References

Akinlotan M, Chen B, Fontanilla T et al (2018) Economic evaluation of dental sealants: a systematic literature review. Community Dent Oral Epidemiol 46:38–46

Amilani U, Carter H, Senanayake S et al (2020) A scoping review of cost-effectiveness analyses of school-based interventions for caries? Community Dent Oral Epidemiol 48(5):357–363

Anderson R (2010) Systematic reviews of economic evaluations: utility or futility? Health Econ 19:350–364. https://doi.org/10.1002/hec.1486

Anopa Y, Conway DI (2020) Exploring the cost-effectiveness of child dental caries prevention programmes. Are we comparing apples and oranges? Evid Based Dent 21:5–7

Australian Institute for Health and Welfare (2019) Oral Health and Dental Care in Australia. https://www.aihw.gov.au/reports/den/231/oral-health-and-dental-care-in-australia/contents/costs. Accessed 20 July 2020

Buck D (2000) Economic evaluation and dentistry. Dent Update 27:66–73

Campain AC, Mariño RJ, Wright FA et al (2010) The impact of changing dental needs on cost savings from fluoridation. Aust Dent J 55:37–44

Centre for Reviews and Dissemination (2009) CRD's guidance for undertaking reviews in healthcare. York Publishing Services, York. https://www.york.ac.uk/media/crd/Systematic. Accessed 20 July 2020

Christell H, Birch S, Horner K et al (2014) Economic evaluation of diagnostic methods used in dentistry. A systematic review. J Dent 42:1361–1371

Coffin D, Craig J, Arber M, Glanville J (2013) Literature review of economic evaluations on oral health improvement programmes and interventions. National Institute for Health and Care Excellence (NICE), York

Critical Appraisal Skills Programme (CASP) (2017) Making sense of evidence. https://casp-uk.net/casp-tools-checklists/. Accessed 20 July 2020

Cunningham SJ (2001) An introduction to economic evaluation of health care. J Orthod 28:246–250

Deery C (1999) The economic evaluation of pit and fissure sealants. Int J Paediatr Dent 9:235–241

Drummond MF, Sculpher M, Torrance GW et al (2015) Methods for the economic evaluation of health care Prorammes, 4th edn. Oxford University Press, New York

Eow J, Duane B, Solaiman A et al (2019) What evidence do economic evaluations in dental care provide? A scoping review. Community Dent Health 36:118–125

Fraihat N, Madae'en S, Bencze Z et al (2019) Clinical effectiveness and cost-effectiveness of Oral-health promotion in dental caries prevention among children: systematic review and meta-analysis. Int J Environ Res Public Health 16:2668

Grant MJ, Booth A (2009) A typology of reviews: an analysis of 14 review types and associated methodologies. Health Inf Libr J 26:91–108

Hawe P, Degeling D, Hall J (1990) Evaluating health promotion: a health worker's guide. MacLennan and Petty, Sydney

Hettiarachchi RM, Kularatna S, Downes MJ et al (2018) The cost-effectiveness of oral health interventions: a systematic review of cost-utility analyses. Community Dent Oral Epidemiol 46:118–124

Higson JF (1976) Caries prevention in first permanent molars by fissure sealing a 2-year study in 6–8-year-old children. J Dent 4:218–222

Husereau D, Drummond M, Petrou S et al (2013) CHEERS Task Force. Consolidated health economic evaluation reporting standards (CHEERS) statement. Value Health 16:e1–e5

Hutubessy RC, Baltussen RM, Torres-Edejer TT, Evans DB (2002) Generalised cost-effectiveness analysis: an aid to decision making in health. Appl Health Econ Health Policy 1:89–95

Källestål C, Norlund A, Söder B, Nordenram G et al (2003) Economic evaluation of dental caries prevention: a systematic review. Acta Odontol Scand 61:341–346

Kroon J, van Wyk PJ (2012a) A model to determine the economic viability of water fluoridation. J Public Health Dent 72:327–333

Kroon J, Van Wyk PJ (2012b) A retrospective view on the viability of water fluoridation in South Africa to prevent dental caries. Community Dent Oral Epidemiol 40:441–450

Laupacis A, Feeny D, Detsky AS, Tugwell PX (1992) How attractive does a new technology have to be to warrant adoption and utilization? Tentative guidelines for using clinical and economic evaluations. CMAJ 146:473–481

Leo M, Cerroni L, Pasquantonio G et al (2016) Economic evaluation of dental sealants: a systematic review. Clin Ter 167:e13–e20

Listl S, Weyant R (2019) For careful consideration: the reporting of health economic evaluations in dentistry. J Public Health Dent 79:273–274

Mariño R, Zaror C (2020) Economic evaluations in water-fluoridation: a scoping review. BMC Oral Health 20:115

Mariño R, Kahn A, Morgan M (2013) Systematic review of publications on economic evaluations of caries prevention programs. Caries Res 47:265–272

Mariño R, Fajardo J, Calache H, Morgan M (2014) Cost-minimization analysis of a tailored oral health intervention designed for immigrant older adults. Geriatr Gerontol Int 14:336–340

Mariño R, Ravisankar G, Zaror C (2020) Quality appraisal of economic evaluations done on Oral health preventive programs-a systematic review. J Public Health Dent 80(3):194–207

Masood M, Sheiham A, Bernabé E (2015) Household expenditure for dental care in low and middle income countries. PLoS One 10(4):e0123075

Morgan M, Mariño R (2012) Economic evaluation of preventive dental programs: what can they tell us? Community Dent Oral Epidemiol 40(s2):117–121

Murray CJ, Evans DB, Acharya A, Baltussen RM (2000) Development of WHO guidelines on generalized cost-effectiveness analysis. Health Econ 9:235–251

Murthy AK, Fareed N (2020) Economic evaluation of school-based caries preventive programs: a systematic review. Community Dent Health 37:1–11

National Advisory Committee on Oral Health (2004) Healthy mouths healthy lives: Australia's National Oral Health Plan 2004-2013. Adelaide, National Advisory Committee on Oral Health, Australian Health Ministers' Advisory Council

O'Brien B, Heyland D, Richardson W et al (1997) Users' guides to the medical literature. XIII. How to use an article on economic analysis of clinical practice. B. What are the results and will they help me in caring for my patients? Evidence-based medicine working group. JAMA 277(22):1802–1806

Platform for Better Oral Health in Europe (2020) The state of oral health in Europe. http://www.oralhealthplatform.eu/our-work/the-state-of-oral-health-in-europe/. Accessed 20 July 2020

Qu Z, Zhang S, Krauth C, Liu X (2019) A systematic review of decision analytic modeling techniques for the economic evaluation of dental caries interventions. PLoS One 14(5):e0216921

Rogers HJ, Rodd HD, Vermaire JH et al (2019) A systematic review of the quality and scope of economic evaluations in child oral health research. BMC Oral Health 19(1):132

Salkeld G, Davey P, Arnolda G (1995) A critical review of health-related economic evaluations in Australia: implications for health policy. Health Policy 31:111–125

Sollenius O, Petrén S, Björnsson L, Norlund A, Bondemark L (2016) Health economic evaluations in orthodontics: a systematic review. Eur J Orthod 38(3):259–265

Srivastava A, Esfandiari S, Madathil SA et al (2020) Willingness to pay for mandibular overdentures: a societal perspective. JDR Clin Trans Res 5(1):30–39

Tan SH, Vernazza CR, Nair R (2017) Critical review of willingness to pay for clinical oral health interventions. J Dent 64:1–12

Tonmukayakul U, Calache H, Clark R et al (2015) Systematic review and quality appraisal of economic evaluation publications in dentistry. J Dent Res:1348–1354
Walker D, Fox-Rushby JA (2000) Economic evaluation of communicable disease interventions in developing countries: a critical review of the published literature. Health Econ 9:681–698
World Health Organisation (WHO) (2020) Oral Health. https://www.who.int/news-room/fact-sheets/detail/oral-health. Accessed 20 July 2020
York Health Economics Consortium (2016) A rapid review of evidence on the cost-effectiveness of interventions to improve the oral health of children aged 0–5 years. Public Health England, London

Chapter 11
Assessing the Quality and Usefulness of Economic Evaluation in Oral Health: A Practical Approach for Clinicians

Carlos Zaror and Alonso Carrasco-Labra

11.1 Evidence-Based Dentistry

Every day we see the emergence of new health technologies and a large volume of research findings. Around 75 clinical trials and 7 systematic reviews are published daily (Bastian et al. 2010). This means that healthcare professionals should read approximately 19 articles a day to keep up. Yet, the time available to health professionals to keep up to date is less than <1 h a week (Sackett et al. 1996).

Although there is currently abundant evidence informing the effectiveness of interventions, it can take anywhere between 17 and 20 years for healthcare professionals and policymakers to finally implement those interventions in clinical practice (Ho et al. 2003).

Healthcare professionals should be aware of the large volume of published scientific information and know strategies to manage and keep their knowledge up to date. Failing to incorporate research findings into practice is to the detriment of the patients, who could have benefited from a readily available intervention if the evidence had been applied quickly.

Another problem that healthcare professionals and decision-makers in healthcare face is that not all evidence is created equal. This means that users of evidence need to appropriately identify more from less trustworthy clinical studies and

C. Zaror (✉)
Department of Paediatric Dentistry and Orthodontics, Faculty of Dentistry, Universidad de la Frontera, Temuco, Chile

Center for Research in Epidemiology, Economics and Oral Public Health (CIEESPO), Faculty of Dentistry, Universidad de La Frontera, Temuco, Chile
e-mail: carlos.zaror@ufrontera.cl

A. Carrasco-Labra
Center for Integrative Global Oral Health, School of Dental Medicine, University of Pennsylvania, Philadelphia, PA, USA
e-mail: alonsocarrascolabra@gmail.com

C. Zaror, R. Mariño (eds.), *Introduction to Economic Evaluation in Oral Health Care*, https://doi.org/10.1007/978-3-030-96289-0_11

bodies of evidence. Ignoring the need to consider methodological rigor when using evidence to inform practice translates into heterogeneous and incorrect clinical decisions, resulting in an increase in clinical complications, costs for health institutions, and a detriment to the quality of patient care.

To respond to this issue and to integrate clinical research into decision-making for patients, in 1981, David Sacket introduced the concept of evidence-based medicine, which was defined as "the conscientious, explicit, and judicious use of current best evidence in making decisions about the care of individual patients" (Guyatt 1991). Later, this approach was expanded to include other areas of health, such as dentistry. The American Dental Association defines Evidence Based-Dentistry (EBD) as "an approach to oral healthcare that requires the judicious integration of systematic assessments of clinically relevant scientific evidence, relating to the patient's oral and medical condition and history, with the dentist's clinical expertise and the patient's treatment needs and preferences"(ADA).

EBD considers the integration of three aspects that are basic for clinical decision-making (Brignardello-Petersen et al. 2014) (Fig. 11.1):

- Evaluation of the best available evidence: the dentist must be able to assess the validity, adequately interpret, and apply the available scientific evidence.
- Recognition of your clinical expertise.
- Understanding, elucidating, and incorporating patient's values and preferences in clinical decisions.

Depending on the nature of the clinical question (e.g., prevention, etiology, diagnosis, treatment, prognosis), the different study designs follow a hierarchy from lowest to highest risk of bias. For example, for questions regarding therapy or prevention, well-designed and conducted randomized controlled trials are the most appropriate designs. For harm, etiology, and prognosis, observational studies are the preferable study designs.

Clinical expertise is the ability to use one's clinical skills, experience, and knowledge to rapidly and correctly diagnose the particular patient state of health and assess the different interventions' benefits and harms considering the particular clinical condition and the clinical setting. Even if the research evidence may

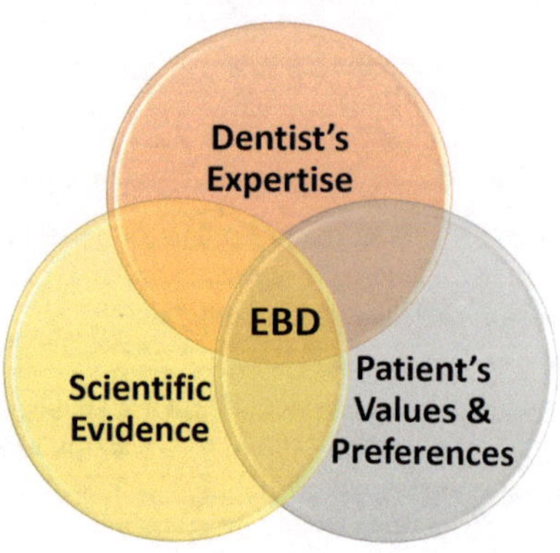

Fig. 11.1 The components of evidence-based dentistry (EBD). (Reprinted from Brignardello-Petersen et al. 2014, with permission from Elsevier)

indicate that an intervention is effective, if clinicians do not have the skills or technology to carry out the procedure correctly, we should offer the patient another alternative.

Finally, the last element to consider is knowing and understanding the preferences and values of our patients to integrate them into any diagnostic or treatment plan. This is relevant since clinical procedures are associated with possible adverse effects and costs for patients. Understanding how much importance patients assign to the desirable and undesirable consequences of planned treatment and using that information to guide the decision-making process is at the essence of evidence-based practice.

11.2 The Process of Evidence-Based Dentistry

The principles of EBD are based on the ability to identify, critically appraise, and apply current best available evidence from relevant research to decisions made in practice in response to a question that arises from clinical practice. There are five steps, also called 5 As, to carry out the EBD process (Fig. 11.2):

- Ask: convert clinical needs or problems into clinical questions so that they can be answered.
- Access: search for the best available evidence to answer the question.
- Appraise: critically appraise the validity (i.e., risk of bias, study limitations) and applicability of the evidence.
- Apply: Apply the results of appraisal in clinical practice, considering clinical experience and patients' values and preferences.
- Assess: assess the process and your performance.

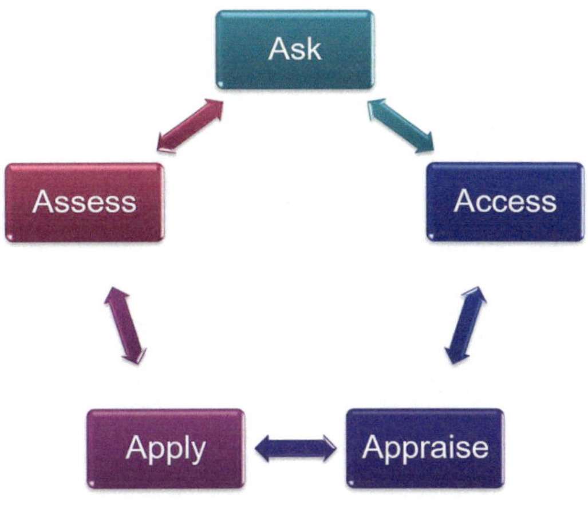

Fig. 11.2 Five steps of EBD process. (Original drawing)

11.2.1 Formulation of Clinical Question

The formulation of a clinical question is a critical step in searching for evidence to inform clinical decisions. There are two main types of clinical questions: background questions and foreground questions. Background questions allow clinicians to contextualize a topic or problem, for example, what is dental caries? Or what are the symptoms of temporomandibular disorders? This information is available in secondary or tertiary sources such as narrative reviews or books, and it shouldn't take more than 10 min to find the evidence to answer these questions. On the other hand, clinicians also have more complex questions or foreground questions because they generally contain several concepts and often reflect the need for information to determine a clinical course of action between a specific set of interventions or clinical tests. For the well-informed clinician, these types of questions require evidence to be answered. Some examples of these questions are: Is water fluoridation more cost-effective than applying sealants at the community level? Are implant-supported prostheses more effective in improving chewing and quality of life than mucosa-supported dentures?

The first step in formulating the question of interest is to identify the nature of the question, which determines the type of evidence the search will target. There are four fundamental types of clinical questions (Brignardello-Petersen 2014):

- Diagnosis: Assess the performance of a test in differentiating between patients with and without a condition or disease.
- Harm or etiology: Evaluate how exposure to risk factors influences patient-important outcomes.
- Therapy: Determine the effect (i.e., benefits and harms) of intervention on patient-important outcomes.
- Prognosis: Estimate a patient's future course of disease based on prognostic factors.

A well-structured clinical question should include four components, also called PICO components:

- Population: key patients' features relevant to the question.
- Intervention: the treatment or prevention strategy or, possibly, the harmful exposure of interest.
- Comparison: the alternative management strategy used as a reference against which to compare the intervention.
- Outcomes: the healthcare consequences of the interventions in which we are interested.

Examples of clinical questions about economic evaluation are:

- What is the cost-effectiveness of a school-based oral health prevention program compared with non-intervention, from the societal perspective?

- What is the cost utility of arthrocentesis using corticosteroids compared with arthrocentesis not using corticosteroids for treatment of temporomandibular joint internal disorders, from the patients' perspective?
- What is the value of a periodontal preventive program in older adults from the healthcare perspective?

11.2.2 Searching Evidence

Finding relevant evidence for foreground questions requires conducting a focused search of the peer-reviewed professional literature based on the appropriate methodology. The PICO components provide the key terms for this step.

There are three categories of information resources:

- Summaries and guidelines: provide updated clinical evidence or guidance/recommendation for patient's management, e.g., UptoDate (www.uptodate.com), DynaMed (https://dynamed.ebscohost.com), International Guideline Library (https://g-i-n.net/library/international-guidelines-library), and GuidelineCentral (https://www.guidelinecentral.com/).
- Pre-appraised research: provides synthesis of evidence like systematic review or structured summaries of main study information (synopses), e.g., Cochrane Clinical Answers (https://www.cochranelibrary.com/cca/about), the journal *Evidence-Based Dentistry* (www.nature.com/ebd/index.html), the *Journal of Evidence-Based Dental Practice* (www.journals.elsevier.com/journal-of-evidence-based-dental-practice/), and the Dental Elf (www.thedentalelf.net).
- Non-pre-appraised research: provides access to primary studies, e.g., Medline (www.ncbi.nlm.nih.gov/pubmed/), Embase (www.elsevier.com/online-tools/embase), and LILACS (https://lilacs.bvsalud.org/es).

There are also some EBD electronic resources specialized in economic evaluations (see Table 11.1). These databases provide not only primary studies but also pre-appraisal and research summaries. Evidence shows that a search in NHS EED along with a supplementary search in Medline through PubMed is an appropriate resource for economic evaluations (Alton et al. 2006).

Finally, there are resources providing access to evidence at all levels, such as the American Dental Association's Center for Evidence-Based Dentistry (http://ebd.ada.org/en/evidence/), Trip (www.tripdatabase.com), SUMSearch (http://sumsearch.org), and Epistemonikos (www.epistemonikos.org).

Table 11.1 Evidence-based dentistry resources for economic evaluation

Database	Content	Availability	Type of resource
Cost-effectiveness analysis registry	Healthcare cost-utility analysis	Free access from https://cevr.tuftsmedicalcenter.org/databases/cea-registry	Pre-appraised resource
COnnaissances et Décision en EConomie de la Sante (CODECS)	Economic evaluation	Free access from https://www.ces-asso.org	Pre-appraised resource
Econlit	Economic evaluation	Subscription access from https://www.aeaweb.org/econlit/	Non-pre-appraised resources
Health economic evaluation database (HEED)	Economic evaluation	Subscription access from https://www.healtheconomics.com/resource/heed-the-health-economic-evaluations-database	Non-pre-appraised resources
Health technology assessment database	Healthcare technology assessment	Free access from https://www.crd.york.ac.uk/CRDWeb/	Non-pre-appraised resources
International health technology assessment database	Healthcare technology assessment	Free access from https://database.inahta.org/about	Non-pre-appraised resources
NHS economic evaluation database (NHS EDD)	Economic evaluation	Free access from https://www.crd.york.ac.uk/CRDWeb/	Comprehensive resources
Pediatric economic database evaluation (PEDE)	Economic evaluation	Free access from http://pede.ccb.sickkids.ca/pede/	Non-pre-appraised resources

11.2.3 Critical Appraisal

Critical appraisal of the scientific literature is the ability to assess the validity, interpret study results, and apply the research findings to practice. This process comprises three stages, which are carried out sequentially: (a) assess the validity of the study, that is, the risk of the study suffering from bias (i.e., systematic error); (b) evaluate and interpret its results; and (c) evaluate its applicability, that is, the generalization of the results to other contexts. In Sect. 11.3, we will describe how to appraise an article addressing economic evaluation.

11.2.4 Applicability of the Results

Once we have assessed the evidence that can answer our clinical question, a crucial step comes to apply it to the patient and clinical scenario that initially triggered the question. At this point, a clinician needs to determine whether the characteristics of the patient and condition of interest are different enough from the participants included in the study that the study's findings cannot be applied back to the clinical scenario. The applicability of research findings not only relates to the similarity of patients' features to the study participants, but it also applies to other barriers regarding the indication of a certain type of dental materials or equipment, technical skills, and cost implications.

Therefore, before applying the results to our patients, we need to ask ourselves the following questions:

- What are the characteristics of the participants of the study? Are the study participants similar to those where the intervention will be applied? It is important to assess the baseline characteristics of participants of the study, as well as the inclusion and exclusion criteria of the study.
- Are the settings of the study similar to the settings where the intervention will be applied? Is the treatment available?
- What alternative interventions are available?
- Are the potential benefits outweighing the harms and burdens?
- Are the outcomes reported in the study patient important?

11.2.5 Evaluation of the Process

Once we have applied the intervention, the final step of the EBD approach is to evaluate the results of our intervention. If a patient's response is different than expected, it is necessary to investigate why they did not respond to the changes and what can be done to address the issue. Therefore, we should ask ourselves a new question and start the EBD process again.

11.3 Critical Appraisal of Economic Evaluation

The process of using an economic evaluation to inform clinical decisions involves assessing the risk of bias (are the results valid?), the results (what are the results?), and the applicability of the results (will the results help in caring for my patients?) (Drummond et al. 2005; Abrahamyan et al. 2015). Below, we will describe the usual structure for critically appraising the scientific literature to inform clinical decisions based on a hypothetical clinical scenario. Table 11.2 summarizes the specific questions to address these three areas.

Table 11.2 User's guides for economic evaluation of clinical practice

Are the results valid?
Did the analysis provide a full economic comparison of healthcare strategy?
Did investigator adopt a sufficiently broad viewpoint?
Are the results reported separately for relevant patient subgroups?
Were consequences and cost measured accurately?
Did investigators consider the timing of cost and consequences?
What are the results?
What were the incremental cost and effects of each strategy?
Do incremental cost and effect differ between subgroups?
How much does allowing for uncertainty change the results?
Will the results help in caring for my patients?
Are the treatment benefits worth the harms and cost?
Could my patients expect similar health outcomes?
Could I expect similar costs?

Source: Abrahamyan et al. (2015)

11.3.1 Clinical Scenario

You are in charge of the dental services within a health department dependent on a municipality in Chile. The director of the health department, your boss, knows about your evidence-based dentistry skills and asks for your help in deciding if they should implement a new oral health preventive strategy. This new strategy consists of a community-wide application of fluoride varnish (FV) in preschool children in rural areas. As financial resources are limited, your boss is particularly interested in learning to what extent the program's benefit would be worth the costs. You decided to conduct a search for a formal economic analysis that compares the application of FV versus the "status quo" to inform a final decision.

11.3.2 Economic Evaluation Identified

You decided to conduct a literature search in MEDLINE via PubMed to answer the following question: What is the cost-effectiveness of a community fluoride varnish application program compared to no intervention, from a public payer perspective? The terms used were "child, preschool" [Mesh] (943,208), fluoride varnish (1638 citations), and "cost-benefit analysis" [Mesh] (84,706 citations). The search identified 13 citations, of which 8 were economic evaluations addressing the cost-effectiveness of FV in preschool children. Two of them were conducted in Chile, and you decided to review both since they seem to match your target population. The first article is an economic evaluation that used a decision-analytic model to evaluate whether FV application increases the proportion of caries-free children in the Chilean preschool population at an acceptable cost (Palacio et al. 2019). The second study is a trial-based economic analysis that assessed the incremental cost-effectiveness ratio of the community-wide application of FV to prevent early childhood caries in non-fluoridated areas (Zaror et al. 2020). The main characteristics of the studies are presented in Table 11.3.

11.3.3 Are the Results Valid?

As with any other study design, the validity of an economic evaluation is determined by the extent to which the study's authors implemented methodological strategies to minimize the effect of bias (Drummond et al. 2005). Aspects such as the target population and subgroups, study perspective, comparators, time horizon, chosen model, methods to determine the effectiveness, and cost, among others, must be stated (Husereau et al. 2013).

Table 11.3 Characteristics of studies identified

Features	Palacio et al. 2019	Zaror et al. 2020
Type of economic evaluation	Cost-effectiveness	Cost-effectiveness
Perspective	Payer (public health system)	Payer (public health system)
Alternatives compared	Five health interventions were compared: Counselling-only intervention, FV application in preschool setting with and without screening, and FV application in primary health care setting with and without screening	The intervention protocol included FV of 5% sodium fluoride, oral health exams, education for the parents, and delivery of a toothbrush and toothpaste kit every 6 months for 2 years The comparator was the same protocol but without FV
Benefit measure(s)	Caries-free child	Caries-free child
Source(s) of effectiveness data	Cochrane systematic review (Marinho et al. 2013)	Randomized clinical trial by Muñoz-Millán et al. 2018
Estimates of resource use	Obtained from different studies and Chilean health source (MINSAL 2012; MINEDUC 2015)	Randomized clinical trial by Muñoz-Millán et al. 2018
Source(s) of cost data	Costing study of health intervention in the national health fund (MINSAL 2010) and Ministry of Treasury (Ministerio de Hacienda 2015)	Randomized clinical trial by Muñoz-Millán et al. 2018 and study of cost-effectiveness of health interventions by the Chilean Ministry of Health (2010)
Time horizon	2 years	2 years
Discount rate	3% cost and benefit	3% cost and benefit
Price year/ currency unit	2015/Chilean pesos (CLP)	2019/Chilean pesos (CLP)
Sensitivity analysis	Univariate deterministic sensitivity analysis	Univariate deterministic sensitivity analysis

Many tools are used to evaluate the validity or risk of bias of economic evaluations (Drummnond et al. 2005; Evers et al. 2005; Husereau et al. 2013) (see Chap. 12). However, for a more simplified approach, we suggest assessing the following criteria: (i) consideration of a relevant alternative, (ii) consideration of subgroups, (iii) accurate measurement of consequences and cost, and (iv) consideration of timing (Guyatt et al. 2008).

11.3.3.1 Did the Analysis Include a Full Economic Comparison of Healthcare Strategies?

As we stated in Chap. 1, a full economic evaluation compares two or more interventions, programs, or strategies, and it must consider both the costs and the outcomes or consequences of these alternatives (Drummond et al., 2005). When only the cost or outcomes are compared (partial economic evaluation), such analysis does not allow a comprehensive assessment to define the extent to which the benefits of the intervention justify the resources allocated. Therefore, this analysis should not be used for decision-making.

Returning to our example, both studies identified were full economic evaluations that assessed the cost-effectiveness of FV in the prevention of caries in preschool populations because they included costs and effect in terms of "caries-free children." Palacio et al. compared five dental interventions: counseling, FV application in a preschool setting with or without screening, and FV application in a primary healthcare setting with or without screening, while Zaror et al. assessed the cost-effectiveness of biannual FV applications versus educational intervention to prevent early childhood caries in children from non-fluoridated rural areas. In addition, both studies considered an educational component as a comparator. At least, an economic evaluation must consider all standard treatment alternatives, including the status quo. Thus, an economic evaluation should consider the relevant strategies in the comparison and include patients with different baseline risks.

11.3.3.2 Did the Investigators Adopt a Sufficiently Broad Viewpoint?

Several perspectives can be viewed in an economic evaluation, including an individual perspective (e.g., patient), an organizational perspective (e.g., hospital), or a payer or societal perspective. When we consider costs and consequences, one should be explicit as to which perspective we are using. The viewpoint chosen should depend on the question that is asked. For example, in our clinical scenario, the relevant viewpoint would be that of the public payer, which corresponds to a local municipality. Then, only direct costs, such as human resources and supplies, are relevant. They considered direct medical costs (dental team's salary, FV, fillings, oral hygiene kit, etc.) and direct nonmedical costs such as transportation of the dental team to and from the preschool institutions. When considering an individual (e.g., patient) or societal perspective, however, indirect costs are relevant. For example, Griffin et al. (2016) evaluated the cost-effectiveness of school-based sealant programs in the United States, using a societal perspective. Together with estimating the direct cost of implementing the program and managing the consequences, they also included the productivity losses for a parent taking a child to the dentist. From a societal perspective, determination of cost should include the therapy's effect on the patient's ability to work.

11.3.3.3 Are the Results Reported Separately for Relevant Patient Subgroups?

Cost and consequences may differ among patient subgroups (e.g., age, sex, illness severity). Thus, it is necessary to establish whether an intervention remains relatively more effective than its comparators across different types of patients (Schuper 2008). For example, a water fluoridation strategy may not be cost-effective in a small community (<1000 habitants); however, it may be a dominant strategy for large size communities (Mariño and Zaror 2020).

Appropriately reflecting subgroups and their heterogeneity has the potential to increase population health gains by focusing on the use of an intervention in people for whom the health gain would be greater. It is implied that ignoring these differences can result in a misleading interpretation of results (Schuper 2008).

In our example, none of the studies reported subgroup analysis. An important subgroup to consider in economic evaluation for oral health prevention is the risk of caries.

11.3.3.4 Were Consequences and Cost Measured Accurately?

In economic evaluations, the evidence on consequences (desirable and undesirable outcomes) may be collected, ideally, from a randomized control trial (RCT) or systematic review (Drummond et al., 2005). The use of other types of design with a lower level of evidence could lead to potential bias in the results. For example, empirical evidence shows that dental economic evaluations frequently use cross-sectional studies as the source of epidemiological data (Mariño et al. 2020).

Although appropriately conducted RCTs provide high validity, their weakness could be in the generalizability of the results when the participants enrolled may not be typical of community practice owing to the specific inclusion criteria set for the RCT. An evaluation based on meta-analyses summarizing the body of evidence from all available RCTs can help to increase generalizability because the pooled estimate of effectiveness is derived from a broader spectrum of patients.

Of the two studies discussed here, Zaror et al.'s (2020) was immersed within the clinical trial in Chilean preschoolers. In contrast, Palacio et al.'s (2019) was a modeling study using an RCT conducted in the United States population (Weintraub et al. 2006). Thus, the first study better represents the relevant scenario since it was based on a Chilean rural population with high caries risk.

As we stated previously, the perspective determines the range of cost and consequences in an economic evaluation. In reporting costs, it is important to report the physical quantities of resources consumed or released by the dental treatments. This allows the reader to calculate the cost in a different setting and come to a conclusion regarding the cost-effectiveness of the new intervention in their context.

The main difference between both studies analyzed for the hypothetical scenario was that the consumption of resources and the cost of the intervention in Zaror et al. (2020) were obtained directly from the clinical trial, whereas Palacio et al. (2019) determined the use of resources and cost from diverse sources. Both studies reported the sources of unit costs and the year of that cost.

11.3.3.5 Did Investigators Consider the Timing of Cost and Consequences?

The consequences and costs of healthcare interventions can occur at different times. For example, although most of the costs to implement a preventive oral health program occur when the program is launched, the benefit of the prevention of oral pathologies can occur years later. Generally, people prefer benefitting from the intervention sooner and postpone costs for the future. This is called "discounting" (Severens and Milne 2004) (see Chap. 1).

In both studies considered here, the author discounted the cost and benefit to occur in the future at a rate of 3% according to Methodological Guidelines for the Economic Evaluation of Health Interventions in Chile (MINSAL 2013).

11.3.4 What Were the Results?

If the answer to the first question was positive, and the economic analysis yields an unbiased assessment of the costs and outcomes of the clinical strategies, then the results are worth examining further.

The guides under this second question consider the size of the expected benefits and costs from adopting the most efficient strategy and the level of uncertainty in the results.

11.3.4.1 What Were the Incremental Cost and Effects of Each Strategy?

As discussed in Chap. 6, the results of economic evaluation are summarized through the incremental cost-effectiveness ratio (ICER), representing the differences between the cost and effectiveness of the evaluated alternatives.

The first step for this analysis is to look at the tables in the publication that list the costs and outcomes of each dental intervention. Keep in mind that the costs are the product of the estimation of resources used by unite price, which should include the cost incurred to produce the treatment and the cost consumed in the future associated with clinical events attributed to intervention or program. Therefore, these costs should be explicitly identified so that a reader can calculate the costs or translate the costs to their particular setting.

In our example, Palacio et al. (2019) did not report details of the resources consumed, which makes it difficult to determine if the costs of the interventions were well calculated and if they could be applied to our scenario. When comparing FV application in a primary care setting without screening with a counselling intervention, they reported an extra cost for FV of Chilean pesos (CLP) 4836 per child. Zaror et al. (2020) reported a total cost per child of CLP 67,739 for the preventive protocol without FV and a total cost of CLP 67,757 for the strategy that included FV at 2-year follow-up (incremental cost of CLP 18).

The effectiveness in both studies was measured in natural units as "caries-free children." Both studies showed higher effectiveness in favor of the FV protocol; however, as the source of effectiveness was different, Palacio et al. (2019) reported higher effectiveness (risk difference 27% vs. 11%).

The second step in this analysis is to interpret the ICER. However, it should be kept in mind that an intervention that is more effective and more costly than a control treatment can have the same ICER as an intervention that is less effective and less costly than the control. Instead, it is key to evaluate whether the differences in costs and effectiveness are large enough to have a clinical and policy-relevant impact (Abranhamayan et al. 2015). For more information on how to interpret the ICER, see Chap. 6.

In summary, both studies concluded that the FV program was more expensive than counseling intervention but provided a more significant number of caries-free children. As expected, the ICER was also higher in the study by Palacio et al. (2019) compared with Zaror et al. (CLP 130,849 vs. CLP 173.84).

11.3.4.2 Do Incremental Cost and Effect Differ Between Subgroups?

A crucial step in the appraisal of economic evaluations is to consider whether cost-effectiveness may differ among subgroups of patients. For example, Schwendicke et al. (2018) assessed the cost-effectiveness of FV application in clinical settings in populations with different caries risks, using a payer perspective. The analyses showed that the cost-effectiveness of FV applied twice a year was a function of the patient's caries risk (i.e., baseline risk for experiencing a new caries lesion). The ICER was 343 Euro spent per single increment in avoided DMFT, becoming less as the risk of dental caries increased (93 Euro/DMFT and 8 Euro/DMFT for medium and high caries risk, respectively). The authors concluded that FV application in the clinic setting was unlikely to be cost-effective in low-risk populations.

Returning to our scenario, the researchers in both studies failed to report the difference in cost-effectiveness per subgroup, mainly according to baseline caries risk. As we saw in the example above, caries risk affects the cost-effectiveness ratio. Therefore, one cannot know whether FV is more cost-effective in Chilean preschoolers with a high risk of caries. Zaror et al. based their analysis on an RCT conducted in a population with an expected high caries risk due to its age, rurality, and lack of access to fluoridated drinking water.

11.3.4.3 How Much Does Allowing for Uncertainty Change the Results?

Although we should always use the best available information in economic analyses, these often combine evidence from different sources to estimate the ICER. This introduces some degree of uncertainty about the accuracy of the underlying data. Incorporating uncertainty into the economic analysis allows us to understand the consequences of decision-making in the presence of uncertainty.

The conventional approach for handling uncertainty in economic analysis is to undertake sensitivity analysis in which key variables are altered one at a time (one-way sensitivity analysis) or in combination with other variables (multiway sensitivity analysis) to explore uncertainty related to methodological (e.g., cost and effectiveness of intervention) or structural uncertainty (e.g., number of branches of the tree, the duration of the cycle in a Markov model, etc.) and determine the robustness of the economic analysis findings to the uncertainty sources (Drummond et al. 2005).

Concerning our case, both articles explored changes in the results of the cost-effectiveness ratio due to possible changes in the values of the main parameters, using a univariate deterministic sensitivity analysis. They concluded that their estimate of cost-effectiveness was most sensitive to the caries rate of the population. For example, Zaror et al. (2020) showed that if the caries rate in the population without varnish was at its lowest limit (47%), the ICER increased considerably from CLP 173 to CLP 188,584 per additional healthy child in a 2-year follow-up. At the other extreme, where the rate in the population without varnish was the highest (64%), everything was in favor of applying varnish since this option is dominant (most economical and more effective).

In addition, Palacio et al. (2019) conducted a probabilistic sensitivity analysis that involved generating a distribution of the possible underlying true values associated with each variable. Repeated simulation (Monte Carlo simulation) generated a large number of cost-and-effect pairs that provided estimates of underlying uncertainty. The results of the probabilistic analysis are usually presented using a cost-effectiveness acceptability curve.

In Palacio et al. (2019), the probabilistic sensitivity analysis for the base-case scenario, all FV simulations were more effective but more costly than counseling only.

11.3.5 Will the Results Help in Caring for My Patients?

If the economic analysis yields valid and relevant results, the next step is to examine how to apply these results to the clinical setting of interest. Therefore, we need to interpret the ICER in the decision-making and to ascertain the extent to which the costs and effects could be applied to your practice setting.

11.3.5.1 Are the Treatment Benefits Worth the Harms and Cost?

As we described previously, when a dental treatment is compared with another, we have four possible outcomes according to the cost-effectiveness plane (see Chap. 6 for more details). Both studies analyzed fell into the quadrant where the intervention is more effective and more expensive than the control. Palacio et al. (2019) reported an ICER of CLP 130,849 and Zaror et al. (2020) an ICER of CLP 173.82 per additional caries-free child. So, how can we interpret this ratio? Is CLP 130,849 an acceptable price to pay for an additional caries-free child?

A first approach to deal with this is to compare the ICER with another similar alternative in practice; however, the specificity of the outcome can make such a comparison impossible. Another option would be to explore how much one is willing to pay for an additional measure of effectiveness, in this case, for a caries-free child. Here, a payment threshold should be established, that is, how much society is willing to pay per unit of outcome. Establishing a monetary threshold for a unit of effectiveness is not an easy task as the threshold values differ by outcomes, they are not always transferrable between countries, they may change over time, and they can vary depending on who decides on the value (Abrahamyan et al. 2015). In such circumstances, plotting the cost-effectiveness acceptability curve (CEAC) allows us to evaluate the probability that a given treatment strategy is cost-effective for different values of the willingness-to-pay threshold. For more information on how to interpret the CEAC, see Chap. 6.

In Chile, there is no available evidence about how much Chilean society would be willing to pay for a caries-free child. Zaror et al. (2020) established an educated threshold of CLP 20,000, which represents the cost for a tooth filling in the Chilean public oral healthcare system (MINSAL 2010). Under this assumption, their estimated ICER (CLP 174/caries-free children) is quite low and assumes high cost-effectiveness.

The last criterion when applying an economic evaluation to a given scenario is to analyze the local opportunity cost, that is, the health decision-maker must determine whether the implementation of a new strategy will decrease the probability of providing or adopting other oral healthcare interventions or how they or the society could have, otherwise, spent this money.

11.3.5.2 Could My Patients Expect Similar Health Outcomes?

The first issue to evaluate is whether the evidence used in the economic evaluation can be applied routinely in our context. To assess whether patients in a specific setting can expect the same health outcomes, one must examine whenever the patients in the study are similar to the patients of interest and if the clinical management applied in the study can be replicated in the local setting.

Examining the RCTs from which the outcome data were taken in both economic evaluations included in our scenario (Muñoz-Millan et al. 2018; Weintraub et al. 2006), their eligibility criteria were similar to the scenario of interest. In the same way, the interventions applied are similar to the recommendations from the Ministry of Health of Chile (MINSAL 2012).

The second issue is determining the extent to which the observed effect and cost data are transferable to other jurisdictions. This issue has been reviewed widely in Chap. 12 (transferability).

11.3.5.3 Could I Expect Similar Costs?

Cost data may not be transferable from country to country. In the same way that clinical practice can vary depending on the setting, resources consumed can also vary as local prices differ from those used in the study. Thus, it is important that authors of economic evaluations report resource use and costs separately, so that readers will be able to ascertain whether practice patterns and prices apply to their setting. If the unit costs are different and the researchers were transparent in their reporting, users of the study can recalculate the total costs by applying the unit costs that are more typical for their setting.

For the scenario of interest, all costs of both economic evaluations were expressed in Chilean pesos and used local and reliable sources to estimate them.

11.3.6 Resolution of the Scenario

Returning to the original scenario, and based on the appraisal conducted, you are ready to inform the director of the health department about the available evidence to inform the decision.

The results of both economic evaluations reported that FV was more expensive but also more effective. The population, effectiveness, resources used, and price data are applicable and relevant to our local situation since both studies were carried out in Chilean preschoolers.

The director of the health department needs to decide if an ICER up to CLP130,849 per caries-free child is acceptable. You emphasize that the cost-effectiveness ratio was highly dependent on the caries rate of the population in the sensitivity analysis. Therefore, a slight change in this parameter can result in a shift in direction of the ICER.

The director tells you that a local study showed that the baseline caries risk is even higher than the one reported in the studies, so the ICER is expected to be even lower for his population. Finally, considering all these antecedents, the director decides to implement the program, as the strategy provides an adequate opportunity cost ratio at the local level.

11.4 Final Remarks

A high-quality economic evaluation and the definition of its framework are the main elements to consider when informing decision-making in oral health. Assessing the validity and applicability of the available evidence is an essential step when using the scientific literature to guide economic evaluation decisions from an efficiency standpoint.

This chapter provides tips to assess the validity and usefulness of economic evaluations. A starting point is that a true economic evaluation should involve at least two interventions. At a minimum, the new intervention or the intervention of interest should be compared with the current state (i.e., status quo). In addition, the study should specify the perspective (e.g., patient, mid-level healthcare provider, health system) to ensure that we can evaluate the relevance of the study to our question. Failing to do so would lead to difficulties with the identification and measurement of costs and benefits.

It is essential that study under assessment provides a comprehensive description of the interventions, costs and benefits included, and the parameters or characteristics of any sensitivity analysis. Limitations in the reporting or depth of these issues seriously threaten the generalization of the study results to practice.

Another important aspect to considered is the time horizon reported of the studies. Not only because it allows evaluating the need for discounting the costs and benefits occurring in the future but because of the importance that the period of time should be long enough for the consequences/benefits/downsides to emerge.

References

Abrahamyan L, Pechlivanoglou P, Krahn M, Carrasco-Labra A et al (2015) A practical approach to evidence-based dentistry: IX: how to appraise and use an article about economic analysis. J Am Dent Assoc 146(9):679–689

Alton V, Eckerlund I, Norlund A (2006) Health economic evaluations: how to find them. Int J Technoly Assess Health Care 22(4):512–517

American Dental Association Center for Evidence-Based Dentistry (ADA) (2019) About EBD. http://ebd.ada.org/en/about. Accessed 5 May 2019

Bastian H, Glasziou P, Chalmers I (2010) Seventy-five trials and eleven systematic reviews a day: how will we ever keep up? PLoS Med 7(9):e1000326

Brignardello-Petersen R, Carrasco-Labra A, Glick M et al (2014) A practical approach to evidence-based dentistry: understanding and applying the principles of EBD. J Am Dent Assoc 145(11):1105–1107

Drummond MF, Sculpher MJ, Torrance GW et al (2005) Methods for the economic evaluation of health care programmes, 3rd edn. Oxford University Press, Oxford

Evers S, Goossens M, de Vet H et al (2005) Criteria list for assessment of methodological quality of economic evaluations: consensus on health economic criteria. Int J Technol Assess Health Care 21(2):240–245

Griffin S, Naavaal S, Scherrer C et al (2016) School-based dental sealant programs prevent cavities and are cost-effective. Health Affairs (Millwood) 35:2233–2240

Guyatt GH (1991) Evidence-based medicine. ACP J Club 114(suppl 2):A-16

Guyatt GH, Rennie D, Meade MO, Cook D (2008) Users' guides to the medical literature: a manual for evidence-based clinical practice. 2 ed.

Ho K, Chockalingam A, Best A et al (2003) Technology enabled knowledge translation: building a framework for collaboration. CMAJ 168(6):710–711

Husereau D, Drummond M, Petrou S et al (2013) Consolidated health economic evaluation reporting standards (CHEERS) statement. Value Health 16(2):e1–e5

Marinho VC, Worthington HV, Walsh T, Clarkson JE (2013) Fluoride varnishes for preventing dental caries in children and adolescents. Cochrane Database Syst Rev 7(CD002279)

Mariño R, Zaror C (2020) Economic evaluations in water-fluoridation: a scoping review. BMC Oral Health 20:115

Mariño R, Ravisankar G, Zaror C (2020) Quality appraisal of economic evaluations done on Oral health preventive programs-a systematic review. J Public Health Dent 80:194–207

Ministerio de educación (MINEDUC) (2015) Analysis of educational indicators of Chile and OECD in the context of the educational reform. In: Chilean Ministry of Education; 2015

Ministerio de Hacienda (2015) ChileCompra. http://www.chilecompra.cl/. Accessed 20 Mar 2021

Ministerio de Salud de Chile (MINSAL) (2010) Estudio Costo-efectividad de Intervenciones en Salud https://desal.minsal.cl/wp-content/uploads/2013/09/04RESUMEN-EJECUTIVO-INFORME-FINAL.pdf. Accessed 5 May 2019

Ministerio de Salud de Chile (MINSAL) (2012) Protocolo de cepillado y aplicación comunitaria de barniz de flúor para intervención en párvulos. https://www.minsal.cl/portal/url/item/b852ac18f3b067fbe04001016401265d.pdf. Accessed 5 May 2020

Ministerio de Salud de Chile (MINSAL) (2013) Guía Metodológica para la Evaluación Económica de Intervenciones de Salud en Chile http://desal.minsal.cl/wpcontent/uploads/2013/09/EE_FINAL_web.pdf. Accessed 5 May 2020

Muñoz-Millán P, Zaror C, Espinoza-Espinoza G et al (2018) Effectiveness of fluoride varnish in preventing early childhood caries in rural areas without access to fluoridated drinking water: a randomized control trial. Community Dent Oral Epidemiol 46(1):63–69

Palacio R, Shen J, Vale L, Vernazza CR (2019) Assessing the cost-effectiveness of a fluoride varnish programme in Chile: the use of a decision analytic model in dentistry. Community Dent Oral Epidemiol 47(3):217–224

Pontificia Universidad Católica (PUC) (2012) Costing study on health interventions in the National Health Fund. Pontifical Catholic University of Chile, Public Health Department, Santiago de Chile, p 2012

Sackett DL, Rosenberg WM, Gray JA et al (1996) Evidence based medicine: what it is and what it isn't. BMJ 13;312(7023):71–72

Schwendicke F, Splieth CH, Thomson WM et al (2018) Cost-effectiveness of caries-preventive fluoride varnish applications in clinic settings among patients of low, moderate and high risk. Community Dent Oral Epidemiol 46(1):8–16

Sculpher M (2008) Subgroups and heterogeneity in cost-effectiveness analysis. PharmacoEconomics 26(9):799–806

Severens JL, Milne RJ (2004) Discounting health outcomes in economic evaluation: the ongoing debate. Value Health 7(4):397–401

Weintraub JA, Ramos-Gomez F, Jue B et al (2006) Fluoride varnish efficacy in preventing early childhood caries. J Dent Res 85(2):172–176

Zaror C, Muñoz-Millán P, Espinoza-Espinoza G et al (2020) Cost-effectiveness of adding fluoride varnish to a preventive protocol for early childhood caries in rural children with no access to fluoridated drinking water. J Dent 98:103374

Chapter 12
Using Economic Evaluations to Inform Decision-Making in Oral Health: Transferability

Marianela Castillo-Riquelme, Bernardo Martorell, and Mauricio Baeza Paredes

12.1 Decision-Making for Resource Allocation of Health Technologies

Ideally, all decisions in healthcare that involve resource allocation should be informed by an economic evaluation. This is especially necessary in resource-constrained settings where the decision to grant coverage to one intervention or program can imply high 'opportunity costs'. That is, deciding to spend on one group of patients or one specific technology means that we will not be able to allocate these resources to another group of patients or to another health technology. However, economic evaluations are lengthy and expensive and require forming multidisciplinary teams with a wide level of competences, such as epidemiology, health economics, mathematical modelling, and biostatistics. For this reason, cost-effectiveness studies are frequently prioritised based on factors such as costs, burden of disease, availability of effective interventions, vulnerability of affected people, and the level of uncertainty around the previous factors.

In many countries, decisions about what studies can be undertaken from a planning perspective fall within the remit of the agencies or institutions responsible for health technology assessment (HTA). HTA has been defined as a broader framework that involves specific actors, methods, and processes to conduct a systematic analysis that goes beyond economic evaluation of health interventions

M. Castillo-Riquelme (✉)
Escuela de Salud Pública, Universidad de Chile, Santiago, Chile
e-mail: marianelacastillo@uchile.cl

B. Martorell
Facultad de Ciencias Médicas, Universidad de Santiago de Chile, Santiago, Chile
e-mail: bernardo.martorell@usach.cl

M. Baeza Paredes
Facultad de Odontología, Universidad de Chile, Santiago, Chile
e-mail: mbaeza.paredes@odontologia.uchile.cl

C. Zaror, R. Mariño (eds.), *Introduction to Economic Evaluation in Oral Health Care*, https://doi.org/10.1007/978-3-030-96289-0_12

and examines social, equity, and other considerations of its implementation (Drummond ct al. 2008). The International Network of Agencies for Health Technology Assessment (INAHTA) defined HTA as ‘a multidisciplinary process that uses explicit methods to determine the value of a health technology at different points in its lifecycle. The purpose is to inform decision-making in order to promote an equitable, efficient, and high-quality health system’ (https://www.inahta.org).

HTA has evolved to become a participative, transparent, and auditable process. The World Health Organisation (WHO) states that HTA is ‘the systematic evaluation of properties, effects and/or impacts of health technologies and interventions. It covers both the direct, intended consequences of technologies and interventions and their indirect, unintended consequences’ (https://www.who.int/health-technology-assessment/en/).

Among several HTA agencies, the most well-known are probable the National Institute for Health and Care Excellence (NICE) in the United Kingdom (UK), the Institute for Quality and Efficiency in Health Care (IQWIG) in Germany, the Pharmaceutical Benefits Advisory Committee (PBAC) in Australia, and the Canadian Agency for Drugs and Technology in Health (CADTH) in Canada (Neumann et al. 2010; Mathes et al. 2013). HTA agencies in different countries dictate the rules, define the processes, and issue technical guidelines for each of the HTA components, including economic evaluation guidelines (Mathes et al. 2013). In the case of economic evaluation – which is probably the main component of an HTA process – these guidelines are known as the ‘reference case’. A reference case gives indications of aspects such as what perspective should be used, what is the preferred outcome measure, what discount rate to use, how to report uncertainty, etc. Although not all countries have an institutionalised HTA agency, most will have national guidelines for economic evaluation.

Despite the development and implementation of HTA worldwide, and an increasing number of economic evaluations published each year, studies are still sporadic at country level. Therefore, policy makers do not always have a ‘de novo’ cost-effectiveness analysis conducted for their specific setting, to make resource allocation decisions (involving coverage, pricing, or reimbursement of health technologies). In this way, the generalisability and potential transferability of published cost-effectiveness or cost-utility studies performed for other contexts play an important role in making an efficient use of the available evidence.

On the other hand, decision-making can make use of economic evaluations in different formats, directly as evidence on costs and effects, as part of an HTA involving deliberative processes, or within a framework of multi-criteria decision analysis (MCDA). Thus, for HTA and MCDA, cost-effectiveness is only one of several criteria which represent the values of each decision setting. In MCDA, criteria are normally weighed by predefined algorithms, to generate an overall performance score for each alternative (Jakab et al. 2020). Although in most settings neither cost-effectiveness ratios nor MCDA scores convey to automatic decisions about incorporating, rejecting, or reimbursing technologies, they are key to informing decision-making.

12.2 Generalisability and Transferability of Economic Evaluations Across Settings

Based on inductive reasoning, the scientific method is constantly testing a hypothesis through observation and experimentation in order to generalise its results to different contexts, in search of models or theories that help predict reality. This same idea of extrapolating results is what motivates generalisability and transferability of economic evaluations. However, the result of any economic evaluation is highly dependent on context and is never expected to carry universal value. Results are especially sensitive to reference case decisions, relative costs, and available comparators, assuming high-quality methods. Not limited to these parameters, the validity of the results in different contexts will be dependent on all input data, such as the baseline prevalence/incidence of the disease, absolute costs, cost-effectiveness thresholds, and even health system organisation and characteristics, among others.

The concepts of generalisability and transferability of cost-effectiveness studies have been found in the literature at least since 1999 (Spath et al. 1999). The basic motivation is that creating de novo economic evaluation studies is a costly and timely endeavour, which might not be feasible in different countries or contexts, especially in view of the ever-growing available health technologies or heath interventions. As such, health systems or health services that wish to efficiently distribute scarce resources might do so by tapping into the wealth of information available from existing economic evaluations. This is not however a simple mechanistic procedure. As mentioned above, results are highly dependent on context and methods, and simply applying results from one setting to another might result in highly inefficient decisions, sacrificing health outcomes or other valuable outcomes. Thus, we must explore the issue of generalisability and transferability in greater detail.

Several terms have overlapping meanings in this issue, for example, generalisability, transferability, applicability, external validity, and extrapolation, among others, might cover the same fundamental problem. We will use primarily the first two of these. Drummond Pang and McGuire (2001) applied the term 'generalisability' to refer to the extent to which the results of an economic evaluation are held true in a context different from the original study. Sculpher et al. (2004) define generalisability of economic evaluations as 'the extent to which the results of a study based on measurement in a particular patient population and/or a specific context hold true for another population and/or in a different context'.

Willke (2003) makes the distinction between 'generalisability' as the generic term for the problem at hand and 'transferability' as the specific task referring to extrapolating study results from one country to another. Welte et al. (2004) published a transferability tool that has been widely used and has been the basis for subsequent work in the field. We discuss this tool in detail in the next section. In 2009, a Pharmacoeconomics and Outcomes Research (ISPOR) taskforce discussed transferability of CE results across different jurisdictions. The taskforce discussed whether cost-effectiveness estimates could be transferred to another specified jurisdiction and, if not, what adjustments of these estimates or even the cost-effectiveness study were possible or necessary (Drummond et al. 2009). The authors made recommendations depending on whether the analyses were multinational trial-based or using modelling approaches. For small countries they recommend collecting data on costs and conducting observational studies to collect baseline risk, since evidence on relative risk is deemed to be more transferable (Drummond et al. 2009). Pichon-Riviere et al. (2012) define transferability as the potential for adjusting an analysis and making results relevant to different contexts.

12.3 Evaluating the Quality of Economic Evaluations

A first step in the transferability of economic evaluations published is checking the quality of the studies of interest to confirm the validity of the results obtained. Nowadays, most journals specialising in economic evaluation have fairly thorough peer-review systems guided by selected quality check instruments, which ensures compliance with methodological standards and an optimal level of reporting. Ultimately, it is a detailed report that allows us to verify the quality and review the methodological correspondence for the transferability of results.

Choosing articles published in journals that expressly publish economic evaluations can be a guarantee of quality and standardised reports. The main journals in this category are Health Economics, Journal of Health Economics, Value Health, PharmacoEconomics, Cost-effectiveness and Resource Allocation, International Journal of Technology Assessment in Health Care, The European Journal of Health Economics, Journal of Medical Economics, and Medical Decision Making.

Another publication worth mentioning is *Health Technology Assessment*, from the National Institute for Health Research in the UK (https://www.nihr.ac.uk/explore-nihr/funding-programmes/health-technology-assessment.htm). This journal, launched in 1997, has been publishing full reports mainly applied to the UK decision-making context.

Regardless of the source of the study published, we need to check the quality of the study as an initial step towards determining transferability to another context. There are currently several instruments for evaluating the quality of economic evaluations; here we present the main ones. Drummond and his collaborators (2005) in their widely known book *Methods for the Economic Evaluation of Health Care Programmes*, first published in 1987, introduced a ten-point checklist to assess the quality and reporting standards.

In the Quality of Health Economic Studies (QHES) published in 2003, 120 international health economists participated in a conjoint analysis, where they developed and validated a grading system of sixteen selected factors weighted, using regression models (Chiou et al. 2003). The Consensus on Health Economic Criteria (CHEC), published in 2005, was derived from three Delphi rounds involving 23 worldwide experts in economic evaluation (Evers et al. 2005).

In 2013 an ISPOR taskforce published the Consolidated Health Economic Evaluation Reporting Standards (CHEERS) (Husereau et al. 2013), which

Table 12.1 Characteristics of instruments to evaluate the quality of economic evaluations

Name/author	Drummond et al. 2005	CHEERS	CHEC	QHES	CAPS
Last reviewed (year)	2005	2013	2005	2003	2018
Number of items	10 (33)	24	19	16	12
Population description		√	√		
Choice and description of alternatives	√	√	√		√
Study design	√	√	√	√	
Time horizon	√	√	√	√	√
Study perspective	√	√	√	√	√
Identification and measurement of costs	√	√	√		√
Identification and measurement of outcomes	√	√	√	√	√
Adjustment of costs for time differences	√	√	√		√
Sensitivity analysis	√	√	√	√	√
Presentation of results	√	√	√	√	√
Researchers' independence		√	√	√	

comprises 24 items (equally weighted). Currently CHEERS is used by the journal of *PharmacoEconomics* in its peer-review process. The UK-based Critical Appraisal Skills Programme (CASP) issues guidelines for different methodologies related to producing and using published evidence, including economic evaluations (Critical Appraisal Skills Programme 2018).

The only instrument that considers a comprehensive assessment of the technical aspects of modelling is Philips et al. (2004). Therefore, this tool should be considered together with one of the previous general instruments, when studies make use of models in the analysis.

Table 12.1 provides an overview of the methodological aspects covered by each instrument, showing that there are many points of agreement across tools.

When using these tools to verify the compliance of the article with each point, it is also necessary to judge the overall assessment. In doing this, some researchers consider the number of points satisfactorily addressed as a score of quality, while sometimes a minimum level of compliance is defined, in terms of a minimum score or threshold. Weighting items differently or considering critical points is also possible.

12.4 Comparing Monetary Values from Different Economies, Currencies, and Time Points

An important aspect of transferability is comparing resource use or costs across different settings and times. Countries have different currencies, and depending on their economic conditions, inflation rates and exchange rates are different too. The challenge of comparing costs and incremental cost-effectiveness ratio (ICER) is firstly to be able to put all values in the same currency and secondly to update these values to a unique point in time. Only in this way can we compare the levels of resources used in healthcare interventions across countries with some level of confidence.

The general recommendations are to use local currencies to firstly update costs to the comparison time point and then exchange rates to convert local currencies to euros or dollars. Of course, other currencies are also possible.

Concerning inflation, there has been extensive debate regarding the use of gross domestic product (GDP) deflators, which translates into using international purchasing power parity (PPP) conversions. However, international US dollars in PPP are not always available for all settings, and when available, sometimes these measures overestimate non-US-based values, thus casting some doubts on the validity of these comparisons. Here we stick to the recommendation of updating the values for the inflation of the country where the intervention took place, and then for the specific time points of comparison, converting the values by the standard exchange rate. Sometimes, when studies have published their results in US dollars (despite being a non-US economy), this involves first converting the values back to the original currency, applying local inflation, and then converting them again to the specific currency for comparison.

12.5 The Main Tools and Approaches for Transferability of Economic Evaluations

At present, several tools and approaches are available for assessing the transferability of economic evaluations in health. A critical point for the design of such tools is the identification of factors that could threaten the transferability of economic evaluations between different countries. Important contributions have been made in the identification and classification of these factors. For example, Goeree et al. (2007) developed a classification system of more than 80 factors grouped into 5 categories, including characteristics of the patient, disease, healthcare provider, and healthcare system.

Based on these factors, several authors have proposed different tools and approaches to evaluate or measure the potential transferability of economic evaluations, including a sequenced flow chart-type approach, an evaluation of critical criteria in a first stage, followed later by an evaluation of other non-critical factors, as well as scoring systems or quantitative indices to measure the potential for transferability (Boulenger et al. 2005, Antonanzas et al 2009, Goeree et al. 2011).

Within these approaches, Welte et al. (2004) created one of the most widely used tools for carrying out the transferability of economic evaluations. For the development of this tool, a systematic review identified potential factors that could influence transferability. Of the factors identified, 14 were finally selected due to their relevance: perspective; discount rate; medical cost approach; productivity cost approach; absolute and relative prices in healthcare; practice variation; technology availability; disease incidence/prevalence; case mix; life expectancy; health status preference; acceptance, compliance, incentives to patients; productivity and work-loss time; and disease spread. Since these factors could be analysed separately, the authors developed a checklist, which was grouped into three categories: methodological characteristics, characteristics of the health system, and characteristics of the population. However, in order to pre-select the studies that would be submitted to this list, the authors included three general knockout criteria: (i) The relevant technology is not comparable to the one that would be used in the decision country; (ii) the comparator is not comparable to the one that is relevant to the decision country; and (iii) the study does not possess an acceptable quality.

The authors present a decision chart that begins with the general knockout criteria to quickly discard studies that are considered non-transferable. Once the knockout criteria have been passed, the transferability checklist is applied to test the specific criteria. For studies that pass all criteria, a model fit to improve transferability will be assessed based on the data availability. For example, if the model does not need to be adjusted because the available data were fully applicable to the local context, the results of the study are fully transferable. For studies where model adjustments are required, the tool also guides the user in identifying whether the study results are transferable after adjustments. If the data of the country to which we want to transfer a study are partially available, it is necessary to replace all the available parameters and calculate a new incremental cost-effectiveness ratio (ICER), which can give two types of results, the study can be qualitatively transferable or not. On the other hand, when data are not available, in relation to the criteria proposed by the authors, both from the local country and from the selected studies, the results of the study would not be transferable.

The transferability tool proposed by Welte et al. (2004) has been applied to various international cost-effectiveness studies covering the areas of interventional cardiology, vaccination, and screening (Goeree et al. 2011). This tool is still considered one of the most useful in the field of transferring economic evaluations. Although in certain cases the authors considered the need to remodel with local data, the application of this tool has allowed significant savings in work time, since the models take much longer to build than to adapt to other contexts.

12.6 Case Application: Transferring the Cost Utility of Caries Preventions Interventions to Chile

To choose an international study to illustrate its transferability to Chile, we first identified the systematic review of economic evaluations of oral health interventions from Hettiarachchi et al. (2018). This review selected 23 cost-utility analyses published between 2000 and 2016, whose quality standards were assessed using the CHEERS checklist. We conducted a transferability analysis following the main features of Welte et al. (2004) decision chart, that is, checking the compliance with the 3 general knockout criteria and then with 12 specific factors (out of 14) as the main guiding tool. To check correspondence in each item we considered Chilean guidelines on cost-effectiveness analysis and unpublished recommendations on transferability of economic evaluations from other settings to the Chilean context (Ministerio de Salud 2016).

12.6.1 Economic Evaluation Guidelines and Health Technology Assessment in Chile

Chile does not have an HTA agency yet, but its functions are performed within the Ministry of Health (Castillo-Riquelme and Santelices 2014). The Health Economic Department within the Ministry of Health published guidelines for economic evaluations in 2013 (Ministerio de Salud 2013), and there are unpublished recommendations for the analysis of transferability of economic evaluation into the national context (Ministerio de Salud 2016).

Methodological guidelines in Chile highlight a reference case that recommends:

- Using a public healthcare perspective.
- QALY gained or DALY averted as measures of outcome.
- A 3% discount rate on costs and outcomes (0–6% for sensitivity analysis).
- Defining the comparator in line with current practice.
- Using modelling for a time horizon representing the survival time of the cohort/ population analysed.
- Exploring deterministic and probabilistic sensitivity analysis on results.

In Chile EQ-5D health state valuations were derived from a sample of adults living in Santiago, the Chilean capital (Zarate et al. 2011), and whenever possible these should be used in building QALY. Regarding the maximum willingness to pay for QALY gained or DALY averted, the guidelines suggest using one GDP per capita, as a reference.

On the other hand, Chile's guidelines for transferability recommend starting by formulating a well-defined research question, in which intervention and comparator are clear. The guidelines continue by identifying the potentially transferable studies through a systematic review of economic evaluations which address the research question. Studies can be identified through recently published systematic reviews of cost-effectiveness analysis. The tool uses Welte et al.'s knockout and specific criteria (Welte et al. 2004), to perform the comparison between each country's methodological features and its correspondence in Chile. For the specific transferability factors, two factors are ignored as they apply only to social perspective ((1) productivity cost approach and (2) productivity and work-loss time). While there is no recommendation to recalculate the costs or the ICER, or rerun the model for the Chilean case, data for Chile is required on the potential costs of the interventions and healthcare, as well as demographic data such as life expectancy, which affect QALY gained, or DALY averted (Ministerio de Salud 2016).

12.6.2 General Context of Oral Health Policy for Children in Chile

Oral health public policy in Chile began in 1978 with a minor program for the restoration of oral health in children. During the 1980s and the 1990s, water fluoridation began, and preventive services for children were set for ages 2 and 4. The decade 2000–2010 saw an important health sector reform, with the creation of National Health Goals and a list of legally binding priority health services (Health Guarantees Regime - GES). Comprehensive dental care for 6-year-old children was included in the GES guarantees regime. Later, preventive strategies for 12-year-old children and a preventive preschool program were initiated with limited coverage (Cartes-Velásquez 2020).

In oral health, programs are developed and financed at a national level, mainly by the Ministry of Health; however, other governmental areas such as JUNAEB, dependent on the Ministry of Education, also contribute. JUNAEB is historically in charge of food programs in schools but also developed a preventive oral health program in public schools with limited coverage. This program is very similar to the ministry of health programs, and efforts are constantly made to not duplicate coverage. From 6 years old and after the complete eruption of permanent molars, the program considers sealing the first permanent molars (FPMs) of all children.

Oral health data shows that in 2010, children aged two had 17.5% prevalence of dental caries, with 19.9% in lower socioeconomic groups versus 6.7% in higher socioeconomic groups. At age 4, 50.4% of children had dental caries, 56.5% in low, versus 24.2% in high socioeconomic groups (Ministerio de Salud de Chile 2010). At age 6, 7% had dental caries, with a decayed-missing-filled (DMF) index of 3.7 teeth (Ministerio de Salud de Chile 2014).

More recently, in 2015, the government made a significant increase in coverage of preschool prevention through the Ministry of Health with the program *Sembrando Sonrisas.* And following this, in 2017, a stratified approach aimed at identifying high-risk children for more intense preventive care (program *CERO*) was inaugurated (Ministerio de Salud de Chile 2019). These programs work in collaboration with other child preventive service programs in public healthcare (PHC) including the early childhood development program *Chile Crece Contigo* (Cornejo-Ovalle et al. 2015). This risk-based preventive approach was incorporated into an existing PHC monitoring system with financial incentives measuring the percentage of children under 3 and 6 years of age free from cavities. Thus, children, from 6 months of age, are screened annually, and a risk measurement tool is used to classify and thus stratify the intensity of preventive controls. These include regular preventive sealing and educating families and parents as crucial caretakers of children's oral health.

Children in publicly funded preschools will also gain access to periodic fluoride applications and additional educational interventions as mentioned and PHC controls at ages 2, 4, 6, and 12 (Ministerio de Salud de Chile 2019).

12.6.3 *Transferability of a Sealing of First Permanent Molar in Iowa (2004) to Chile*

Bhuridej et al. (2007) reported an economic evaluation comparing sealed and non-sealed first permanent molars in children under 6, in the Iowa Medicaid Program. We use this study as an academic exercise to transfer the results of an intervention that was not widely used in Chile before 2005, as it was in the USA, which is now (as 2021) covered by the GES program.

The evaluation included the clinical study based on a retrospective cohort of Medicaid-enrolled children in a dental program between 1996 and 2000. Eligible children needed to be 6 years old and continue in the program during the study period. The time horizon was 4 years, and they reported a special type of cost-utility analysis, from a societal perspective. They sought to identify the group of children for whom sealant was most cost-effective. Fees by the American Dental Association were used (assuming these represent better societal costs), while families direct costs or productivity losses were omitted.

The outcome measure used in the study was quality-adjusted tooth years (QATYs), which basically represents 1 year of a tooth free of caries and restorative treatment, a measure deemed easily transferable between settings. However, states and utilities could be defined and valued locally to accommodate for other potentially relevant tooth states. Utilities were derived by dentists and the general population in a previous study. Although there are no universal threshold values or maximum willingness to pay for outcomes such as QATY, valid comparisons are possible within the remit of cost-effectiveness alone or cost-utility analysis when utilities for teeth states are validated.

Table 12.2 shows the application of the knockout criteria as well as the other 12 specific factors from Welte et al. (2004). As pointed out before, 2 out of the 14 critical factors are omitted, since they do not apply to a public healthcare provider perspective, being only relevant for the societal perspective.

To compare costs, we present Table 12.3 where the unit costs published in the study were updated to 2021 US dollars and are compared to the most equivalent dental services in Chile. As in the published study where they used ADA fees, we used fees from the Chilean College of Dental Surgeons (published in 2018) as baseline costs. Although in Chile there are fees from the National Health Fund (FONASA) in the so-called institutional modality, these fees do not represent real opportunity costs for the public healthcare system since they are usually outdated reference costs not used for reimbursement. Besides, treatment such as Pulp/root canal therapy (RCT) and crowns are rare in children, since sealant for the four

Table 12.2 Transferability analysis of Bhuridej et al. (2007) to the Chilean context

Knockout criteria reformulated	Criteria/ score	Transf.	Commentary
The evaluated technology is relevant for the Chilean context	Knockout 1	Yes	In Chile dental sealant is and has been available, but it was not included in national programs at the time of publication
The comparator used in the study is valid for Chile	Knockout 2	Yes	No dental sealant (of the first molars) was the comparator, which was also a valid comparator for Chile at the time of the study
The study has acceptable quality (using CHEERS in this case)	Knockout 3	Yes	See **appendix 1** for the full application of CHEERS instrument. Twenty-two of the 24 items were applicable, the two points alluding to modelling were deemed not applicable The authors did not fulfil 2 out of the 22 remaining factors. They did not disclose the source of funding nor the potential conflicts of interest
Relevant specific criteria for the transferability to Chile's reference case			
Perspective	2	2	A societal perspective was declared in the paper, despite only direct healthcare costs were included, patients' costs (normally included in social perspective) were omitted. Chile uses a public healthcare perspective. From this point of view, the perspective finally implemented is transferable, as Medicare is a public sector provider
Discount rate	2	2	The study uses 3% on costs and effects, similar to Chile's EE guidelines
Approach to costing (direct costs)	2	2	Direct costs to Medicaid were considered, using a 2001 survey of dentist fees by the American dental association (ADA) for unit costs. Medicaid costs were used in sensitivity analysis. Chile's approach to costing is considering direct cost to healthcare too, and the fees of the dentist college are likely to represent real opportunity costs, especially when these services are covered within the general budgets, without a fee reimbursement system
Absolute and relative prices of healthcare	2	1	See Table 12.3 for cost comparison. After adjustments for inflation, the costs in the USA are higher than current costs in Chile (converted to US dollars as of May 2021). Relative costs are not very different, but in Chile, restorative care services are slightly less expensive in relation to sealant costs
Clinical practice variability	1	1	Sealant teeth in children seem to be a very standard procedure across countries, especially by 2021
Technology availability	1	1	This technology is available in Chile

(continued)

Table 12.2 (continued)

Knockout criteria reformulated	Criteria/ score	Transf.	Commentary
Incidence and prevalence	1	–	The study does not describe epidemiological features of the condition in the USA. In Chile, in 2010 children aged 2 had a 17.5% prevalence of cavities, 50.4% at age 4, and 70% at age 6 (Ministerio de Salud de Chile 2014)
Case mix	1	1	Presumably, the case mix of caries profile in children under 6 years is not too different between Medicaid and Chilean public health users
Life expectancy	N/A	N/A	The study defined a time horizon of 4 years, and the outcome measured does not consider standard life years or QALY gains
Health states preferences	1	1	Outcome measure for QATY calculation uses three values: 1 for healthy tooth, 0.81 for treated tooth, and 0 for lost tooth. These utilities could be validated and replicated in Chilean studies
Incentives to patients	1	1	Not addressed in the paper, but presumably as Medicaid is a public program, there are not such incentives to patients
Disease spread	1	1	Caries is not contagious, and its spread, beyond potential differences in incidence and prevalence, is unlikely to affect the study results
Total	15	13	

EE economic evaluation, *N/A* not applicable, *QATY* quality-adjusted tooth years

permanent molars (and some non-permanent teeth too) have existed since 2006. To compare to Medicaid fees, used in sensitivity analysis, we considered two services covered by FONASA in the free-choice modality (Modalidad Libre Elección, MLE), which constituted real reimbursement fees. For the other services not covered through this modality, we kept the fees from the Chilean College of Dental Surgeons as better proxies for real healthcare system costs. For the baseline comparison, relative costs were estimated taking the sealant costs as reference. The details of the cost update and conversion are included as Appendix 2. To arrive at only one value in procedures where more than one code exists, we averaged the closest alternatives found, validated by clinical experts.

We can see that unit costs based on dentist fees are lower in Chile than in the US ADA fees in today's values. However, costs for sensitivity analysis are more similar between countries, these are slightly higher in Chile, but crowns are more expensive in Chile, while root canal therapy is more expensive in the USA. Differences in private costs can be due to changes in human resources costs, which tend to be higher in more developed countries and, due to changes in the cost of technologies over time, becoming more affordable as time passes. Importantly, relative costs (in reference to sealant costs) show that costs of restorative treatments are slightly lower in Chile today, than these were in the USA around 2001.

Table 12.3 Comparison of unit costs (Bhuridej et al. 2007) updated to 2021 US dollars

Charges	Baseline costs (private fees)				Sensitivity analysis (public fees)	
	American Dentist Association (US)		College of Dental Surgeons (Chile)		MEDICAID (US)	FONASA (Chile)
	Absolute costs	*Relative costs*	Absolute costs	*Relative costs*	Absolute costs	Absolute costs
Sealant	48.50	*1.00*	34.71	*1.00*	29.51	34.70
1-surface restoration	111.35	*2.30*	69.41	*2.00*	66.39	69.40
2-surface restoration	138.58	*2.86*	92.55	*2.67*	84.10	92.50
3-surface restoration	166.00	*3.42*	104.12	*3.00*	101.80	**113.30**
Crown	958.53	*19.76*	323.93	*9.33*	162.29	323.9
Root canal therapy	930.44	*19.18*	251.62	*7.25*	568.02	**185.10**
Extraction	133.48	*2.75*	69.41	*2.00*	73.46	69.40

Inflation rate in the USA, for the period 2001–2021, was 52.1% (Bureau of Labor Statistics). Chilean costs are the most updated values in Chilean pesos (CLP), converted to USD by the mean daily exchange rate observed between Jan and May 2021. One USD equal 719 CLP (Chilean Central Bank).
For FONASA MLE, fees were available for 3-surface restoration (code 2503001 diagnosis, prevention, and obturation for a tooth) and PULP/RCT (mean values of codes 2,503,004, 2,503,005, and 2,503,006 referring to uni-, bi-, and multi-radicular endodontic treatment).

The potential ICER for Chile could be recalculated for each first molar as in the study, using Chilean costs and assuming the same utilisation data published in the study (ignoring the fact that costs are already discounted). The ICER is the result of dividing incremental costs with incremental QATYs when comparing sealing versus non-sealing first molars. In other words, the costs of the intervention (dental sealants) are contrasted with costs averted because of the effectiveness of the sealant program. In the study, sealed versus non-sealed first permanent molars were compared in terms of the observed probabilities of occurrence of subsequent treatment (teeth restoration, crown, endodontic therapies, and extractions).

The authors report a cost per QATY averted for each first permanent molar and stratifying low- to high-level users. Sealant placement was most cost-effective for tooth 19 in low utilisers (cost/QATY ratio of $171.1) and least cost-effective per tooth 3 in high utilisers (cost/QATY ratio of $510.3). Based on this pattern, non-utilisers (children who did not attend preventive dental services and were not part of the study) might show even better cost-effectiveness. In sensitivity analysis using Medicaid fees the cost/QATY ranged from $134.1 for tooth 19 to 265.8 for tooth 3. The authors also present the ICER for a change from a restored tooth year (utility 0.81) to a non-restored tooth year (utility of 1), that is, 0.19 QATY. This ICER ranges from $36.7 to $83.5 by sealed molar.

Without doing further estimations for the Chilean context, we can say that lower unit costs would yield lower cost/QATY (as demonstrated by the authors in the sensitivity analysis when they use Medicare fees), but on the other hand, lower relative cost (to dental sealant) will increase pressure in the opposite way, that is, increasing the ICER. Overall, we may conclude that the results are transferable to the Chilean context, since the transferability is quite high, with a score of 13 out of 15 points (87%) as shown in Table 12.2.

How can a policy maker in Chile use these results? In light of the high level of transferability, this study might inform a Chilean policy maker as to the benefits of a sealant program, saving precious time and resources in generating similar local data. Beyond cost comparison, could the effectiveness of a sealant program be more or less effective in Chile? Prevalence data are lacking from the study context, which is fundamental to understanding whether both settings (Iowa and Chile) show similar levels of dental damage or not. However, if the level of dental damage were similar, one would expect similar effectiveness of a sealant program. On the other hand, if we consider that at the time of the study in Chile coverage for restorative treatment was scarce, teeth extracted as consequence of lack of prevention were probably higher than in the USA; thus potential gains in terms of QATY would be higher for Chile, reducing the ICER. One difficult point to assess in this transferability exercise is the willingness to pay for a healthy tooth year. Though in Chile, the WTP for a *QALY* has been set at 1 GDP per capita, no such threshold has been considered for a QATY. However, cost per QATY would be a relevant argument for both health and finance ministry officers when negotiating health budgets. If universal coverage of sealant programs were a decision-making problem in Chile, it would be useful to check whether better effectiveness studies (hopefully randomised) were available and preferably using QALYs. These, together with good quality and highly transferable cost-effectiveness studies, would be highly useful in a country context where novel clinical trials and economic evaluations are relatively infrequent.

12.7 Final Remarks

Economic evaluations in healthcare are very useful for informing decision-making about efficient allocation of resources. This is more relevant for countries with centralised systems, where healthcare is funded by general taxes collected from all citizens. In this chapter we have reviewed and applied a practical instrument to evaluate the potential transferability of an economic evaluation performed originally in a country or province, different to the one that is requiring this information to make a decision. In the case of dental interventions which can be considered standardised procedures, transferability analysis could be a valid option where the possibility of doing a 'de novo' study is scant. The existence of country-published guidelines facilitates this analysis as well as adherence to cost-utility analysis with universal outcomes such as QALY. In this example we have analysed a study published for the

USA in the year 2007, which used an intermediate measure of outcome validated in dental preventive programs.

As demonstrated here, the potential transferability of the results of studies from one place to another depends greatly on the quality of the study, the adherence to economic evaluation guidelines, the level of detail when reporting, and the possibility for recalculating ICER if necessary. Having information on absolute and relative costs is key but cannot always allow for recalculating an ICER. This is especially true when complex modelling and longer time horizons are used.

Appendices

Appendix 1: Evaluation of Quality Standards of Bhuridej et al. (2007) Using CHEERS Checklist

Section/item	Item no	Recommendation	Reported on page no/ brief description
Title and abstract			
Title	1	Identify the study as an economic evaluation or use more specific terms such as 'cost-effectiveness analysis', and describe the interventions compared	Page 191 / The title explicitly states that the study is a cost-utility analysis (CUA) and describes the interventions compared. 'Four-year cost-utility analyses of sealed and nonsealed first permanent molars in Iowa Medicaid-enrolled children'
Abstract	2	Provide a structured summary of objectives, perspective, setting, methods (including study design and inputs), results (including base case and uncertainty analyses), and conclusions	Page 191 / The study presents a structured summary with the corresponding components
Introduction			
Background and objectives	3	Provide an explicit statement of the broader context for the study.	Page 191–192 / 'The purposes of this study were to a) assess the 4-year incremental cost utility of treatment outcomes of sealed first permanent molars, compared with nonsealed molars, of 6-year-old children enrolled in the Iowa Medicaid program, using a societal perspective and b) identify the group of children for whom sealants are most cost-effective'

Section/item	Item no	Recommendation	Reported on page no/ brief description
		Present the study question and its relevance for health policy or practice decisions	Page 191–192 / The study tacitly presents the question and its relevance for health policy in the context of Medicaid (a state and federal healthcare program in the USA)
Methods			
Target population and subgroups	4	Describe characteristics of the base case population and subgroups analysed, including why they were chosen	Page 192–193 / The characteristics of the population (a group of children enrolled in Iowa Medicaid) and subgroups are described. The children socioeconomic status and their patterns of dental services utilisation are reported
Setting and location	5	State relevant aspects of the system(s) in which the decision(s) need(s) to be made	Page 192 / The study is set in Iowa USA, with Medicaid as provider. Medicaid is widely known as the public health funder/ provider for the poor and the unemployed in USA
Study perspective	6	Describe the perspective of the study and relate this to the costs being evaluated	Page 192 / They use social perspective but only direct costs of services are included
Comparators	7	Describe the interventions or strategies being compared and state why they were chosen.	Page 192 / The study describes and explains the interventions being compared (sealed and non-sealed first permanent molars)
Time horizon	8	State the time horizon(s) over which costs and consequences are being evaluated and say why appropriate	Page 192 / The time horizon was 4 years, which was the follow-up of each children. In the discussion the authors acknowledge that longer follow-up could have yield better outcomes but may be, also, additional costs of treatment

Section/item	Item no	Recommendation	Reported on page no/ brief description
Discount rate	9	Report the choice of discount rate(s) used for costs and outcomes and say why appropriate	Page 193 / Using the shadow price-of-capital approach, costs and *quality-adjusted* tooth years (QATYs) were discounted 3%, which approximates the 'social rate of time preference' that transforms the future consumption losses and gains into the present value of current investments and benefits
Choice of health outcomes	10	Describe what outcomes were used as the measure(s) of benefit in the evaluation and their relevance for the type of analysis performed	Page 192 / Outcomes measures were QATYs, which represents a healthy tooth-year (i.e. a tooth free of restoration and extraction). This is a validated measure of outcome in the prevention of dental caries
Measurement of effectiveness	11a	*Single study-based estimates:* Describe fully the design features of the single effectiveness study and why the single study was a sufficient source of clinical effectiveness data	Page 192 / The description is adequate and measurement are shown in tables. 'A retrospective cohort study was used to assess the costs and outcomes of treatments rendered to sealed and nonsealed first permanent molars in a group of Iowa Medicaid-enrolled children'
	11b	*Synthesis-based estimates:* Describe fully the methods used for identification of included studies and synthesis of clinical effectiveness data	Not applicable
Measurement and valuation of preference based outcomes	12	If applicable, describe the population and methods used to elicit preferences for outcomes	Page 192 / The preferences to determine the relative values of the different teeth states (three states) used to calculate QATYs were obtained from Fyffe and Kay 1992 (a Scottish study)

Section/item	Item no	Recommendation	Reported on page no/ brief description
Estimating resources and costs	13a	*Single study-based economic evaluation:* Describe approaches used to estimate resource use associated with the alternative interventions. Describe primary or secondary research methods for valuing each resource item in terms of its unit cost. Describe any adjustments made to approximate to opportunity costs	Page 192 / The identification and measurement of costs is based on the observational study. Then, to price the costs, they use the ADA 2001 Survey of Dentists Fees, which was the most current published schedule of average dental fees in the USA at the time of analysis
	13b	*Model-based economic evaluation:* Describe approaches and data sources used to estimate resource use associated with model health states. Describe primary or secondary research methods for valuing each resource item in terms of its unit cost. Describe any adjustments made to approximate to opportunity costs	Not applicable. The study is based on an observational study
Currency, price date, and conversion	14	Report the dates of the estimated resource quantities and unit costs. Describe methods for adjusting estimated unit costs to the year of reported costs if necessary. Describe methods for converting costs into a common currency base and the exchange rate	Page 193 / The currency used is American USD of 2001. Inflation adjustments were not reported
Choice of model	15	Describe and give reasons for the specific type of decision-analytical model used. Providing a figure to show model structure is strongly recommended	Not applicable
Assumptions	16	Describe all structural or other assumptions underpinning the decision-analytical model	Not applicable
Analytical methods	17	Describe all analytical methods supporting the evaluation. This could include methods for dealing with skewed, missing, or censored data; extrapolation methods; methods for pooling data; approaches to validate or make adjustments (such as half cycle corrections) to a model; and methods for handling population heterogeneity and uncertainty	Page 192–194 / All these aspects are described in the context of the observational study, which was the basis of the analysis

Section/item	Item no	Recommendation	Reported on page no/ brief description
Results			
Study parameters	18	Report the values, ranges, references, and, if used, probability distributions for all parameters. Report reasons or sources for distributions used to represent uncertainty where appropriate. Providing a table to show the input values is strongly recommended	Page 196 / Baseline values (from 2001 ADA survey of fees and utility values suggested by Fyffe and Kay 1992) and sensitivity analysis ranges (obtained from 2001 Iowa Medicaid reimbursement rates) were reported and presented in a table
Incremental costs and outcomes	19	For each intervention, report mean values for the main categories of estimated costs and outcomes of interest, as well as mean differences between the comparator groups. If applicable, report incremental cost-effectiveness ratios	Page 195 / Mean annual discounted costs and QATYs, total annual costs and QATYs of each first permanent molar, and incremental cost-effectiveness ratios are reported
Characterising uncertainty	20a	*Single study-based economic evaluation:* Describe the effects of sampling uncertainty for the estimated incremental cost and incremental effectiveness parameters, together with the impact of methodological assumptions (such as discount rate, study perspective)	Page 197 / A deterministic sensitivity analysis was used. A one-way sensitivity analysis was conducted to evaluate the stability of the conclusions of the CUA and to identify the most critical parameters of analysis
	20b	*Model-based economic evaluation:* Describe the effects on the results of uncertainty for all input parameters and uncertainty related to the structure of the model and assumptions	Not applicable
Characterising heterogeneity	21	If applicable, report differences in costs, outcomes, or cost-effectiveness that can be explained by variations between subgroups of patients with different baseline characteristics or other observed variability in effects that are not reducible by more information	Page 195 / A table shows the relevant differences between subgroups

Section/item	Item no	Recommendation	Reported on page no/ brief description
Discussion			
Study findings, limitations, generalisability, and current knowledge	22	Summarise key study findings and describe how they support the conclusions reached. Discuss limitations and the generalisability of the findings and how the findings fit with current knowledge	Page 196–198 / These aspects are detailed in the discussion. A paragraph that summarises the main findings and their implications is presented below. 'Given the limited resources available to most public health programs, these results support policies that target dental sealants to those in most need and are least likely to utilize other dental services'
Other			
Source of funding	23	Describe how the study was funded and the role of the funder in the identification, design, conduct, and reporting of the analysis. Describe other non-monetary sources of support	No
Conflicts of interest	24	Describe any potential for conflict of interest of study contributors in accordance with journal policy. In the absence of a journal policy, we recommend authors comply with International Committee of Medical Journal Editors recommendations	No

Appendix 2: Procedure for Updating and Comparing Costs for Transferability Analysis

Step 1	**Updating the study unit costs**				
Charges	**2001 ADA fees**	**2001 Medicaid**	**Inflation factor**	**2021 ADA fees**	**2021 Medicaid**
Sealant	31.89	19.4	1.52	48.47	29.49
1-surface restoration	73.21	43.65	1.52	111.28	66.35
2-surface restoration	91.11	55.29	1.52	138.49	84.04
3-surface restoration	109.14	66.93	1.52	165.89	101.73
Crown	630.2	106.7	1.52	957.90	162.18

Pulp/RCT	611.73	373.45	1.52	929.83	567.64
Extraction	87.76	48.3	1.52	133.40	73.42

The factor 1.52 allows for the update of the cumulative rate of inflation of 52.1%, determined between 2001 and 2021, by the US inflation calculator available at https://www.usinflationcalculator.com/inflation/current-inflation-rates/ whose source is the US Bureau of labor statistics.

Step 2	**Identifying similar unit costs for the Chilean costs**			
Sources	Fees from the Colegio de Cirujano Dentistas, in 2018 values, still valid for 2021. Available from https://dentonet.cl/uco/			
Treatment	**Original name/ description**		**Chilean pesos (CLP)**	
Sealant	Sealant application			$24,954
1-surface restoration	Restoration class I – 1 surface			$49,908
2-surface restoration	Restoration class II – 2 surface			$66,544
3-surface restoration	Restoration class III – 3 surface			$74,862
Crown	Full metal crown			$216,268
	Three-quarter metal crown			$216,268
	Complete perforated crown			$232,904
	Plural fixed prosthesis insertion crown			$266,176
Root canal therapy (RCT)	Incisor and vital canine endodontics (UCO 6)			$99,816
	Endodontics in vital premolars (UCO 7)			$116,452
	Endodontics in incisors and vital canines (UCO 8)			$133,088
	Endodontics anterior teeth (incisors and canines) with apical lesion (8.5)			$141,406
	Endodontics vital premolars (UCO 9)			$149,724
	Tri-radicular premolar endodontics (without lesion)			$216,268
	Tri-radicular premolar endodontics (with lesion)			$249,540
	Endodontics premolars with apical lesion			$166,360
	Endodontics in vital upper molars			$216,268
	Endodontics in vital lower molars			$199,632
	Endodontics in upper molar with lesion			$249,540
	Endodontics in lower molar with lesion			$232,904
Extraction	Simple extraction tooth			$49,908

UCO are units that express different complexities of interventions

Step 3	**Getting mean or final values for each service and transforming them to USD of 2021**				
	Final cost in CLP	Exchange rate	USD 2021		
Sealant	$24,954	719	$34.71		

1-surface restoration	$49,908	719	$69.41		
2-surface restoration	$66,544	719	$92.55		
3-surface restoration	$74,862	719	$104.12		
Crown	$232,904	719	$323.93		
Pulp/RCT	$180,917	719	$251.62		
Extraction	$49,908	719	$69.41		
The exchange rate of 719 CLP per one USD corresponds to the mean value obtained from the daily observed rate between the first and 31st of May 2021. Available from the Central Bank of Chile at https://si3.bcentral.cl/indicadoressiete/secure/IndicadoresDiarios.aspx					
Step 4	**Comparing absolute and relative costs in 2021 USD**				
	US ADA fees		**Chilean dentists' fees**		
Charges	**Absolute costs**	**Relative costs**	**Absolute costs**	**Relative costs**	
Sealant	48.47	1 (ref)	34.71	1(ref)	
1-surface restoration	111.28	2.30	69.41	2.00	
2-surface restoration	138.49	2.86	92.55	2.67	
3-surface restoration	165.89	3.42	104.12	3.00	
Crown	957.90	19.76	323.93	9.33	
Pulp/RCT	929.83	19.18	251.62	7.25	
Extraction	133.40	2.75	69.41	2.00	
Relative costs were calculated taking the sealant cost as the reference					
We need to replicate this procedure for the Medicare costs to compare them to Chilean equivalent fees by the National Health Fund (FONASA).					

References

Antonanzas F, Rodriguez-Ibeas R, Juárez C et al (2009) Transferability indices for health economic evaluations: methods and applications. Health Economics Health Econ 18(6):629–643

Bhuridej P, Kuthy RA, Flach SD et al (2007) Four-year cost-utility analyses of sealed and non-sealed first permanent molars in Iowa Medicaid-enrolled children. J Public Health Dent 67(4):191–198

Boulenger S, Nixon J, Drummond M et al (2005) Can economic evaluations be made more transferable? Eur J Health Econ 6(4):334–336

Cartes-Velásquez R (2020) Salud bucal en Chile, situación actual y desafíos futuros. Odontol Sanmarquina 23(2):189–196

Castillo-Riquelme M, Santelices E (2014) Foundations for the institutionalization of health technology assessment in Chile. Rev Med Chil 142(suppl 1):50–54

Chiou CF, Way JW, Wallace JF et al (2003) Development and validation of a grading system for the quality of cost-effectiveness studies. Med Care 41(1):32–44

Cornejo-Ovalle M, Brignardello-Petersen R, Pérez G (2015) Pay-for-performance and efficiency in primary oral health care practices in Chile. Rev Clin Periodoncia Implantol Rehabil Oral 8(1):60–66

Critical Appraisal Skills Programme (2018) CASP Economic Evaluation Checklist. https://casp-uk.net/wp-content/uploads/2018/01/CASP-Economic-Evaluation-Checklist-2018.pdf. Accessed 21 Feb 2019

Drummond M, Pang F, Mcguire A (2001) Transferability of economic evaluation results. In: Drummond MF, McGuire A (eds) Economic evaluation of health care: merging theory with practice. Oxford University Press, New York

Drummond MF, Schulpher M, Torrance G et al (2005) Methods for the economic evaluation of health care Programmes. Oxford University Press, New York

Drummond MF, Schwartz SJ, Jönsson N et al (2008) Key principles for the improved conduct of health technology assessments for resource allocation decisions. Int J Technol Assess Health Care 24(3):244–258

Drummond M, Barbieri M, Cook J et al (2009) Transferability of Economic Evaluations Across Jurisdictions:ISPOR Good Research Practices Task Force Report 12(4): 409–418

Evers S, Goossens M, Vet H et al (2005) Criteria list for assessment of methodological quality of economic evaluations: consensus on health economic criteria. Int J Technol Assess Health Care 21(2):240–245

Goeree R, Burke N, O'Reilly D et al (2007) Transferability of economic evaluations: approaches and factors to consider when using results from one geographic area for another. Curr Med Res Opin 23(4):671–682

Goeree R, He J, O'Reilly D et al (2011) Transferability of health technology assessments and economic evaluations: a systematic review of approaches for assessment and application. Clinicoecon Outcomes Res 3:89–104

Hettiarachchi RM, Kularatna S, Downes MJ et al (2018) The cost-effectiveness of oral health interventions: a systematic review of cost-utility analyses. Community Dent Oral Epidemiol 46(2):118–124

Husereau D, Drummond M, Petrou S et al (2013) Consolidated health economic evaluation reporting standards (CHEERS)-explanation and elaboration: a report of the ISPOR health economic evaluation publication guidelines good reporting practices task force. Value Health 16(2):231–250

Jakab I, Németh B, Elezbawy B et al (2020) Potential criteria for frameworks to support the evaluation of innovative medicines in upper middle-income countries—a systematic literature review on value frameworks and multi-criteria decision analyses. Front Pharmacol 11:1203

Mathes T, Jacobs W, Morfeld JC, Pieper D (2013) Methods of international health technology assessment agencies for economic evaluations- a comparative analysis. BMC Health Serv Res 13(1):371

Ministerio de Salud de Chile (2010) Informe consolidado:diagnóstico nacional de salud bucal de los niños y niñas de 2 y 4 años que participan en la educación parvularia. Chile 2007–2010. https://diprece.minsal.cl/wrdprss_minsal/wp-content/uploads/2015/05/Informe-consolidado-2-y-4-años.pdf. Accessed 15June 2019

Ministerio de Salud de Chile (2014) Diagnóstico Nacional de Salud Bucal de los niños de 6 años. Análisis por macrozona. https://diprece.minsal.cl/wrdprss_minsal/wp-content/uploads/2015/05/Diagnostico-Nacional-6años_analisis-por-macrozona.pdf. Accessed 15 Jun 2019

Ministerio de Salud de Chile (2019) Orientación Técnico Administrativa Población en Control con Enfoque de Riesgo Odontológico. Programa CERO. https://diprece.minsal.cl/wp-content/uploads/2019/02/Orientacion-Tecnica-Programa-CERO-2019.pdf. Accessed 15 May 2020

Ministerio de Salude de Chile (2013) Guía Metodológica para la Evaluación Económica de Intervenciones en Salud en Chile. http://desalminsalcl/wp-content/uploads/2013/09/EE_FINAL_webpdf- Accessed 15 Jun 2019

Ministerio de Salude de Chile (2016) Propuesta de la Herramienta de Transferibilidad de Evaluaciones Económicas en Salud. Santiago

Neumann PJ, Drummond MF, Jönsson B et al (2010) Are key principles for improved health technology assessment supported and used by health technology assessment organizations? Int J Technol Assess Health Care 26(1):71–78

Philips Z, Ginnelly L, Sculpher M et al (2004) Review of guidelines for good practice in decision-analytic modelling in health technology assessment. Health Technol Assess 8(36):1–158

Pichon-Riviere A, Augustovski F, García S et al (2012) Transferability of health technology assessment reports in Latin America: an exploratory survey of researchers and decision makers. Int J Technol Assess Health Care 28(2):180–186

Sculpher MJ, Pang FS, Manca A et al (2004) Generalisability in economic evaluation studies in healthcare: a review and case studies. Health Technol Assess 8(49):1–192

Spath H et al (1999) Analysis of the eligibility of published economic evaluations for transfer to a given health care system methodological approach and application to the French health care system. Health Policy 49:161–177

Welte R, Carrère MO, Fervers B, Philip T (2004) A decision chart for assessing and improving the transferability of economic evaluation results between countries. PharmacoEconomics 22(13):857–876

Willke RJ (2003) Tailor-made or off-the-rack? The problem of transferability of health economic data. Expert Rev Pharmacoecon Outcomes Res 3(1):1–4

Zarate V, Kind P, Valenzuela P et al (2011) Social valuation of EQ-5D health states: the Chilean case. Value Health 14(8):1135–1141

Chapter 13
Economic Evaluation: Uses and Potential Uses in Oral Health Policy Development

John Rogers

13.1 Oral Health Policy and Economic Evaluation

The World Health Organization (WHO) defines health policy as 'decisions, plans and actions that are undertaken to achieve specific health care goals within a society' (World Health Organization 2020). In the broadest sense health policy is a strategic outline of priorities for action to improve the public health. Health policy includes legislation, regulation, strategic plans, policy papers, budget papers and funding protocols. It can also include initiatives at a dental clinical level such as clinical guidelines.

At the government level, health policy is concerned with decisions that direct public resources in one direction and not another. In effect, choices about who gets what, where, how and why.

Economic evaluation is the 'comparative analysis of alternative courses of action in terms of both their costs and consequences' (Drummond et al. 2015) and can assist in shaping health policy by determining the most effective and efficient use of resources. Being 'concerned with maximising people's health and well-being given available resources' (Listl and Weyant 2019), it is therefore intimately linked to the making of health and oral health policy.

Such research can provide details about the cost of commencing or expanding a program or evidence for advocacy for a new program or technology (Morgan et al. 2012). Economic evaluation can assist policy makers to answer questions of health program efficacy (is it working?), effectiveness (is it working well?) and equity (is it reaching those it is supposed to reach?). These questions are related to allocative efficiency (what to do) and technical efficiency (how to do it).

Oral health policy is a subset of health policy and comprises activities undertaken to achieve community oral health goals – hopefully within the dental/oral

J. Rogers (✉)
University of Melbourne, Melbourne, Australia
e-mail: jgogers@unimelb.edu.au

C. Zaror, R. Mariño (eds.), *Introduction to Economic Evaluation in Oral Health Care*, https://doi.org/10.1007/978-3-030-96289-0_13

public health endeavour of preventing oral disease and promoting oral health through organised community efforts. These efforts may be via legislation (community water fluoridation, workforce regulation), budget decisions (funding of public sector prevention and treatment programs), strategic plans (development of national oral health plans) or best practice guidelines (at the clinical level). Economic evaluation can provide evidence to inform decisions in all of these areas as will be outlined in the following sections.

13.2 Economic Evaluation's Influence on Oral Health Policy

There is limited literature on the impact that overall oral health research has on influencing oral health policy (Bell et al. 2014; Crocombe et al. 2016). Crocombe and colleagues' review of the oral health research literature determined that analysis of how policy is formed is a very small research area within oral health. They found that the issues of evidence translation into policy were seldom studied with just a few studies reviewing evidence-practice translation (Rogers 2012), improving the translation of evidence from clinical trials (Barnett and Pihlstrom 2004) and clinical guidelines (Clarkson et al. 2010). Apart from the issue of community water fluoridation, their conclusion was that most oral health research evidence is not policy-relevant, and most of the time, policy is not drawing on the evidence (Bell et al. 2014, Crocombe et al. 2016).

As in broader oral health research, there has been little study of the impact that economic evaluation in dentistry has had on policy. As outlined in other chapters, economic evaluations have been conducted across a broad range of oral health areas encompassing prevention and dental care. The systematic reviews of these studies conducted over the last 5 years (Murthy and Fareed 2020; Marino et al. 2020; Marino and Zaror; 2020; Eow et al. 2019; Fraihat et al. 2019; Rogers et al. 2019; Tonmukayakul et al. 2015a, b) have not identified whether any of the research has actually influenced oral health policy.

A scoping literature review was undertaken for this chapter to determine the impact that economic evaluation has had on influencing oral health policy. Details about the search are presented in Appendix 1.

The searches of the databases identified over 300 studies when using the economic evaluation and dentistry terms. Less than 20 studies were identified when 'and policy' was added to the search. However, the references to 'policy' were predominantly that the results of the study should be considered by policy makers. No study actually stated that the evidence did in fact influence oral health policy.

The search of grey literature identified studies in three areas where economic evaluation had led to the introduction of policy or support for the implementation or continuation of programs. These initiatives were in the areas of extension of community water fluoridation (Australia, see case study in Sect. 13.5), prevention interventions for preschool children (Scotland, see (Anopa et al. 2015; Macpherson et al. 2019; Althous et al. 2020); Australia, see case study in Sect. 13.5) and clinical guidelines (e.g. Public Health England, *Delivering better oral health: an evidence-based toolkit for prevention 2017* (Public Health England 2017)).

Opportunities to use evidence from economic evaluation to influence policy will be highlighted in the following sections. A third case study from the general health policy research will also be included in Sect. 13.5.

13.3 How Economic Evaluation Can Further Contribute to Influencing Oral Health Policy

It has been said that there are two things that should not be watched – the making of sausages and the making of laws or policy. This remark has been attributed to the nineteenth-century German Chancellor, Otto von Bismarck, but others have made similar comments. It refers to the often-messy process of making laws and policy, as distinct from the systematic, evidence-based process favoured by researchers (Lewis 2005).

The making of health policy is a complex, dynamic, social and political process based on ideas and values (Lewis 2005). It can be unpredictable and chaotic. On the other hand, the policy development process may follow a rational comprehensive approach and include specific stages, if not sequential, within a policy cycle (Althous et al. 2020). The process typically involves many players and can be highly contested. Lewis notes that it involves a complex network of continuous interactions (Lewis 2005).

Two frameworks will be presented that outline the key components and stages of making public health policy: Kingdon's agenda-setting theory (Kingdon 2010) and the policy cycle model (Althous et al. 2020). The relevance of these frameworks to making public oral health policy, and examples of how economic evaluation has been, or could have been, incorporated will be explored. Case studies of policy processes that successfully used economic evaluation research will be presented in more detail in Sect. 13.5.

The key players in making oral health policy are the same across each of the policy frameworks. Politicians make the final decisions about major budget matters, legislation and workforce planning. They are advised by ministerial advisors and public servants (in health departments but also in finance departments) and also consider input from oral health professional groups, oral health researchers, private dentists, community members, health and welfare advocacy groups and industry lobbyists. The media can be an important player as can a politician's own dentist. These key players are likely to have different values, political goals and perceptions of oral health issues.

Kingdon's Agenda-Setting Theory

Kingdon's agenda-setting theory is particularly useful in understanding, developing and gaining acceptance of policy as the theory focuses on a set of processes (Kingdon 2010). Kingdon proposes a multiple policy streams analysis in which policy solutions can only be reached at a 'window of opportunity' when the problem, the policy change required to resolve it and the desire of the politicians to do so all align (Fig. 13.1). The streams develop and operate largely independent of one another but come together at critical times (Kingdon 2010).

For Kingdon, agenda setting is a key factor in the policy process. The policy agenda is the list of issues or problems to which government officials, or those who make policy decisions (including the community), pay serious attention. Each problem must compete for official attention because of limited time and resources. According to Kingdon, moving an idea onto, or higher up, the agenda involves the three processes: problems, proposals and politics (Kingdon 2010).

Problems refer to the process of persuading policy decision-makers to pay attention to one problem over others. The chances of a policy proposal rising on the agenda are better if the associated problem is perceived as serious and the issue strikes an emotional chord. Decision-makers about health policy need to see the issue as real and be able to relate to it. They are always considering how a problem compares to the myriad of other health problems.

The problem of poor oral health might be framed to include the economic and emotional costs: for example, the prevalence of very young children having general anaesthesia to treat dental caries and the impact on quality of life of poor oral health (ability to eat, speak and socialise, impact on schoolwork and employment). Also relevant are inequality in oral health; long waiting lists for public dental care; the high cost of dental care; and prevention being better than cure with possible cost savings.

Economic evaluation can contribute to framing the problem by clearly identifying the economic impact of poor oral health, thereby strengthening the case for policy change. The high prevalence of dental caries and periodontal disease means that the mouth is among the most expensive parts of the body to treat (Listl et al.

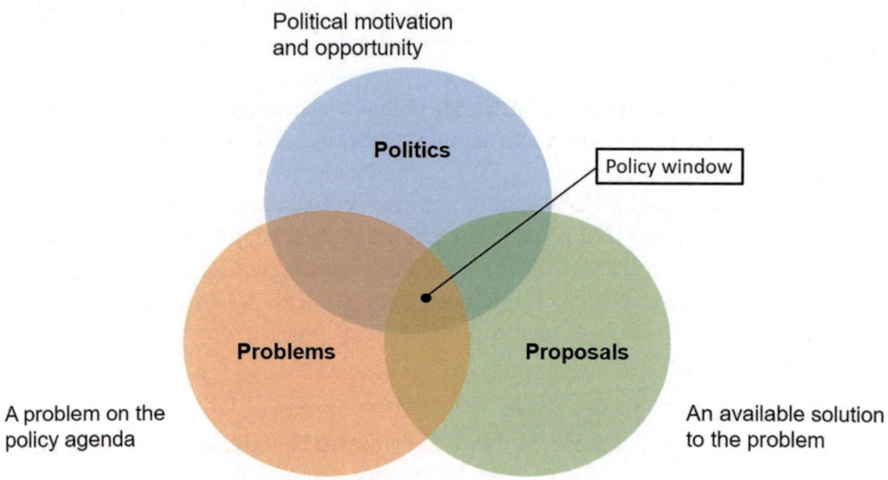

Fig. 13.1 Kingdon's agenda-setting theory. (Source: Kingdon 2010)

2015). There are financial impacts on the health system through pressure on hospital emergency departments and operating theatres. Costs are also incurred through workers' lost productivity and school children's days lost from school (Australian Government 2015). The impact on families of dental treatment costs and the inconvenience of working parents taking children for care were reasons for a recent expansion of school dental services in Australia (Victorian Labor Government 2018).

The definition of the problem and economic impacts should also recognise that there are common risk factors (CRF) between oral and other chronic conditions such as obesity, diabetes, cancers, cardiovascular disease and respiratory diseases. These CRFs include poor dietary practices (particularly excessive sugar consumption), smoking and excessive alcohol intake in addition to the broader social determinants of health. An integrated approach to the promotion of both oral and general health is more efficient and effective than just targeting a single disease or condition (Watt and Sheiham 2012; Sheiham and Watt 2000).

Proposals represent the process by which policy proposals are generated, debated, revised and adopted for serious consideration. Policy proposals are likely to be more successful if they are seen as technically feasible, compatible with decision-maker values, reasonable in cost and appealing to the public (Kingdon 2010). Values matter because some politicians value reduction of inequality highly, whereas others focus more on decreasing public expenditure.

Economic evaluation has contributed to the adoption of policies that benefit oral health in a range of countries as identified by the scoping review (Sect. 13.2). Policy makers agreed to extend community water fluoridation to rural areas in Victoria, Australia, partly on the economic 'killer fact' that 25 years of community water fluoridation in the capital, Melbourne, had led to a $1 billion saving in dental treatment costs (as detailed in the first case study in Sect. 13.5). In Scotland, cost-effectiveness research on the impact on future dental treatment costs of supervised toothbrushing in preschool settings, as part of a program called Childsmile, determined that estimated savings would be more than two and half times the costs of program implementation within 8 years (Anopa et al. 2015). This evidence, combined with other successful impacts of Childsmile, has contributed to national UK oral health policy (Macpherson et al. 2019).

Economic and oral health status data to support a proposal will be more persuasive if the decision-maker has seen direct evidence of the impact of poor oral health and has an emotional involvement. The personal can become political when policy makers have an experience with the oral health system. For example, an Australian senior policy maker became a supporter of a public dental program after he paid for expensive private dental care for his daughter and so became aware of how treatment costs can be a significant barrier for low-income families.

Oral health proposals can gain more support if they involve the integration of oral and general health promotion through cross-sector CRF approaches. Also necessary is the integration of oral and primary care treatment services for the provision of preventively focused oral healthcare. The integration of oral health and general health can be progressed by developing 'oral health in all policies' (Sheiham et al. 2015; Watt et al., 2019) and integrating oral health into international policies and frameworks such as the Sustainable Development Goals (SDGs) and the WHO global action plan on non-communicable diseases (NCDs) (Watt et al. 2019).

For Kingdon, *politics* are political factors that influence agendas, such as election commitments, changes in elected officials, political climate or mood (e.g. a conservative and tax averse climate), budget crises and the voices of advocacy or opposition groups. The likelihood of successful agenda setting substantially increases if all three elements (problem, proposal and politics) are linked in a single package and come together at a critical time, that is, when a 'policy window' opens (Kingdon, 2010). These occasions can be elections or budgets when politicians can propose new public health policies. It is critical at these times that oral health advocates have problems and proposals (including economic evaluations) prepared that they can promote.

Kingdon's agenda-setting theory is particularly useful to the process of understanding, developing and gaining acceptance of policy as it focuses on a set of processes. The policy cycle model assists by outlining the key stages of the policy process.

Policy Cycle Model

As mentioned, the development of public health policy can be a messy process. On the other hand, the policy development process involves specific stages, even if not sequential, within a policy cycle (Althous et al. 2020). The 'policy cycle' model of the policy process specifies eight stages and associated activities as outlined in Box 13.1.

Box 13.1: Stages of the Policy Process (Althous et al. 2020)

1. Identify issues.
2. Policy analysis – consider alternatives and consequences of each option including relating to values.
3. Policy instruments – consider how to lock in policies for implementation.
4. Consultation with key stakeholders.
5. Coordination across government portfolios.
6. Decision-making.
7. Implementation.
8. Evaluation.

These stages may not occur sequentially.

What is relevant to economic evaluation research is recognising that there are many steps before policy decisions are made. The first stage is identification of the issues, which Kingdon identifies as getting on the policy agenda. Researchers who want their research to be policy-relevant need to discuss with policy makers what their policy questions are and engage with them during the research process. Possible research areas are discussed in Sect. 13.6.

Economic evaluation can assist in the policy analysis stage (Stage 2) by identifying what is the most effective and efficient use of resources. Designing implementation practicalities (Stage 3) may also be explored through economic evaluation research. Researchers are key stakeholders and should be part of Stage 4 – consultation with stakeholders. Economic evaluation is crucial in the eighth stage of the process – evaluation of implementation of the policy. This evaluation can then feed into a continuing review of issues as part of the policy cycle. Translating research into policy and practice will now be addressed.

13.4 Translating Research into Policy and Practice: Bridging the Gap

As discussed earlier, much research is never translated into policy and practice. Contexts, motivation, reward systems, time frames, priorities and language can be different for policy makers and researchers (Bell 2010). In completing the jigsaw of all the factors that are part of making health policy, it is as though researchers and decision-makers each have different pieces and are in different rooms trying to fit the pieces together.

Economic evaluation researchers can assist in bridging the gap between policy and practice by understanding the policy process as outlined in Sect. 13.3. What can also be useful is for them to appreciate what is driving policy makers: to understand levels and presentation of evidence; to engage with health department officers; and to be policy advocates. These four approaches will now be briefly outlined.

Understand what is driving policy makers. Policy making is a sociopolitical process. For enhanced success in influencing policy, it is useful to understand what is driving policy makers and to point out how your issue is relevant to them. For more policy-persuasive research there is a need to discuss with policy makers the research questions for which they want answers in order to understand their context and timeframes (Crocombe et al. 2016).

There are considerable time pressures on senior decision-makers. Ministers in particular have to manage myriad issues. Former Victorian deputy premier and health minister, John Thwaites, on leaving government, noted that generally, ministers want to deliver election commitments and deliver good policies. They also want to get on with stakeholders, leave a legacy of good government and get re-elected (Thwaites 2008b). Public opinion is key to the latter.

Appreciate different levels and presentation of evidence. Policy decision-makers take a wider view of what might be considered evidence compared to researchers' more 'scientific' lens (Catford 2009). Researchers often want to know beyond reasonable doubt, in contrast to policy makers who are interested in the balance of probabilities and a clear message (Lin 2003). The research evidence is the technical aspect that can be trumped by the cultural (values and ethics) and the political (distribution and management of power and the creation of legitimacy) (Lin 2003).

Decision-makers use stories, metaphors and analogies to persuade others. Researchers, including those with an economic evaluation focus, can also use human interest stories to help prosecute their case in addition to presenting clear and succinct economic 'killer facts'. Recognise the importance of emotion in decision-making – sometimes hot emotion and fixed beliefs can overcome cold logic. It is important for researchers wanting to influence policy to appreciate both the 'p value' and the 'PR value' of their research findings.

Engage with health department officers. Health department officers work within a context of political imperatives and administrative hierarchies and have an understanding of what policy relevant research is required. They have privileged access to decision-makers and, like researchers and other oral health advocates, should have problems and proposals (informed by economic evaluation) prepared and ready to present and advocate for when a policy window opens. Researchers and health department officers can assist each other in translating research into policy and practice (Dwan and McInnes 2013).

Advocate. Thwaites, mentioned above, outlined 'ten commandments' for influencing government to make good public policy (Thwaites 2008a). These can be categorised under the three areas of political awareness, framing of the problem and proposal, and communication style (Box 13.2).

Box 13.2: Commandments of Influencing Government

(John Thwaites, Victorian Deputy Premier and Minister for Health 1999–2002)

Political awareness.

Know what the government wants to achieve.

Understand government policies.

Framing of problem and proposal.

Provide alternatives and priorities.

Say something new.

Identify key stakeholders.

Collaborate – with broad range of sectors and organisations and be prepared to be part of a team.

Communication style.

Be clear in your advice.

Get the timing right.

Put effort into communication.

Be honest.

Researchers can be potent oral policy advocates who can transmit the central message clearly as oral health champions. They can be more policy-effective if they collaborate and form coalitions with a broad range of sectors and organisations. It can be useful for those advocating for policies to prepare for a 'lift conversation' (elevator pitch) with a health minister by having pertinent statistics, a brief relevant story or a clear proposal ready in case of a chance meeting.

Watt has identified that oral health advocates need to mobilise social power through engagement with civil society and community organisations in order to raise public health awareness and influence policy decisions that will reduce oral health inequalities (Watt 2017). Further key aspects of advocacy are use of the media, working with those politicians who have an interest in oral health and being persistent.

Ultimately, there are a myriad of factors that influence policy making (Fig. 13.2). A positive outcome for good oral health policy may require good fortune – colloquially speaking for 'all the stars to be aligned'. This is especially the case for government policy decisions that result in the allocation of significant resources. Policy decisions about dental clinic interventions occur at a lower level and can be more straightforward.

Nutbeam's analysis is that health policy is derived from a balance between what is scientifically plausible (evidence based), politically acceptable (fits with the vision of the government and the balance of interests), and practical for implementation (powers and resources are available; systems, structures and capacity for action exist) (Nutbeam 2003).

13.5 Case Studies of how Economic Evaluation Has Influenced Oral Health Policy

Examples of where economic evaluation has helped move oral health up the policy agenda and shape oral health policy include in the areas of community water fluoridation and in oral health improvement programs for 0–5-year-olds. These will now be outlined. A case study in policy development in early childhood development will also be described.

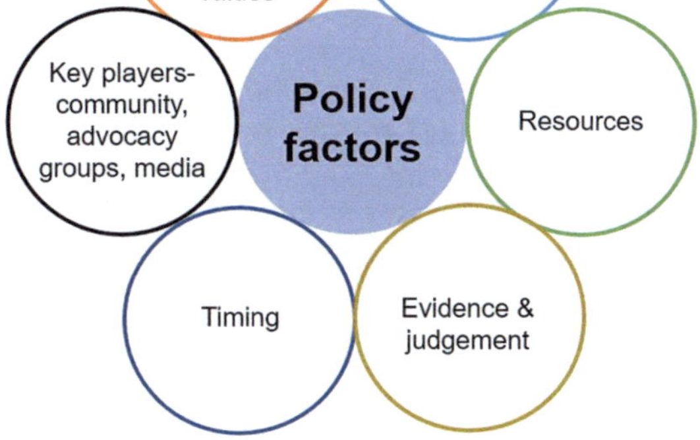

Fig. 13.2 Factors influencing policy

13.5.1 The Extension of Community Water Fluoridation

A review of the evidence of the impact of community water fluoridation by the influential Australian National Health and Medical Research Council (NHMRC) concluded that water fluoridation is a safe, cost-effective and ethical way to help reduce dental caries (NHMRC 2017a). The review determined that the costs of establishing and maintaining a fluoridated water supply are significantly lower than the savings from reduced dental treatments and less time lost from work for dental-related reasons. Four economic evaluations from Australia (NHMRC 2017b) and a systematic review of CBAs undertaken in the United States were identified in the NHMRC review (Ran and Chattopadhyay 2016).

The Australian studies on the cost-effectiveness of water fluoridation found that for every dollar spent on fluoridation, between $7 and $18 is saved in avoided treatment costs. As mentioned in Sect. 13.3, it is reported that a CEA found that over 25 years, water fluoridation had saved Victorians about $1 billion through avoided dental costs, days away from work or school and other costs (Department of Health and Human Services 2020).

These economic 'killer' facts have been influential in continuing broad political support for community water fluoridation in most states and territories in Australia. Health ministers from all jurisdictions approved the National Oral Health Plan 2015–2024 which proposes that communities of more than 1000 people should have access to reticulated fluoridated water supplies (Australian Government 2015). The plan also notes that the improved design and reducing cost of fluoridation plants mean that extending coverage to smaller communities may be cost-effective.

13.5.2 Oral Health Improvement Programs for 0–5-Year-Olds

Public Health England commissioned the York Health Economics Consortium (YHEC) to undertake a rapid review of evidence on the cost-effectiveness of interventions to improve the oral health of children aged 0–5 years. The review (Public Health England 2014) found that five prevention programs reduced dental caries in 5-year-olds and determined the cost-effectiveness and return on investment (ROI) of five oral health initiatives:

- Targeted, supervised tooth brushing with fluoride toothpaste.
- Targeted fluoride varnish.
- Water fluoridation.
- Targeted provision of toothbrushes and toothpaste by post.
- Targeted provision of toothbrushes and toothpaste by post and by health visitors.

Returns on investment after 5 and 10 years were identified. The ROIs ranged from 1:1.03 and 1:3.06 for 5 and 10 years for targeted provision of toothbrushes by post to 1:12.71 and 1:21.98 for water fluoridation, as shown in Fig. 13.3.

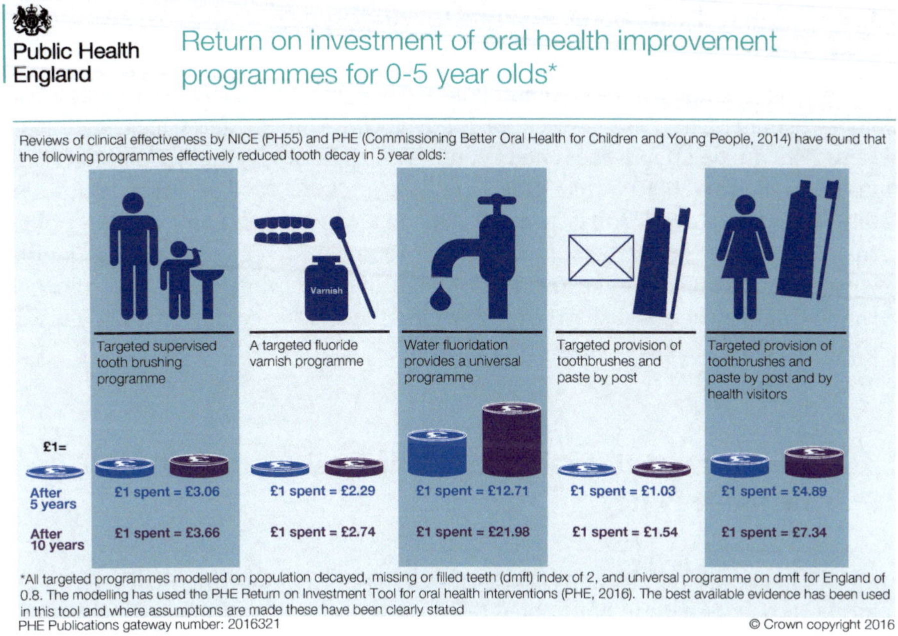

Fig. 13.3 Return on investment for oral health improvement programs for 0–5-year-olds. (Reprinted from Public Health England (2016), with permission from Public Health England)

The review informed the development of a modelling tool which can be used by commissioners of oral health improvement programs to determine the cost-effectiveness of the five initiatives. The calculator allows effectiveness data on interventions to be used to estimate the potential economic benefits from specific interventions using tooth decay prevalence rates and treatment costs specifically for England.

A limitation of the review is that there is a paucity of studies on ROI for 0–5-year-olds. As the data are specific for England, the approach would need to be replicated with relevant local country data.

The summary infographic developed as part of the project (Fig. 13.3) proved useful in discussing interventions for 0–5-year-olds with policy makers in the Victorian Department of Health and Human Services. The infographic provided a clear and succinct summary of the ROI research for policy decision-makers without an oral health background. While there was recognition that the data are relevant for England and ROIs may not be directly transferable to Australia, the information helped push oral health up the policy agenda for enhanced access to additional resources.

13.5.3 Early Childhood Policy Development

A CBA helped shape early childhood policy development in New South Wales and South Australia. The Perry Preschool Study in the United States identified cost-benefit data on the effectiveness and economic benefit of early childhood interventions (Bowen et al. 2009). A particularly influential 'killer fact' was that there was a return of $7.16 for every dollar invested. This fact was used and promoted by politicians, bureaucrats, researchers, practitioners, journalists and participants in parliamentary inquiries and was restated in a range of policy documents. Its influence resulted from its short and sharp nature, with dollars at the core, signalling a sensible use of public resources (Bowen et al. 2009).

13.6 Future Directions for Economic Evaluation Research to Shape Policy

As mentioned in Sect. 13.3, to ensure that economic evaluations will be policy-relevant, it is important to understand the priorities of policy makers. What is their 'problem setting'? What are their goals and objectives? Is there concern for providing universal access to services, for example, or for providing greater priority to a specific population or group?

Recently published economic evaluation research which shows promise for influencing public policy includes studies that show the cost-effectiveness of school-based interventions for caries (Amilani et al. 2020) and treating children with severe childhood caries under conscious sedation rather than general anaesthesia (Burgette and Quinonez 2018). Other studies that could influence policy are the use of oral health professionals in residential aged care facilities (Munzenmayer et al. 2019) and the use of silver diamine fluoride to arrest dental caries in young children from disadvantaged families (Johhnson et al. 2019).

Policy-persuasive economic evaluations that would be useful include reviews of public dental programs to determine their impact on quality of life. Generic outcome measures are needed such as quality-adjusted life years (QALYs), so that comparison between programs can be more readily made (Amilani et al. 2020). It is important to determine impacts beyond improvements in oral health, for example, in programs that tackle common risk factors such as diet and smoking. These cross-disciplinary programs include diabetes management, the reduction of sugar consumption, impact on obesity and smoking cessation. Highlighting the impact of oral health programs on broader social costs such as time lost from work and school can be policy persuasive. Identifying the broader impact of oral health programs will assist in having oral health included in other health promotion programs: moving closer to placing 'oral health in all policies' (Watt et al. 2019).

Further economic evaluation research is needed to develop policy about reducing inequalities in oral health, reform of oral healthcare systems and addressing the commercial determinants of oral health (Watt et al. 2019). Evaluations are also required in areas such as the optimum recall periods for dental visits, use of teledentistry and the management of asymptomatic third molars.

In addition, economic evaluation is required to inform oral health value-based policy and practice. An approach gaining momentum among decision-makers, value-based healthcare (VBHC), is a patient-centric approach to designing and managing healthcare systems. It has the potential to deliver improved health outcomes that matter most to patients and at a lower cost (Porter 2010).

An aspect of VBHC is developing funding reforms that maximise value and outcomes for patients, funders and the health system. Robust economic evaluation can provide economic evidence to identify payment systems with incentives to improve oral health outcomes that matter to patients, limit low value services, emphasise prevention and utilise an optimal workforce skill mix (Hegde and Haddock 2019).

The particular emphasis should be on conducting CBAs which can provide the most relevant information for making decisions about policy (Listl and Weyant 2019). It is also necessary to address the identified limitations in conducting, reporting and publishing economic evaluations in dentistry. A universal approach to reporting economic evaluation research results has been proposed via use of the Consolidated Health Economic Evaluation Reporting Standards (CHEERS) checklist (Listl and Weyant 2019).

Finally, there is also a need to study the impact of economic evaluation on policy and practice. That is, to identify the enablers and barriers for the translation of economic evaluation into making good oral health policy and its implementation.

13.7 Final Remarks

Public oral health policy covers a range of initiatives, from legislation, budget decisions and strategic plans to best practice guidelines. Economic evaluation has been influential in shaping oral health policies, but there is further scope for more policy-persuasive research. The impact has been predominantly on the development of clinical guidelines, with less impact, apart from evidence to support water fluoridation, on broader government policy.

Economic evaluation can provide policy decision-makers with information that helps them make difficult decisions about competing use of limited resources. Evidence can be provided to advocate for new programs and to inform decisions about shaping existing programs. Economic evaluation can assist policy makers to answer questions about health program efficacy (is it working?), effectiveness (is it working well?) and equity (is it reaching those it is supposed to reach?).

Governments pursue their objectives by implementing policy. Many factors influence policy making at the government level. Kingdon's three Ps is a useful approach for understanding, developing and gaining acceptance of policy. What is required is to appropriately frame the problem, to develop proposals to address these and to engage in the politics, so as to be prepared for when a policy window opens. This may be prior to an election or a budget or a change of minister.

Public policy making at the highest level is based on ideas and values, is dynamic and can involve many players and be highly contested. There can be a cultural gap between researchers and policy makers that needs to be bridged for research to be translated into policy. Contexts, language, motivation, incentives, time frames and priorities are different for each group.

Economic evaluation is required that is timely and relevant to policy makers' questions. This will assist in placing oral health on the policy agenda – those issues and problems to which policy makers pay attention. It is important to appreciate what is driving policy makers – to have empathy and understand their interests and motivation. Understanding the values and policies of a government is key.

Economic evaluation research can produce succinct economic 'killer facts' that can be policy persuasive, particularly when combined with scenarios and stories that capture the human impact of the policy proposal. It can be helpful to engage with health department officers early on in a research project to gain their interest.

Integrated approaches that efficiently address CRFs to promote oral and general health may be received more favourably than stand-alone oral health-focused interventions. Take opportunities to link with smoking cessation, nutrition interventions, diabetes programs or oral cancer screening and prevention. Policy proposals are more likely to be accepted by decision-makers if there is a coalition of supporters including the community. Researchers have opportunities to be policy advocates and oral health champions.

Policy-persuasive economic evaluation is needed in areas such as reducing inequalities in oral health, CRF approaches, VBHC and the effective use of the dental team. Evidence for shaping clinical guidelines is also required, for example, identifying the optimal recall period for dental visits, use of teledentistry and the management of asymptomatic third molars. There is a need for high-quality CBAs because they can provide the most relevant information for making decisions about policy as they translate outcomes into quality of life metrics to allow comparison across programs.

Economic evaluation researchers who want their research to be translated into policy and practice need to understand the policy-making process and be prepared to step out of what can be an academic research bubble to engage more with policy makers. The ability to influence broad oral health policy will likely to involve coordinating and working with health department staff and politicians on their goals and information needs. Influencing policy and practice at the clinical level will require closer relationships at the dental service level.

Acknowledgements Thank you to Rodrigo Marino, Pauline Sanders and Clare Lin for helping shape this chapter.

Appendix 1: Scoping Review of the Literature

The systematic database search carried out in May 2020 included MEDLINE, ERIC and CINAHL via the EBSCOhost platform; PubMed, EMBASE, DARE, NHSEED, HTA, Cost-Effectiveness Analysis Registry, PEDE and Cochrane reviews via EMBASE Classic and Evidence-Based Medicine Reviews; Scopus; Science Direct; and Google Scholar.

Grey literature including government plans, papers and reports were sourced through content experts in oral health policy. Reference lists of these documents were also searched. General health policy makers also provided information about policy decisions in oral health in which they were involved.

Search terms included 'economic evaluation or cost-effectiveness or cost-benefit or cost-utility' and 'oral health' or 'dental health' or 'dentistry' or 'dental care' and 'policy'. Inclusion criteria were peer-reviewed studies in English published between 1990 and May 2020.

References

Althous C, Bridgman P, Davis G (2020) The Australian policy handbook: a practical guide to the policy making process. Routledge, New York

Amilani U, Carter HE, Senanayake S, Hettiarachchi RM, McPhail SM, Kularatna S (2020) A scoping review of cost-effectiveness analyses of school-based interventions for caries. Community Dent Oral Epidemiol 48:357–363

Anopa Y, McMahon AD, Conway DI, Ball GE, McIntosh E, Macpherson LM (2015) Improving child Oral health: cost analysis of a National Nursery Toothbrushing Programme. PLoS One 10:e0136211

Australian Government (2015) Healthy families healthy lives: Australia's National Oral Health Plan 2015–2024. Adelaide, Council of Australian Governments (COAG) Health Council

Barnett ML, Pihlstrom BL (2004) Methods for enhancing the efficiency of dental/oral health clinical trials: current status, future possibilities. J Dent Res 83:744–750

Bell E (2010) Research for health policy. Oxford University Press, Oxford

Bell E, Crocombe L, Campbell S, Goldberg LR, Seidel BM (2014) Understanding the research–policy divide for Oral health inequality. Healthcare Policy 10:64–78

Bowen S, Zwi AB, Sainsbury P, Whitehead M (2009) Killer facts, politics and other influences: what evidence triggered early childhood intervention policies in Australia? Evidence & policy 5:5–32

Burgette JM, Quiñonez RB (2018) Cost-effectiveness of treating severe childhood caries under general anesthesia versus conscious sedation. JDR Clin Trans Res 3:336–345

Catford J (2009) Advancing the 'science of delivery' of health promotion: not just the 'science of discovery'. Health Promotion Int 24:1–5

Clarkson JE, Ramsay CR, Eccles MP, Eldridge S, Grimshaw JM, Johnston M, Michie S, Treweek S, Walker A, Young L, Black I (2010) The translation research in a dental setting (TRiaDS) programme protocol. Implement Sci 5:57

Crocombe L, Bell E, Campbell S, Goldberg L, Seidel B (2016) Oral health policy: international implications for Australia. Final Report. Centre for Research Excellence in Primary Oral Health Care, Launceston

Department of Health and Human Services. (2020). Water fluoridation: Questions and answers - The impact of water fluoridation. https://www2.health.vic.gov.au/public-health/water/water-fluoridation/fluoride-information. Accessed 10 Aug 2020

Drummond MF, Sculpher MJ, Claxton K, Stoddart GL, Torrance GW (2015) Methods for the economic evaluation of health care programmes. Oxford University Press, Oxford

Dwan KM, McInnes PC (2013) Increasing the influence of one's research on policy. Aust Health Rev 37:194–198

Eow J, Duane B, Solaiman A, Hussain U, Lemasney N, Ang R, O'Kelly-Lynch N, Girgis G, Collazo L, Johnston B (2019) What evidence do economic evaluations in dental care provide? A scoping review. Community Dent Health 36:118–125

Fraihat N, Madae'en S, Bencze Z, Herczeg A, Varga O (2019) Clinical effectiveness and cost-effectiveness of Oral-health promotion in dental caries prevention among children: systematic review and meta-analysis. Int J Environ Res Public Health 16:2668

Hegde S, Haddock R (2019) Re-orienting funding from volume to value in public dental health services. Deeble Institute for Health Policy Research, Canberra

Johhnson B, Serban N, Griffin PM, Tomar SL (2019) Projecting the economic impact of silver diamine fluoride on caries treatment expenditures and outcomes in young U.S. children. J Public Health Dent 79:215–221

Kingdon J (2010) Agendas, alternatives and public policies. Longman, United States

Lewis J (2005) Health policy and politics: networks, ideas and power. IP Communications, Melbourne

Lin V (2003) Competing rationalities: evidence-based health policy? In: Lin V, Gibson B (eds) Evidence-based health policy: problems and possibilities. Oxford University Press, Oxford

Listl S, Weyant R (2019) For careful consideration: the reporting of health economic evaluations in dentistry. J Public Health Dent 79:273–274

Listl S, Galloway J, Mossey PA, Marcenes W (2015) Global economic impact of dental diseases. J Dent Res 94:1355–1361

Macpherson LM, Rodgers J, Conway DI (2019) Childsmile after 10 years part 2: programme development, implementation and evaluation. Dent Update 46:238–246

Marino R, Zaror C (2020) Economic evaluations in water-fluoridation: a scoping review. BMC Oral Health 20:115

Mariño R, Ravisankar G, Zaror C (2020) Quality appraisal of economic evaluations done on oral health preventive programs-a systematic review. J Public Health 80(3):194–207

Morgan M, Mariño R, Wright C, Bailey D, Hopcraft M (2012) Economic evaluation of preventive dental programs: what can they tell us? Community Dent Oral Epidemiol 40(Suppl 2):117–121

Münzenmayer MA, Mariño R, Hsueh A (2019) Cost-effectiveness of professional oral health care in Australian residential aged care facilities. Gerodontology 36:107–117

Murthy AK, Fareed N (2020) Economic evaluation of school-based caries preventive programs: a systematic review. Community Dent Health 37:1–1

NHMRC (2017a) NHMRC public Statment on water fluoridation and human health in Australia., National Health and medical research. https://www.nhmrc.gov.au/about-us/publications/2017-public-statement-water-fluoridation-and-human-health. Accessed 12 Aug 2020

NHMRC (2017b) Water fluoridation and human health in Australia: questions and answers. In: National Health and Medical Research Council Canberra

Nutbeam D (2003) How does evidence influence public health policy? Tackling health inequalities in England. Health Promot J Austr 14:154–158

Porter ME (2010) What is value in health care? N Engl J Med 363:2477–2481

Public Health England (2014) Local authorities improving oral health: commissioning better oral health for children and young people: an evidence-informed toolkit for local authorities. Public Health England, https://assets.publishing.service.gov.uk/government/uploads/system/uploads/attachment_data/file/321503/CBOHMaindocumentJUNE2014.pdf. Accessed 10 Aug 2020

Public Health England (2016) Return on investment of oral health improvement programmes for 0–5 year olds. https://assets.publishing.service.gov.uk/government/uploads/system/uploads/attachment_data/file/560973/ROI_oral_health_interventions.pdf Accessed 20 Sept 2020
Public Health England (2017) Delivering better oral health: an evidence-based toolkit for prevention. https://assets.publishing.service.gov.uk/government/uploads/system/uploads/attachment_data/file/605266/Delivering_better_oral_health.pdf Accessed 3 Aug 2020
Ran T, Chattopadhyay SK (2016) Economic evaluation of community water fluoridation: a community guide systematic review. Am J Prev Med 50:790–796
Rogers J (2012) Building the links between surveillance, research, and policy and practice--dental public health experiences in Australia. Community Dent Oral Epidemiol 40(Suppl 2):82–89
Rogers HJ, Rodd HD, Vermaire JH, Stevens K, Knapp R, El Yousfi S, Marshman Z (2019) A systematic review of the quality and scope of economic evaluations in child oral health research. BMC Oral Health 19:132
Sheiham A, Watt RG (2000) The common risk factor approach: a rational basis for promoting oral health. Community Dent Oral Epidemiol 28:399–406
Sheiham A, Williams DM, Weyant RJ, Glick M, Naidoo S, Eisele JL, Selikowitz HS (2015) Billions with oral disease: a global health crisis--a call to action. J Am Dent Assoc 146:861–864
Thwaites J (2008a) Ten commandments of influencing government. Melbourne
Thwaites J (2008b) What are the drivers for ministers?. Melbourne
Tonmukayakul U, Calache H, Clark R, Wasiak J, Faggion CM Jr (2015a) Systematic review and quality appraisal of economic evaluation publications in dentistry. J Dent Res 94(10):1348–1354
Tonmukayakul U, Sia KL, Gold L, Hegde S, de Silva AM, Moodie M (2015b) Economic models of preventive dentistry for Australian children and adolescents: a systematic review. Oral Health Prev Dent 13:481–494
Victorian Labor Party (2018) Bringing back the free dental van to public schools.. https://static1.squarespace.com/static/5b46af5a55b02cea2a648e93/t/5bf0b3bb032be406b199399d/1542501313849/181118+-+Bringing+Back+The+Free+Dental+Van+To+Public+Schools.pdf. Accessed 3 August 2020
Watt RG (2017) Addressing oral health inequalities - where do we stand? In: Peres M, Watt RG (eds) Policy solutions for oral health inequalities. Australian Research Centre for Population Oral Health, The University of Adelaide, Adelaide, pp p2–p4
Watt RG, Sheiham A (2012) Integrating the common risk factor approach into a social determinants framework. Community Dent Oral Epidemiol 40:289–296
Watt RG, Daly B, Allison P, Macpherson LM, Venturelli R, Listl S, Weyant RJ, Mathur MR, Guarnizo-Herreño CC, Celeste RK, Peres MA, Kearns C, Benzian H (2019) Ending the neglect of global oral health: time for radical action. Lancet 394:261–272
World Health Organisation (2020) Definition of health policy.. https://www.who.int/topics/health_policy/en/. Accessed 3 Aug 2020

Index

C. Zaror, R. Mariño (eds.), *Introduction to Economic Evaluation in Oral Health Care*, https://doi.org/10.1007/978-3-030-96289-0

E

P

Q

GPSR Compliance

The European Union's (EU) General Product Safety Regulation (GPSR) is a set of rules that requires consumer products to be safe and our obligations to ensure this.

If you have any concerns about our products, you can contact us on ProductSafety@springernature.com

In case Publisher is established outside the EU, the EU authorized representative is:

Springer Nature Customer Service Center GmbH
Europaplatz 3
69115 Heidelberg, Germany

Batch number: 10777422

Printed by Printforce, the Netherlands